The Governance of Cyberspace

That information and communications technologies (ICTs), such as the Internet, are challenging the very fabric of our political systems can no longer be doubted. Yet the nature of such technologically driven changes and their desirability is hotly contested. *The Governance of Cyberspace* critically focuses upon the alleged transformations in power relationships between individuals, government and social institutions as they are emerging in what is becoming known as cyberspace: a computer-generated public domain that has no territorial boundaries, is controlled by no single authority, enables millions of people to communicate around the world and maybe encourages post-hierarchical control of populations.

The ability of computer networks to transcend modern conceptions of time and space has considerable consequences for governance based upon the nation-state. Thus traditional forms of government are said to be weakened by an increasing lack of control over global communications in cyberspace. Hence issues of surveillance, control and privacy in relation to the Internet are coming to the fore as a result of state concern with security, crime and economic advantage.

By advancing this debate, the authors steer a course between those proclaiming cyberspace as a liberating technology and the alternative prophesies of those opposed to technological change. In this way, *The Governance of Cyberspace* aims to encourage a more informed discussion about the nature of the changes heralded in by the new ICTs, and should be of considerable interest to all those who are concerned about the technological shaping of our political future.

Brian D. Loader is Co-Director of the Community Informatics Research and Applications Unit (CIRA), University of Teesside, Middlesbrough, UK.

The Governance of Cyberspace

Politics, technology and global restructuring

Edited by Brian D. Loader

London and New York

First published 1997
by Routledge
11 New Fetter Lane, London EC4P 4EE

Simultaneously published in the USA and Canada
by Routledge
29 West 35th Street, New York, NY 10001

Reprinted 1998

© 1997 selection and editorial matter, Brian D. Loader;
individual chapters, the contributors

Typeset in Palatino by Routledge
Printed and bound in Great Britain by
T.J. International, Padstow, Cornwall

British Library Cataloguing in Publication Data
A catalogue record for this book is available from the
British Library

Library of Congress Cataloging in Publication Data
A catalog record for this book is available from the
Library of Congress

ISBN 0–415–14723–9 (hbk)
ISBN 0–415–14724–7 (pbk)

Dedicated to the memory of Kieron Walsh
(1949–1995)

Contents

Contributors

Simon Baddeley is a lecturer at the University of Birmingham, where he has pursued an interest in the application of information technology to local government and most recently he has been exploring ideas of internal psychological governance through the work of Michel Foucault.

Roger Burrows is Assistant Director of the Centre for Housing Policy at the University of York, UK. He recently co-edited (with Mike Featherstone) *Cyberspace/Cyberbodies/Cyberpunk: Culture of Technological Embodiment* (Sage, 1995).

Dave Carter is the Economic Development Officer for Manchester City Council, where he has been involved in the development of the Manchester Host and 'Electronic Village Halls'. He is currently involved with the European electronic cities initiative.

Dorothy E. Denning is professor of Computer Science at Georgetown University, Washington, DC, where she is currently working on policy and technical issues related to encryption and law enforcement

Paul Frissen is professor of Public Administration at Tilburg University in the Netherlands and also acts as a private consultant on informatisation for the Dutch government and local authorities. He is Co-Director of the joint Tilburg–Rotterdam research programme on 'informatisation in public administration'. He is author, co-author and editor of ten books and over one hundred articles, contributions to books and conference papers.

Gwyneth Jones is a science fiction novelist and critic, with a particular interest in the metaphors of science, and the relationship between imagined futures and emergent technologies. Recent books include: *White Queen*(1991), *North Wind* (1994) and *Kairos* (1995), all published by Cassell/Gollancz.

Klaus Lenk is Professor of Public Administration at the University of Oldenburg, Germany. He has published extensively in the field of IT and governance.

Brian D. Loader is Co-Director of the Community Informatics Research and Applications Unit (CIRA) at the University of Teesside. He is joint-editor of *Towards a Post-Fordist Welfare State?* (Routledge, 1994).

David Lyon is professor of Sociology at Queen's University, Kingston, in Canada. His research and publications have dealt with a range of issues concerned with the social consequences of new ICTs, including *The Information Society* (Polity, 1988) and *The Electronic Eye* (Polity, 1994). His most recent book is *Postmodernity* (OUP, 1994).

Charles D. Raab is a senior lecturer in Politics at the University of Edinburgh, UK. He is a member of the ESRC study group on informatics and public policy and has written extensively on issues relating to privacy and data protection.

Ralph Schroeder is a lecturer in the Department of Social Policy and Social Sciences, Royal Holloway–University of London. He is the author of numerous articles on virtual reality and is currently working on a book entitled *Worlds in Cyberspace*.

Puay Tang is a Research Fellow at the Centre for Information and Communication Technologies, University of Sussex, UK. Her current research interests are in telecommunications policy and globalisation.

Michael Whine has been Executive Director of the defence and group relations department at the Board of Deputies of British Jews since 1986. He is a Member of the Royal Institute of International Affairs, the European Jewish Congress Commission on anti-Semitism, and a consultant to the Institute of Jewish Affairs.

Preface

This collection is the outcome of a small conference held at the University of Teesside in April 1995 which was devoted to exploring the changing nature of governance as a property of that emergent techno-domain which has commonly come to be known as cyberspace. All the papers have been extensively revised both as a consequence of the debate conducted at the event and as a result of the continuing public interest in the issues and themes raised by the transforming qualities of the new information and communications technologies (ICTs).

That the developments of ICTs are challenging the post-war political order can no longer be doubted, but the nature of the changes and their desirability is hotly contested. The contributors to this book have attempted to advance the debate about the governance of cyberspace by avoiding the hyperbole of both the Utopian exhortations of the cyber-libertarians and the dystopian prophesies of the digital Luddites. It is hoped by the authors that this may help to engender a more informed discussion of the nature of the changes which the new ICTs are heralding in and that this collection will make a valuable contribution to that debate.

A significant attraction of the debates surrounding cyberspace is that they appeal to a wide range of individuals associated with a disparate host of disciplines, organisations and locations. Thus it is no surprise that this eclectic dimension should find expression in this volume with contributions from science fiction writers, sociologists, psychologists, political theorists, computer scientists, policy analysts and others drawn from Europe, Canada and the USA. Such diversity, we believe, contributes a great deal to the vibrancy and quality of the debate and will appeal to a wide readership. It also has to be acknowledged, however, that interested parties speak different professional and cultural languages. Furthermore, there is always the risk in such an undertaking that the social theorist may wish to see more conceptualising whilst the techno enthusiast may be disappointed by insufficient material on ICTs. The view of the contributors to this volume is that the issues addressed are too important for fragmentary analysis. Cyberspace and ICTs may indeed be redefining the way we think about traditional subject boundaries. Much may be gained by embarking upon the enterprise of sharing discourses and seeking to understand the value of looking at an issue from different vantage points, that is, of bridging the cleavage of the technical and non-technical perspectives.

My thanks go to all the participants at the conference who helped make it such an enjoyable and stimulating occasion and thereby reminding one that face-to-face interaction still takes some beating. I am indebted to them also for the forbearance shown towards the attentions of the media and to the co-operation of those who helped us to try to meet the demands of the press reporters, radio presenters and TV interviewers.

Such events are of course only possible when academics are assisted by the sensible disposition and organising abilities of our administrative colleagues. It is thus with heartfelt gratitude that I thank Nikki Emmerson and Suzanne Raine as the people most responsible for enabling us to pursue our intellectual pleasures; June Murphy for her invaluable help with accommodation bookings; and Jo Brudenell, who assisted with the word processing and compilation.

Special thanks are due to my friend and former colleague Roger Burrows, whose unerring enthusiasm and support has been a constant source of personal inspiration and but for whom, and a few pints of real English Ale, the idea for the conference would not have materialised. Mention also needs to be made of John Taylor, Christine Bellamy and the other members of the ESRC study group in informatics and public policy who raised my interest in ICTs in the first place.

Lastly, but by no means less significantly, I would like to thank Kim Loader for her valued comments not only on the conference arrangements and the resulting volume but also for bearing an extra burden with such good grace at a time when the attentions of our very young children William and Christopher were more than enough to cope with.

An earlier version of Chapter 11, 'The Future of Cryptography', by Dorothy E. Denning, was published in *Internet Security Review* (October 1995) and is reproduced here by kind permission of the publishers.

Chapter 1

The governance of cyberspace
Politics, technology and global restructuring

Brian D. Loader

INTRODUCTION

Much of the burgeoning literature on the economic and social restructuring of the advanced capitalist societies is predicated upon the notion that such transformations are driven by the revolutionary developments in a range of information and communications technologies (ICTs). Through their potential capacity to transcend the time and space delimiters of modernist organisation and technique some commentators have suggested that ICTs are facilitating the emergence of new forms of human interaction in what is becoming known as cyberspace: a computer-generated public domain which has no territorial boundaries or physical attributes and is in perpetual use. To date its most potent manifestation is that matrix of electronic telecommunication and computer networks, usually referred to as the Internet, which links millions of people globally, is growing at a rapid rate daily, is taking new shape and direction as a consequence of the voluntary actions of its participants, and, it is claimed, is not controlled by any single authority.

What is becoming of increasing interest and forms the central focus of this collection is the possibility of cyberspace giving rise to new forms and expressions of governance: a paradigmatic change in the constellation of power relations between individuals, governments and social institutions. Such a contention arises from the transcending qualities of ICTs as a means to facilitate the demise of modernist forms of governance based upon territory, hierarchical managerial control of populations, and policing. Thus nation-state boundaries are said to be weakening both from the development of global economies where 'cyberspace is where your money is'[1] and also from the lack of control by national governments over communications in cyberspace. Furthermore, the changing politics of identity characterised by the breakdown of social class, patriarchal and racial modes of political organisation and their replacement by a diverse range of movements championing social difference may also be finding expression in cyberspace. In this context cyberspace is regarded as the medium through which to explore concepts of emancipation, empowerment and the transcendence of physical subjugation (Haraway, 1985).

To some this disjuncture heralds a libertarian future of self-expression freed from the impositions of government domination. Yet cyberspace is not an uncontested domain and stakeholders in the politics of the modern nation-state are not so easily displaced. Hence issues of surveillance, control and privacy in relation to the Internet have preoccupied the world's media in recent years, ostensibly as a result of a renewed state concern with security, crime and economic advantage.

This chapter is intended to provide, albeit briefly, a contextualisation for the debates, issues and themes surrounding the governance of cyberspace and thereby further act as an introduction to the more detailed contributions which follow.

CONCEPTUALISING CYBERSPACE

One of the problems which besets analysis of this new techno-domain is the difficulty of clarifying what exactly is being described when cyberspace is being talked about. Its antecedence is a curious mixture of science fiction literature in the cyberpunk genre most commonly epitomised by the work of William Gibson; those whom I will describe as cyber-libertarians, such as John Perry Barlow and Mitch Kapor; international commercial computer interests; and cyber-enthusiasts like Howard Rheingold. Thus it has been variously described as 'the conceptual space where words, human relationships, data, wealth and power are manifested by people using CMC [computer-mediated communications] technology' (Rheingold, 1994: 5). It is this interactivity between millions of people around the globe using email, Usenet newsgroups and BBSs which gives rise to Rheingold's notion of the creation of 'virtual communities' on the Internet. Alternatively, as the originator of the term itself,

William Gibson, has famously described it, cyberspace can be regarded as

> a consensual hallucination . . . . A graphic representation of data abstracted from the bank of every computer in the human system. Unthinkable complexity. Lines of light ranged in the nonspace of the mind, clusters and constellations of data. Like city lights receding.
>
> (1984: 51)

It can be claimed that in at least two important respects William Gibson's depiction of cyberspace in his novels such as *Neuromancer* (1984) and *Virtual Light* (1993) has acted to prefigure the debate about the governance of cyberspace. In the first place some commentators have suggested that his and other cyberpunk science fiction literature can be regarded as more insightful about the present condition of the world than more conventional social theory (Burrows, 1996; Kellner, 1995). Kellner, for example, asserts that

> it is my contention that Gibson is mapping our present from the vantage point of his imagined future, demonstrating the possible consequences of present trends of development. In particular, he is charting the ways that new technologies are impacting on human life creating new individuals and new technological environments.
>
> (1995: 299)

As a cultural movement cyberpunk has probably been even more influential by evoking the use of technology for anti-authoritarian and libertarian stances. As Kellner remarks,

> In Gibson's work and other cyberpunk fiction, technology and communications systems are represented as a fundamental means of power and hence as something important for democratic control. There is thus a kind of populism in the cyberpunk movement which advocates individuals using technology for their own purposes and engaging in media and technological activism.
>
> (1995: 323)

In the hands of John Perry Barlow, who popularised Gibson's term, it came to denote the emergence of an alternative virtual world, an 'electronic frontier' (Sterling, 1994: 247). In this conception, cyberspace becomes something qualitatively more than a network of computer linked telephony. The matrix itself gives form to a virtual space behind the computer screen where physical presence is replaced by incorporeal relationships which take place increasingly in computer-simulated environments. Thus Barlow claims that what cyberspace heralds is nothing less than

> the promise of a new social space, global and antisovereign, within which anybody, anywhere can express to the rest of humanity whatever he or she believes without fear. There is in these new media a foreshadowing of the intellectual and economic liberty that might undo all the authoritarian powers on earth.
>
> (1996a)

John Perry Barlow has played a significant role both in the development of 'on-line' culture and the fight to defend free speech in cyberspace (Sterling, 1994: 235–6). A former lyricist for the American band the Grateful Dead, a cattle rancher and Wyoming Republican, Barlow has been at the forefront of campaigning for civil liberties on the Internet.[2] He has thus been important for establishing some important perimeters of the debate concerning the governance of cyberspace. Given his fascinating history we should perhaps not be surprised that his depiction of the electronic frontier seems to draw upon the imagery of a virgin territory where all frontiers-people are free to roam, establish their own virtual communities, are all equal and are unimpeded by the agents of the state: a veritable digital Eden where politics needs no existence.

Barlow is particularly vehement in his castigation of nation-states. He rightly identifies that 'the Internet is too widespread to be easily dominated by any single government. By creating a seamless global-economic zone, borderless and unregulatable, the Internet calls into question the very idea of a nation-state' (1996a). In this new virtual world politics is replaced by self-policing using such activity as flaming and placing greater emphasis upon parental control; mutual self-help through virtual communities such as the WELL[3] and the emancipation of the national subject by people choosing their own identities.

It is clear from Barlow's 'declaration of the independence of cyberspace' (1996b), that he believes that an alternative civilisation of the mind is naturally evolving in cyberspace which will eventually replace the politics of the flesh, sovereignty, military force and national boundaries. Thus he proclaims to the old order that 'our identities have no bodies, so, unlike you, we cannot obtain order by coercion. We believe that from ethics, enlightened self-interest, and the commonweal, our governance will emerge.'

DEMYSTIFYING THE ELECTRONIC FRONTIER

Such Utopian characterisations of cyberspace have and continue to be a powerful contribution to the debate about the governance of cyberspace. They have, however, been charged with mystifying CMC and thereby contributing to a more general misunderstanding of the relationship between ICTs and global restructuring (Bennahum, 1996; Brook and Boal, 1995; Robins, 1995). The very discourse of those proselytising about cyberspace can often be mistaken for a kind of exhortation to enter an alternative reality freed from the encumbrances of a decaying and discredited late modernist society (Rheingold, 1991). Such linguistic reverberating between the future and present often makes it difficult to distinguish between what is being claimed for current behavioural practice and what is prophesy for a future as yet unrealised. Such ambiguity demands further attempts at clarification.

In the first place cyberspace is frequently portrayed as a kind of homogenous virtual public or common space. But this is surely to cloak the multifarious usages of ICTs. More accurately cyberspace should perhaps be regarded as a collection of different multimedia technologies and networks which whilst they may be held together by standard computing protocol (TCP/IP) do not necessarily imply that visitors to cyberspace can access all of its domains. Thus whilst some usages of the Internet, such as encrypted person-to-person electronic mail, invited Internet relay chat or video conferencing and password protected file transfer protocol or World Wide Web (WWW) sites may be relatively private, others, such as electronic mail-based distribution lists, Usenet groups and WWW pages, are more public in orientation (Bennahum, 1996).

Moreover, since it is a defining feature of cyberspace that it is a global facility accessible to many millions of people from different countries, it is important to be clear about both the degree to which the Internet may act to homogenise the world's historical cultures and the desirability of doing so. Herbert Schiller (1995) has alluded, for example, to the US government's possible role in colonising global culture through the Global Information Infrastructure (GII). Whilst Barlow is eager to see the creation of wealth-producing marketplaces (1996b), he has little to say about his advocacy of free speech seemingly requiring the world to speak English on the electronic frontier. Yet, as we shall see later in the chapter, the 'political' struggle between competing cultural identities seems unlikely to diminish as we approach the next millennium.

The cyber-libertarians' apolitical stance may be further limited by their preoccupation with what they regard as the authoritarian domination of nation-states. Governance is surely not simply authoritarian control by the nation-state over its subjects, as Barlow and his associates seem to imagine. Rather, it is concerned with a complex pattern of interrelationships between social institutions and individuals. By concentrating on what they regard as government control they also fail to consider the importance of free enterprise in restricting individual actions and thought. Yet an analysis of the disjuncture between the old world order and the rapidly emerging global economy has at its core the power of multinational corporations (MNCs) vis-à-vis nation-states and their citizens (Frieden, 1991; Held, 1995; O'Brien, 1992). It is perhaps instructive in this context that some of the contending organisations for MNC status are the very computer and software companies responsible for driving the visions of the information age.

A further weakness of the cyber-libertarian formulation of cyberspace is the notion that it comprises a virtual reality which is somehow alternative and unrelated to the 'real' world. Yet such an understanding is surely to ignore the fact that the very technologies enabling 'virtuality' have been developed for military, educational, public and increasingly commercial use. The Internet itself was the product of the United States' desire to build a military communications system which would be secure from terrorist and nuclear attack. As a research and civilian communications network it continued to be funded directly by the US government through the National Science Foundation until April 1995, and although now privately operated it continues to be indirectly funded by public finance. The origins, development and co-operative ethos of cyberspace are therefore directly related to the real world of government policy-making and public expenditure.

Finally, it is necessary to address the cyber-libertarian assertion that they 'are creating a world that all may enter without privilege or prejudice accorded by race, economic power, military force, or station of birth' (Barlow, 1996b). Again, such sweeping assertions surely need to be embedded within the social context of access to the Internet. Although data on usage are at present limited, they do not indicate that anything more than a small percentage of the world's population is on-line and that the majority probably come from affluent countries and have professional backgrounds. The degree to which a wider range of people may become 'wired' is likely to be heavily dependent upon public policy-making and corporate planning, which once more invokes the role of politics in the development of cyberspace.

The elucidation of such conceptual shortcomings is not intended to deny the significance that ICTs pose as a challenge to traditional models of governance but rather to contend that cyberspace can only be understood in relation to the techno-social restructuring which is occurring in the real world: ICTs are both driving that restructuring and responding to it; they are not creating an imagined realm separate from it.

POSTMODERNITY, IDENTITY AND GOVERNMENTALITY

The relationship between the dramatic changes occurring in contemporary societies and the transforming qualities of ICTs has been a recurrent theme in postmodernist literature. Whilst many commentators do not always wish to make the link between post-industrial society and postmodern cultural theory explicit, the two strands have been usefully merged in more recent accounts. David Harvey, for example, has been prepared to consider 'the condition of postmodernity' (1989) as a comprehensive social account of structural change, and Mark Poster's 'second media age' synergises postmodern culture with wider political, economic and social change through the mediation of ICTs (1995a, 1995b).

Notorious for the difficulty of finding an analytical vantage point from which to clarify the notion of postmodernism, we shall none the less run the risk of drawing upon a selection of the more familiar contentions that its leading exponents postulate. To do so is to consider the idea that cyberspace is in some sense a manifestation of the postmodern world: a domain where postmodern cultural theories fuse with the post-industrial information society thesis.

'Little narratives', fragmentation and pluralism in cyberspace

One of the high priests of postmodernity, the French social critic Jean-François Lyotard, foregrounds the importance of information and computerisation in the development of what he describes as 'the knowledge society' (1984). A post-industrial context where knowledge becomes commodified through the use of ICTs. Distinct from such social transitions, but developing in tandem, are cultural transformations which Lyotard characterises as the discreditation of the 'grand' or 'meta-narratives' which define modernity. Universal proclamations of social progress based upon the elucidation of rational laws and rules of interaction associated with such movements as the Enlightenment are being increasingly discarded. Instead, according to Lyotard, they may be replaced by 'little narratives' which invoke the creative, playful and self-defining validation of local discourse which has no reference to claims of external scientific universality.

It is precisely these postmodernist little narratives which may be characteristic of discourse in cyberspace. As Poster remarks, 'the Internet seems to encourage the proliferation of stories, local narratives without any totalising gestures and it places senders and addressees in symmetrical relations. Moreover, these stories and their performance consolidate the "social bond" of the Internet "community" . . . ' (1995b: 92).

This view, the postmodernists would contend, is consistent with the growing disenchantment with political ideologies and the retreat from participation in mass political parties to be witnessed in all contemporary capitalist societies, and particularly amongst the younger generations (Wilkinson and Mulgan, 1995). Moreover, it may be that the emergence of 'new social movements', based not on modernist socio-economic groupings, but rather on the contingencies of lifestyles and ephemeral global issues, can find expression in cyberspace through little narratives.

However, while such discourse may reflect the fragmentation and pluralism of the postmodern political age it is not clear that such narrations are heralding the emergence of electronic democracy much beloved by many celebrants of cyberspace. ICTs may indeed make possible individual participation, for some, and facilitate interactive communication between millions around the globe. But does this necessitate the creation of computer-mediated public spaces? Much that is currently narrated on the Internet has more in common with the sound-bite politics which epitomises the commodification of political discourse rather than informed political dialogue. In a postmodern world where information and knowledge are said to be power this is surely not without significance.

The rise of the global and local, and fall of the nation-state

Governance in the postmodern world is further characterised by the weakening of the nation-state through the accentuation of the local and global dimensions of human interaction. ICT networks such as the Internet facilitate the deconstruction of national financial and cultural boundaries which are an intrinsic attribute of modernism. Instead, it is maintained that power is decentralised as the traditional functions of the modern state – external defence, internal surveillance and the maintenance of citizenship rights – have been challenged (Crook *et al.*, 1992; see also Lenk, this volume).

The globalising qualities of the Internet are thus responsible for producing new formulations of governance at the local level which are expressed through the notions of enhanced participatory democratic activity and economic regeneration on the one hand and the re-emergence of local cultural identities on the other. The former are characterised by the use of multimedia networks to enable the development of post-bureaucratic public service organisations with their decentralised flexible forms facilitating entirely new interfaces with communities and citizens. Local governments in the USA and Europe have enthusiastically embraced ICTs as a means of improving public information services. Cyberspace now abounds with web pages portraying the logos of cities, regions and other sub-national administrations each proclaiming their missions to serve their cyber-citizens. Such technologies are also increasingly the cornerstone of economic regeneration schemes. Through the development of training and access opportunities local governments hope to gain competitive advantage for their localities in the global information economy (see Carter, this volume).

Here again we see a threat to the position of the nation-state as urban communities seek a digital autonomy as nodal points in the matrix of communications networks. Whilst it may not produce the imminent demise of nation-states, the rise of electronic cities such as Singapore, Tokyo, London or New York (Sassen, 1991) could be regarded as a significant reconfiguration of international political and economic relations.

These developments are matched by the growing interest in local cultural identities which have been subsumed within modern nation-state identities. As David Held reminds us, ICTs 'both stimulate new forms of cultural identity and rekindle and intensify old forms' (1995: 125).

'Hyperreality' and virtual reality

Perhaps most notable within the debates about postmodernism and CMC has been the prominence of Jean Baudrillard's exposition of 'hyperreality' (1988) as it relates to the development of cyberspace and especially the potential capabilities of virtual reality technologies. Although based primarily upon mass communications media, Baudrillard's contention that such technologies are constructing an entirely new social environment, an electronic reality, has clear resonance for those proclaiming that cyberspace represents an alternative, virtual reality. In contrast to cyber-libertarians, Baudrillard is unlikely, however, to find solace in the electronic frontier: his is a dystopic view of future technological change.

For Baudrillard and his followers, media communications technologies have been responsible in the past for hiding reality behind a veil of signs, images and symbols which constitute such processes of commodification, propaganda and advertising. The immense persuasiveness of such media have contributed to the condition of what he describes as the 'ecstasy of communication': an environment composed of simulations of images which have no base in reality: a 'hyperreality' (1983). The fantasy worlds of Disneyland and Disney World and the American cities of Las Vegas and Los Angeles are for Baudrillard examples of hyper-reality where copy and fabrication become reality.

In the hyperreality of cyberspace it is contended that time, place and individual identity are separated from modernist physical locations. That virtual reality technology, at present in its infancy, will develop to enable computer-generated simulated environments where individuals will be able to interact through iconic identities which they may change at will. Feminists such as Donna Haraway have been eager to explore how such hyper-reality may enable 'imagining a world without gender' (1985: 66). Such virtual empowerment further offers the opportunity for emancipation from the domination of other physical attributes such as disability and skin colour.

Such visions however have been treated with caution concern-ing technological capabilities (see, for example Schroeder, this volume) and even rejected as psychotic in their desire to con-struct and inhabit a fantasy world. Kevin Robins points out that 'such empowerment entails a refusal to recognise the substantive and independent reality of others and to be involved in relations of mutual dependency and responsibility.' He continues later that 'it is the continuity of grounded identity that underpins and underwrites moral obligation and commitment' (1995: 144–5). As has already been suggested, such self-referential individuality seems unlikely to lead to the kind of mutual supporting virtual communities based on equality which some celebrants of virtual reality proclaim.

Instead, Baudrillard's analysis may suggest that the gover-nance of cyberspace at one level is essentially bound up with the creation, maintenance and contestability of the metaphors, icons, symbols and mores which influence the conduct of computer-mediated communication (CMC). I am reminded here of the ubiquitous Microsoft toolbars and icons which are instantly recognisable around the world and which with the launch of Windows 95 will doubtless attempt to colonise the Internet. Indeed, it is somewhat ironic that many of those who champion the libertarian credentials of the new ICTs now find themselves engaged in a kind of Habermasian contest to defend the earlier text-based interaction, which they believe promulgates democra-tic participation, against commercial interests which are portrayed as hell-bent upon commodifying political discourse in cyberspace (Habermas, 1989; Rheingold, 1994).

Governmentality and identification

We will conclude this section by further exploring the relation between identity and governance in cyberspace through Michel Foucault's work on 'governmentality'. Although a poststructuralist rather than a postmodernist theorist, Foucault devoted a significant amount of his energies to analysing the power relationship between the state and individual in modern society. His insights are therefore pertinent to any discussion about significant changes in governance as a consequence of ICTs. It may even be contended that the present attempts to utilise the new technologies for control and surveillance purposes can best be understood through the Foucauldian notion of governmentality.

In his studies Foucault examines how as nation-states developed during the eighteenth century with the rise of capitalism and demographic increases the nature of government became increasingly concerned with the management of populations.

> In contrast to sovereignty, government has as its purpose not the act of government itself, but the welfare of the population, the improvement of its condition, the increase of its wealth, longevity, health, etc.: and the means that the government uses to attain these ends are themselves all in some sense immanent to the population.
>
> (1991: 100)

Governmentality is a kind of power, therefore, which arises from the process by which the state seeks to improve the wealth of the nation and the happiness of its citizens by means of the systematic identification of individual needs and characteristics whilst at the same time regulating and policing their actions in ways which act to strengthen the role of the state. Such practices enable the individual interest to become subsumed in the summation of interests.

> The population . . . is . . . the object in the hands of government, aware, vis-à-vis the government, of what it wants, but ignorant of what is being done to it. Interest at the level of the consciousness of each individual who goes to make the popu-

lation, and interest considered as interest of the population regardless of what particular interests and aspirations may be of the individuals who compose it, this is the target and the fundamental instrument of the government of population.

(Foucault, 1991: 100)

But governmentality should not be confused with coercion by the state or centralised state control. It is, rather, a set of tactics or heterogeneous techniques. This is made clearer in Foucault's assertion that

this form of power applies itself to everyday life which categorises the individual, marks him by his own individuality, attaches him to his own identity, imposes a law of truth on him which he must recognise and which others have to recognise in him.

(1980: 186)

This internalisation of individual identity according to external classifications implies that governmentality can also involve manipulation of the subject. Foucault continues,

this form of power cannot be exercised without knowing the inside of people's minds, without exploring their souls, without making them reveal their innermost secrets. It implies a knowledge of the conscience and an ability to direct it.

(1980: 214)

Thus it is through this process of individual collusion with state techniques of confession, identification, classification and regulation in the pursuit of economic prosperity that the social domain has become immersed in the 'pastoral' practices of governmentality.

It is a form of power which makes individuals subject: subject to someone else by control and dependence, and tied to his own identity by a conscience or self knowledge. Both meanings suggest a form of power which subjugates and makes subject to.

(Foucault, 1980: 212)

Foucault's explorations of governmentality are important for discussions about the governance of cyberspace on at least two counts. First, they foreground quite clearly the liberating potential of electronic domains where subjects may be able to free themselves from identities which have not been chosen but rather given. Second, it may help us to understand the response of nation-states who appear threatened by cyber-interactions.

In his writings, Foucault suggests that resistance to subjugation is possible and liberty should be pursued by denying the identities imposed upon us.

> The political, ethical, social, philosophical problems of our day is not to try to liberate the individual from the state, and from the state's institutions, but to liberate us both from the state and from the type of individualization which is linked to the state. We have to promote new forms of subjectivity through the refusal of this kind of individuality which has been imposed on us for centuries.
>
> (1980: 216)

Whilst such comments may appear to echo the cyber-libertarian arguments for independence in cyberspace, there are some important distinctions to be made.

Unlike the cyber-libertarians, Foucault does not dispense with politics and power relations. For Foucault, power is a precondition for freedom rather than a barrier to its attainment.

> Power is exercised only over free subjects, and only insofar as they are free. By this we mean individual or collective subjects who are faced with a field of possibilities in which several ways of behaving, several reactions and diverse compartments may be realized.
>
> (1982: 221)

Whilst cyberspace may introduce new possibilities for interaction which may in turn enable individuals to promote alternative identities, it is difficult to imagine how such subjectivity can exist outside of Foucault's conception of power relationships. Here, as in other ways, it is the 'real world' mental baggage and social conditions which disputants take with them when they enter cyberspace.

The prospect of cyberspace facilitating the emergence of new forms of power relations is also important for considerations of whether the nation-state can continue to exercise power over its subjects and manage its populations through traditional policing and regulatory methods of governmentality (see Lenk, this volume). The response to date of governments around the world has tended to be attempts to control use of the Internet through legislation such as the Communications Decency Act passed in the USA, encryption technology such as the Clipper chip (see Denning, this volume) and restriction of use in such countries as Germany and Singapore. The need for traditional government regulation is defended on grounds of security, commerce and law enforcement (see Tang and Whine, this volume).

Of equal interest, however, is how the technology may be used to reconstruct cyber-identities through electronic surveillance technologies capable of building highly sophisticated profiles of individuals which are as detailed as anything constructed by the nation-state (Davies, 1996; Lyon, 1994b). As with the earlier forms of governmentality data, subjects are not the product of state coercion but rather the voluntary and everyday activity of electronic transactions and the individual surrender of some privacy and autonomy in return for quality of life. That is, governmentality in cyberspace suggests that power relationships based upon public compliance and subject identity will continue to play an important part in human interaction.

EXPLORING THE DEBATE FURTHER

The volume is structured in such a way as to advance the debate by first critically examining the nature of cyberspace before going on to consider how this techno-domain may be affecting the territories, organisation and policy processes of traditional nation-states and concluding with an exploration of cyberspatial policing strategies. Thus the book is divided into three sections. Part I is devoted to the objective of conceptually clarifying the nature of cyberspace and thereby provide a critical framework for the more specific considerations of governance which come later.

The contributors to the first section undertake their task by exploring some of the key facets of this techno-domain. It begins with David Lyon's consideration of the contention that classical sociological approaches to social relationships are limited in their understanding of the emerging computer-mediated social interactions in cyberspace. ICTs are accelerating the shift towards an expanding sphere of indirect relations, making remoteness (but not necessarily impersonality) their predominant feature. ICTs are also facilitating virtual relations, some of which are visible on the Net (cross-dressing and 'mudding'), while others are less visible but more pervasive and are products of surveillance. Whilst not advocating the abandonment of traditional sociological analysis, Lyon contends that the burgeoning remote and virtual relations emerging in cyberspace demand a consideration of postmodern theory for its explanatory value.

The chapter by Roger Burrows attempts to frame contemporary issues of urban governance through the genre of cyberpunk, the literary concomitant of cyberculture. His aim is to encourage a (re)reading of cyberpunk as social and political theory. The contention is that with the postmodern demise of the meta-narrative many of the themes and processes which a symptomatic reading of cyberpunk reveal are a good deal more insightful than those offered by what now passes for the theoretical and empirical mainstream.

The role of literary sources as a means of theorising CMC is further explored by Gwyneth Jones. Her chapter attempts to conceptualise cyberspace by using metaphors developed in the separate spheres of science fiction and scientific understanding and considering the notion that in cyberspace these different perspectives are merging. Gerald Edelman's work on neuroscience is adopted to examine the extent to which science fiction metaphors of networks and matrices are becoming central to our understanding of behaviour and social relations in cyberspace. Edelman is intent upon putting our understanding of the mind and consciousness back into nature by expressing it as the evolutionary product of complex neurological connections. In cyberspace, mind and consciousness merge within an electronic matrix.

The concept of governmentality which Michel Foucault developed to describe how individuals, amid great changes in the past, became aware of new problems and redefined their self-understanding and their responsibilities to themselves and the world is used by Simon Baddeley to pursue his interest in the government of the psyche in the imagined territories of cyberspace.

Schroeder concludes the first section by examining the significance of 'virtual reality' (VR) in understanding the future of human–computer interaction in cyberspace. He proposes that VR systems are likely to play a part in the convergence between various new information and communication technologies, and thus become a widespread tool for interacting with computer-generated worlds. Whatever shape these technologies may take, VR provides a good example of the social implications of different options within cyberspace, which range from pre-manufactured virtual worlds over which users have little control, to imaginative virtual worlds which allow manipulation and exploration.

Part II of the volume provides a consideration of how ICTs are challenging nation-state boundaries and re-emphasising the local interest through such devices as economic regeneration schemes. Paul Frissen's chapter relates developments in ICTs to recent changes in (Dutch) public adminstration. His underlying contention is that a fundamental transition is taking place from bureaucratic forms of public administration based upon territorial organization towards a postmodernist network model of governance facilitated by ICTs. Politics is developing into a sort of 'broker' politics, in which ideology plays a secondary role. Horizontal relations in policy domains are becoming more prominent, which produces tensions with the vertically integrated, territorially organised, hierarchical political system.

In general, Frissen suggests that we may observe a process of fragmentation. The world is becoming multi-centred; social and electronic networks are converging; and cyberspace is to some extent an anarchistic world. A grand narrative cannot be told and the pyramid of politics disappears in the archipelago of policy domains. No longer is politics a matter of content, but a question of grammar: designing decision-making arrangements for societal self-steering, equipping them with ICT. The core of politics, then, may become an aesthetic of styles.

Such claims are countered somewhat by Klaus Lenk's contention that we should reconsider the classical functions of the nation-state in order to afford at least some protection and security against crime and violence. Whilst recognising that ICTs may be undermining this traditional role, Lenk contends that we need to consider regulation over the design and use of our technological artefacts.

Dave Carter's chapter outlines the strategic importance of exploiting the opportunities offered by ICTs to support economic regeneration and urban development. It aims to identify ways in which the applications and services being developed using advanced telecommunications and telematics should be made more accessible to local people and organisations. It highlights the potential for new projects to be developed which will enable the benefits of the development of the 'information superhighway' to be maximised at a local level.

The third and final part of the book looks more closely at specific issues of privacy, surveillance and policing cyberspace. Charles Raab commences by addressing the question: can 'cyberspace' promote democracy? If so, he asks, can it preserve privacy to the same extent as more conventional democratic processes have done? Must the informational openness of democracy and the individual's or group's need to control the flow of personal data be seen, as is customary, as zero-sum alternatives that may (or may not) be 'balanced', or are there sufficient grounds for thinking that they can support each other, as many democratic theorists assert, albeit in conditions of 'informatisation' that were unforeseen by the theory of democracy?

Dorothy Denning provides a thorough analysis of the role of encryption in the debate about regulating the Internet and Puay Tang addresses the problems that electronic information services and products pose for copyright. The final chapter, by Mike Whine, asserts that since the neo-Nazi Far Right has targeted the Internet as the communications medium of the future, it makes it difficult to see such usage as an acceptable cost in return for free speech in cyberspace.

CONCLUDING REMARK

The transforming qualities of ICTs are rapidly altering the political composition of our planet and posing fundamental questions for governance in the next millennium. A primary aim of this collection has been to attempt to clarify the nature of such change and foster participation in what the authors regard as a fundamental debate about liberty, identity, privacy, democracy and surveillance in the 'information polity' (Taylor and Williams, 1991). As is often the case, the extent to which we have been successful will be evidenced by the level of discourse which we hope will follow.

NOTES

1 Attributed to John P. Barlow in Rheingold's *The Virtual Community* (1994: 75).
2 Together with Mitch Kapor and others Barlow established the Electronic Frontier Foundation (EFF).
3 See Howard Rheingold's *The Virtual Community* (1994) for a more detailed exposition of the WELL and social interaction in cyberspace.

Part I

Theorising cyberspace

Chapter 2

Cyberspace sociality
Controversies over computer-mediated relationships

David Lyon

INTRODUCTION

The advent of the Internet helps to focus a question that has been asked for over a decade: what do computer-mediated communications (CMCs) mean for social relationships? Answers may be offered in a highly contentious form, as in: 'the Internet portends new kinds of networks and a transformation of society as we know it.' There is no shortage of such extravagant claims, especially in the pages of those magazines that aim to sell new equipment and software. Nor is there any shortage of those who believe such a transformation is taking place and who exhibit what Kroker and Weinstein whimsically call the 'will to virtuality' (1994: 163).

More soberly, but no less interestingly, the question may be asked in sociological terms: 'What happens to social relationships when other factors – economic, political, religious, technological – undergo change? In nineteenth-century Europe and North America, where the modern nation-state was emerging, and where market-oriented economies and the growth of cities seemed to reshape social relations, many sociologists noted (what they read as) a shift away from face-to-face communities. In the later twentieth century, the context of the so-called advanced societies is one of rapid technological change, involving information and communication technologies (ICTs) above all, which in turn are implicated in economic and political restructuring on a global level. In this context some, like Howard Rheingold (1993), foresee a re-emergence of community, compensating for past losses.

To ask the question about new ICTs and social relationships

sociologically, then, is to focus on the kinds of relations that obtain in different settings. At first glance, so far from fostering community, CMCs might seem to contribute to further remoteness of contact and the proliferation of indirect relations. Indeed, some early research on CMCs gave the impression that they were simply a 'socially impaired' medium (see Baym, 1995: 140). Beyond this, however, CMCs raise other kinds of questions. For one thing, self-identity, taken for granted in earlier sociological accounts, is now in question. Some suggest that self-identity is becoming mutable, indistinct. The so-called data image circulating within surveillance systems or the personae involved in Multi-User Dimensions (MUDs) are not easily correlated with the modern 'self' that participated in 'society'.

The upshot of this is that more than one sociological account of CMCs is available. The rise of CMCs challenges sociology to explain its implications for social relationships conventionally understood, that is, within a modern framework of assumptions. This is the first account. But CMCs also contribute to the questioning of those very assumptions. ICTs are chronically bound up with the (contested) condition of *post*modernity, and thus the very language of 'self' or 'society' that once served sociology no longer seems adequate. This second account of CMCs relates to current debates over discourse, human–machine relations, and how humans represent the world to themselves (for example, Harvey, 1989; Poster, 1995a).

In what follows these two accounts are described and discussed with a view both to assessing their adequacy and to exposing the assumptions woven through them. Can they be considered in any way as compatible or complementary, or are they simply competing accounts between which a choice must be made? Such questions are crucial, both for understanding the social aspects of ICTs and for reframing sociology in the era of cyberspace.

MODERNITY, TECHNOLOGY AND SOCIAL RELATIONS

In a sense, modernity is all about the stretching of social relationships. Writing, print and new modes of transport and communications are the technologies that enabled the corporation, the bureaucracy, the nation-state and now the globalised world. Relationships were stretched in time – the office filing cabinet, for example, holds histories together in folders – and in space – the telegraph and telephone facilitated administration and business links over broad territories.

But not all relationships exhibit the same qualities. This stretching process was frequently read as loss, especially 'loss of community'. A shift was taking place, argued Ferdinand Tönnies, from societies characterised primarily by community (*Gemeinschaft*) type relationships of kinship and face-to-face contact, to more associational (*Gesellschaft*) relations where contracts, and tokens such as money, held people together. Though illuminating in some important ways, such analysis also had its limits. For one thing, it tended to exaggerate the differences between traditional and modern societies such that, for example, the persistence of community became a puzzle to be explained. It also tended implicitly to foreclose the question of what other sorts of relationships might develop as modernisation continued.

Theorists such as Émile Durkheim saw these shifts less negatively. He posited a new organic solidarity forming within industrial society that would eventually replace its earlier 'mechanical' counterparts. Despite this, it is fair to say that the strongest sense gained from classical sociology is that modernisation spelled a regrettable loss of community. More recently, this thesis has been questioned on several scores. Craig Calhoun argues, for example, that direct, face-to-face relations, though they may not predominate, certainly do not disappear. Rather, they tend to become compartmentalised, and thus alter their sociological significance (Calhoun, 1992: 208). Moreover, people involved in such relationships may use the very means of communication that support indirect relations, most obviously, the telephone, but now also CMCs, in order to maintain the quality of their direct relationships.

The language of 'community-lost' reappears perennially, but, more recently, globalisation has lent weight to the 'stretching' metaphor in the last few decades of the twentieth century. Popular concepts such as Marshall McLuhan's 'global village' help to capture the sense of stretching, especially in its spatial aspects. Others, such as Harold Innis's 'time-binding' and 'space-binding' technologies (1964), Anthony Giddens's 'time–space distanciation' (1985) or David Harvey's 'time–space compression' (1989), do so more sociologically. Each tries in different ways to grasp theoretically the massive expansion of indirect relationships technologically enabled above all by new ICTs.

Craig Calhoun (1992) offers a set of ideal types that classify these relationships in order to demonstrate just how far-reaching are the alterations that have characterised modernity. He argues that contemporary conditions require some further sociological sophistication in considering indirect relations. If primary relations are thought of as direct, face-to-face and typical of traditional and early modern societies, then the prevalence of secondary, indirect ones may be thought of as constitutive of modern societies. But, he continues, today both 'tertiary' and even 'quaternary' relationships are also evident as emergent types of indirect relation.

'Tertiary relations need involve no physical copresence,' he suggests, ' . . . they may be mediated entirely by machines, correspondence or other persons, but the parties are well aware of the relationship' (1992: 218). Calhoun has in mind contacts such as those of customers with personnel in a remote bank headquarters, or voters with their political representatives. Mutual recognition and intention exist, in principle, as does the possibility of identification. Active, rational subjects are clearly involved within these relationships even though the physical body of the other may be permanently absent.

What, then, of 'quaternary' relationships? These contrast with all the other types in that they occur beyond the attention and awareness of at least one party. They are, says Calhoun, 'the products of surveillance and exist wherever a sociotechnical system allows the monitoring of people's actions and turns these actions into communications, regardless of the actors' intentions' (1992: 219). Obvious cases of listening in to a cellular telephone call or hacking into a computer database must now be placed alongside the routine use of personal data for purposes other than that for which it was collected. Details gleaned from warranty forms and incorporated into marketing databases that then show up as junk mail would be a case in point (Lyon, 1994b). Such relationships are indirect and generally invisible, but not insignificant.

Calhoun's argument about the extension of social integration to a larger scale is mobilised against those theorists – especially of 'post-industrialism' – who suggest that the advent of new

ICTs marks a break with modernity. Due to the new interaction between the global and the local, issues such as ICT and social–political control become crucial, he asserts, but this still does not amount to a qualitative shift of power or social formation. Concrete social relationships, he maintains, should be analysed at the level of both the life-world and large-scale international organisation. This is essential, he says, 'even if they are based on relationships over which participants have little control, of which they may not even be aware, and the results of which they may tend to reify' (1992: 232).

Quaterniary relationships, for Calhoun, are seen primarily in surveillance situations. His analysis does not touch upon other examples of relationships which seem to have similar characteristics, enabled by the same ICTs. On the Internet, for instance, relationships are found not unlike those produced by surveillance. These are discussed in the next section. Calhoun's complaints against post-industrialism being viewed as a break with modernity are justified, on the level that he makes them. But by extending his earlier comments on how participants may identify each other to the analysis of what is now called cyberspace, the broader argument about continuity is challenged in new ways.

POSTMODERNITY, VIRTUAL COMMUNITY AND THE TECHNOSOCIAL SPHERE

Cyberspace evokes the sense of being 'wrapped in media' (Gibson, 1984). The term provides a useful shorthand for social experiences in an era of electronic communication. Whereas other communication technologies have, at least after their initial novelty, become 'normal' add-on devices to ease or enhance human contact, CMCs seem in some senses to engage human and machine more directly. The telephone, for instance, simply extended human capacities to converse over distances, whereas CMCs, especially in their emerging multimedia forms, increasingly oblige some users to pause and reconsider the 'reality' of their experiences. Hence the need to distinguish 'real time' from the asynchronous world of, say, email or computer conferences, or 'virtual reality' from the bodily experiences of physical space. The term 'cyberspace' itself hints at a 'space' being created where previously none existed.

The significance of cyberspace arises from the convergence and interactivity of media. Whereas a crucial development in modern ICTs was the separation of transport and communication – the coming of the telegraph meant that messages no longer had to be carried personally – cyberspace seems to take this a stage further. Certain environments and experiences can already be shared without physical presence. The crude harbingers of this may be seen in telepresence, in which workers can see each other and work 'together' despite geographical remoteness. Televirtuality is the stage at which the settings themselves become 'virtual' and where participants interact in computer-generated environments. Hence the appropriateness of Gibson's fictional description of such participants being 'wrapped in media'.

The phenomena associated with virtuality in cyberspace have stimulated debates well beyond the pages of 'fiction' as to whether the converging, interactive electronic technologies can still be discussed within conventional sociological terms. The contributors to a volume on *CyberSociety* (Jones, 1995b) approach the matter by testing the limits of existing social theory. They note, for example, the difficulties of establishing identities in some cyberspace settings, where anonymity or the lack of clear, single authorship is increasingly common. This may be perceived negatively, as in Eudora, an early email software that allowed 'impersonation' by using other's addresses, and which was modified to prevent abuse. Or alternatively, the chance to exploit opportunities for exploring new 'selves' may be welcomed by those who value anonymity and who wish to play in a world of ephemeral personae. Either way, the stable self, construed as central to social relationships in most modern sociology, is now in question.

This becomes abundantly clear in the case of MUDs, or Multi-User Dimensions. In MUDs, users create what are in effect virtual environments, which, though text-based, are not quite like speech or writing. Though participants may share nothing more than access to a common computer system, authors in the *CyberSociety* collection insist that the 'social realities' created in MUDs may properly be thought of as 'communities' (for instance, Baym, 1995: 161). Yet at the same time, such 'communities' appear to be somewhat self-referential. As Elizabeth Reid notes, MUD webs of communication 'are substitutes for and yet distinct from the networks of meaning in the wider community'. Yet they bind 'users into a common culture whose specialised meanings allow the sharing of imagined realities' (Reid, 1995: 183).

Jones rightly notes that such 'new social formations may require new forms of inquiry' (1995a: 7). And he quotes James Carey, to the effect that 'a sociology of border crossing, of migration across the semipermeable membranes of social life', may be called for (Carey, 1993: 179). Such border crossing is accomplished in the *CyberSociety* book but it is most usually done – effectively – through conventional techniques of participant observation and other forms of ethnography. Connections with 'postmodern' discourses are made: Ted Friedman, for instance, sees computer simulations as providing 'a radically new quasi-narrative form through which to communicate structures of interconnection' following the failure of language to hold together postmodern subjectivity (1995: 86). But in the main, these are detailed surveys of relatively uncharted cultural terrain. Mark Poster, on the other hand, thinks he has found at least sketches for the map.

In contrast with most of the approaches of the *CyberSociety* authors, Poster (1995a) argues directly that a 'second media age' is intimated by the interactive and converging multi- and hyper-media of cyberspace. While avoiding the error of seeing technological prototype as future workplace and domestic 'necessity', his thesis depends heavily on the assumption that the 'broadcast model' of communication cannot last long in an era of electronic media that allow for *many* producers, distributors and consumers. His work continues the line of thought begun in *The Mode of Information* and also expressed in his sympathetic critique of poststructuralism (Poster, 1989, 1990).

Central to Poster's argument is the idea that subjects are constituted differently in modern and postmodern contexts. Whereas in print culture the author – literally – had authority, and the reader a capacity to criticise, these fixed points are blurred in electronic communication. The distance between communicating partners accentuates certain features of language. Such partners, though remote, are brought together through various kinds of 'interfaces'. Language, so far from representing reality, now serves to reconfigure it. This in turn has huge implications for the nature of social relations in cyberspace.

Poster's work also finds a single theoretical means of grasping

what has, until now, been separate in this paper – the participants, or personae, of cyberspace 'communities' such as MUDs,
and the data images circulating within surveillance systems. In
both cases, Poster argues, subjects are being constituted within
the mode of information, the second media age. Through an
analysis of CMCs in the light of work by Jacques Derrida, Michel
Foucault and Jean Baudrillard, Poster suggests that electronic
culture actually promotes theories (especially poststructuralism)
'that focus on the role of language in the process of the constitution of subjects' (1995a: 59). This underlies how the social realm
should be understood in the second media age.

Gone, in this account, is the centred, rational, autonomous
individual of modern times. But it is not surprising that this individual should have dominated modern social theory. Classical
sociologists of modernity, observing the market economy and
the growth of bureaucracies, missed the communicative aspects
of social life, says Poster, and in so doing diverted attention from
what is now central. Though theorists such as Karl Marx and
Max Weber made great contributions, they focused on action and
institutions, not language. Trapped as they were in the world of
print culture, they could only show how the rational individual
might be liberated through class struggle or how instrumental
rationality was making social organisations one-dimensional,
lacking spirit.

In place of the modern, rational individual, suggests Poster, is
a subject that is 'multiplied, disseminated and decentred, contin-
uously interpellated as an unstable identity' (1995a: 57), and this
subject is seen *par excellence* in CMCs. Getting away from the
notions that rationality is the final ground of human experience
and that authority is reality defined by the author has social and
cultural implications of some consequence. Electronic communication may encourage participation by and protest from those
excluded and marginalised by modern rationality and authority,
thus presenting challenges to modern social institutions. This
emerging social order could then be thought of as 'a social form
beyond the modern, the possibility of a postmodern society'
(1995a: 59).

If this were indeed so, then numerous further questions might
be raised, regarding democratic involvement, the governance of
and resistance within cyberspace, along with manners and social
ethics. Nagging questions remain, however. The emerging 'post-

modern society' may well display features that distinguish it qualitatively from the familiar world of modernity. But it is not clear how resistance, for example, even if it becomes 'immanent critique', as in Kroker's work, could operate without the involvement of something equally familiar, namely, the intending agent. Empowerment would depend on agents' ability to use highly rational communication formats, not to mention their access to them, and, via them, to others who might be appropriately influenced. Electronic resistance to date has entailed just such aspects (Lyon and Zureik, 1996).

So how does Poster's analysis bring together the personae of cyberspace and the data images of surveillance? On the one hand, the virtual communities of cyberspace are populated by subjects constantly in process of constituting themselves, for example, in MUDs. This, the fastest-growing aspect of the Internet, is easily misunderstood, warns Poster, if the real/virtual distinction is strongly maintained. Such communities may well be formed in novel ways but they are not somehow 'unreal' because of that. What makes a community 'vital to its members is their treatment of the communications as meaningful and important' (1995a: 36). The real/virtual distinction turns out, in this account, to be a further – regrettable – instance of the binary oppositions typical of modernity, and which show up in first media age logic as sender/receiver, ruler/ruled, and so on. Dispose of the equation 'real equals fixed, stable identities' and one enters the logic of the second media age.

On the other hand, consider data images, digitised personal traces, dispersed through surveillance spaces, but triggered by 'real-world' transactions such as telephone calls, credit card purchases or health insurance claims. Once again, subjects are constituted, this time in the 'discourses' of databases. In this case, as noted by Calhoun, the process takes place partly beyond the conscious action of those whose data has been garnered, but this is just what makes the process amenable to a Foucauldian analysis of discourses, to which Poster treats it. Thus when personal data are specified in a classificatory grid – such as those used by taxation departments or marketing companies – subjects are being 'interpellated' or 'hailed' in a particular way. The grid, seen as a kind of electronic language, constitutes subjects by interpellation, but they remain, as do other CMCs subjects, 'unstable, excessive, multiple' (Calhoun, 1992: 79).

In these surveillance spaces, created to track anyone from criminals to hairspray purchasers to those who fail to return library books, new social identities appear, constituting individuals as social agents. Poster takes issue with those who see emancipation in terms of resisting the power of capitalist organisations that subordinate the weak through surveillance, of protesting privacy invasions from governments, or even of putting databases in the hands of the people. All these assume the 'autonomous individuals' of modernity. Rather, in the mode of information, strategies of resistance have to be sought in counter-definitions of individuals. Likewise, if 'community' be sought it should 'resist nostalgia' for 'face-to-face intimacy', taking into account these new modes of identity and communication.

Various analysts and theorists of CMCs, then, express some frustration with the apparent limits of conventional sociology for understanding the social relations of cyberspace. In focusing on issues of virtuality/reality, and pleading for fresh ways of grasping who 'selves' and the 'social' might be, contributors to the *CyberSociety* volume point up some issues unexplored by Calhoun. But none makes the direct claims about a 'second media age', best understood poststructurally, that Poster does.

Assuming rational, autonomous social agents, Calhoun's analysis doubts that a break with modern conditions can seriously be countenanced. Pondering the experiences of those agents in actual CMCs situations, Jones and his colleagues are much less sure that continuity is so obvious. By altering the mode of analysis to one that engages with discourse and language, Poster not only looks for a break, but finds it, between the first and the second media age.

COMPLEMENTARY OR COMPETING PERSPECTIVES ON CYBERSPACE SOCIALITY?

The sociology of cyberspace raises some crucial questions, not only about the emergence of new forms of community and sociality, but also of how these are best understood. The forms of social interaction observable within CMCs, especially on the Internet, appear to push social theory beyond the simple dichotomy of direct and indirect relationships – hence Calhoun's further subcategories of tertiary and quaternary – but also beyond the scope of modern notions of self and society. The debate on real versus virtual reality of cyberspace communities will no doubt continue for some time, as will that on the kinds of power and resistance within CMCs. That cyberspace challenges time-honoured notions of social reality is not in doubt, and to that extent media of Poster's 'second age' are implicated in reality transformation.

So what is the relationship between the modern and the post-modern account of cyberspace sociality? Is one being displaced by the other within a broader social scientific revolution, or can they offer different angles on the same phenomena, such that cyberspace is better understood by combining the two perspectives? For Calhoun, who is dubious about the salience of terms like modernity and post-industrialism, let alone postmodernity, the answer seems clear. Conventional sociological analysis will suffice. For Jones, serious difficulties confront the sociologist trying to encapsulate cyberspace 'realities' within existing conceptual and theoretical frameworks. For Poster, while he acknowledges that other views have much to offer, he hints strongly that abandoning them for poststructuralist accounts has more.

One difficulty here, then, is that it is hard to separate the social and cultural phenomena under discussion from debates over acceptable theory. While Calhoun is a reluctant sociologist of 'modernity', Jones and Poster are caught between a sociology of postmodernity and a postmodern sociology (see Bauman, 1992: chap. 4). Jones and his collaborators seek sociologically to describe and explain processes and relationships of emergent 'cybersociety', including some features that might be described as 'postmodern'. Poster, on the other hand, not only analyses 'postmodern' phenomena, but he does so taking a self-consciously 'postmodern' stance. For him, classical sociological theorists of modernity were trapped within the outlook of the 'first media age' and so the contemporary challenge is to find new conceptual frameworks equal to the task of understanding the new configuration. Thus the debate over the social transformations associated with new electronic media is also a debate over transformations of the social.

Seen this way, certain issues stand out. In relation to cyberspace sociality, they may be considered under the headings of the technosocial subject and the reality of the social. But because they hang in tension between modern and postmodern discourses, much more is at stake than is the case with some other sociological disputes. As we have seen, at least two assumptions of modern social theories – rational, acting subjects, and the universality of some basic features of social relationships – are called into radical question. Does the apparent blurring of the distinction between human and machine, and the ephemeral, mutable character of virtual communities, spell the end of meaningful action, once central to most mainstream sociological theories?

This is not the place to try to provide an answer, although I shall close with a couple of observations on the matter. The point is that the debate over cyberspace and postmodern conditions is more radically reflexive than some earlier debates about an appropriate sociology of the present. Virtual communities are appearing at just that juncture when universality and essentialism are locally if not widely in doubt, and when the notion that local discourses are the only grounds remaining for understanding identities or forming moral critique. When virtual communities are justified in terms of the meaningfulness to participants of their communications, they appear to confirm further the positions already taken by self-referential local discourses of ethnicity, region, gender or sexuality. That is, dominant forces of colonial, patriarchal, capitalist or other forms of domination have excluded those at the margins for too long, and opportunities at last appear, not for new 'metanarratives' but for equality between multiple narratives (see, for example, Vattimo, 1992).

The question of a sociology of cyberspace is part of a much larger debate. Without mentioning cyberspace, for instance, Steven Seidman discusses the shift in social theory from fixed accounts of self and agency, to what he advocates, namely, 'conceiving of the self as having multiple and contradictory identities, community affiliations, and social interests' (1992: 133). Cyberspace becomes a further vehicle for just such debates. Within this process are both potential gains and potential losses. The limitations of earlier social theory, not only of fixed views of agency and identity, but also of matters discussed above, the relative neglect of time, space and the role of communications in stretching of social relationships, are brought more clearly into view. But the potential disadvantage of the debates, as construed at present, is that in the haste to abandon previous positions, some aspects of modern accounts may be neglected.

The technosocial self that appears in the above account as a digital persona or as a data image serves to highlight some significant questions in contemporary social theory. The self as a project to be constructed, rather than a psychological given, is one aspect of this. Self-identity is being construed in fresh ways (see Giddens, 1991) and this helps social theory break free from the fixity of previous construals. In cyberspace opportunities abound for such self-construction, which accelerate the process from that seen, for instance, in consumption. At the same time, the process of self-construction cannot be seen in an asocial or an a-technological vacuum.

Several reasons for this may be adduced. One is that CMCs have some specific empirical referents. Although not much reliable data are available on Internet use, indications are that the majority of users are operating within rather conventional modern, rational frames, in university research, business corporations, and the like. Among domestic users, higher income homes in large urban areas tend to have the highest density of computers, which again suggests particular kinds of uses.

Many CMCs are highly institutionalised for specific instrumental transactions between agencies and the 'populations' they construct, whether for marketing, distance-education, computer-supported co-operative work or welfare benefits. In contrast with our relative ignorance about digital personae of fantasy worlds, we know that these identity categories *are* highly influential (see, for example, Gandy, 1993). Moreover, the discursive features of 'quaternary' relations may interact with the bureaucratic (or other modern) features of 'tertiary' ones, for instance in CMCs-oriented workplaces where *both* data images *and* physical presences are available (see Clarke, 1994).

A second, more theoretical argument is that the self also takes on new relations to the body. Modernity often depicted the body (anatomically defined) as the shell housing the self. The postmodern turn – especially assisted by feminism – reconnects body and self, bringing them into closer unity (see Haraway, 1990). At the same time, if the boundaries of the body blur as the 'machine' and the 'human' interact more profoundly and intimately, then the self has to be thought of in more 'technosocial' terms. Rationality and action may not define the self, as in some modern social theoretical accounts, although it would be hard to do sociology with no reference at all to these (albeit contested) categories.

Which brings me, lastly, back to the reality of the social. As I have indicated, it is no mere coincidence that debates over cyberspace sociality and about postmodern shifts in social theory are being pursued at the same time. They are implicated in each other. Issues concerning 'local discourses' and 'neo-tribalism' simply find further instances in the virtual communities of cyberspace, although they may have some special features, as noted above. This will become a fascinating and important site for sociological investigation. One might be forgiven for thinking that virtual communities, with their self-referentiality and, sometimes, their self-absorption, could be highly vulnerable to political manipulation; a classic Marxian opiate (Woolley, 1992). On the other hand, certain kinds of virtual communities might become highly effective agencies of political resistance, as has already been demonstrated in cases of protest against environmental or surveillance abuse.

Whatever the eventual trajectory of virtual communities, the extent to which they are able to be consequential will depend on how subjectivity and meaning are understood and mobilised within them. And if they are to be politically consequential, questions of access, participation and co-ordination would also have to be addressed. The shift from a centred subject or from predominant rationality does not have to lead to a vanishing or irrational subject. Poster, for example, does not want to jettison the notion that human beings can make a difference and alter their situations. But the world of cyberspace may militate against recognising reasons for doing so.

While it is likely that instrumental and utilitarian meanings are as prevalent as ever within many CMCs, it is more difficult to imagine how larger frames of meaning – which might catalyse resistance for example – would not tend to drain out of increasingly remote relations, especially those mediated by computer languages and interfaces (Steiner, 1991: 230). Kroker, following Jean Baudrillard, thinks that critique is still possible from within, by embracing technoculture, but it is not clear to me how this would work without *some* broader narrative to inform it. Postmodern theorists are of course supposed to be incredulous towards such broader narratives. My question is: can a social world exist without them?

Lastly, then, one might ask whether the category 'social' does not require some 'subject', some 'self', (technosocial or otherwise) to be involved. Even cyberspace sociality seems to need some notion of participation between those who recognise each other's identities. As Scott Lash and James Urry observe, postmodern discourses are often guilty of infinitely deferring meaning. But they argue that within new electronic networks, communities of shared *meanings*, rather than just those of shared interests or properties, may be available (Lash and Urry, 1994: 168). Surely, unless a self is free enough to recognise another – the other – it makes little sense to speak of community, at least one of shared supra-instrumental meanings. This, I grant, is to refer to a particular narrative in which to locate and critique cyberspace sociality. But without such a narrative, I suggest, neither sociology nor, for that matter, ethics is possible.

For the present, I propose that neither the modern nor the postmodern accounts of cyberspace sociality simply be discarded, despite what some see as the straightforward incompatibility between them. Each has important insights to offer; each has serious flaws and shortcomings, at least as I have expounded them. The reason for retaining some aspects of each, however, is not a mere pragmatic eclecticism but rather a conviction that each is at best (and again, despite their frequent pretensions to adequacy) a very partial picture. Moreover, those working within the two frameworks would do well to communicate with each other. Though the modern is, palpably, still very much in evidence, it is at the very least tinged with the postmodern, in ways that invite systematic analysis.

At the same time, each perspective contains important elements that could be yoked with a larger narrative, one whose ontology of the social is bound up with its ethic, and yet is not tied to either modern or postmodern categories. In this story, communities involve shared meanings between participants – subjects – who recognise each other's identities, and, indeed, recognise that each has claims on the other. If cyberspace sociality can illuminate this matter, either by contrast or by example, exploring what it means to be 'wrapped in media' will be worthwhile.

Chapter 3

Virtual culture, urban social polarisation and social science fiction

Roger Burrows

In our hyper-aestheticised world it is perhaps no surprise that we are increasingly coming to know ourselves through ideal types derived not through analytic social science but through the discourses of social science fiction. In this brief chapter I attempt to frame contemporary issues of urban governance through the genre of cyberpunk, the literary concomitant of much of cyberculture. My contention (Burrows, 1996), although certainly not an original one (Kellner, 1995), is that with the demise of the meta-narrative many of the themes and processes which a symptomatic reading of cyberpunk reveal are a good deal more insightful than are those offered by what now passes for the theoretical and empirical mainstream (Hamnett, 1994; Mollenkopf and Castells, 1991; Sassen, 1991).

For the most part the literature on cyberculture invokes the development of a world in which two societies co-exist. As Virilio views it: 'One is a society of "cocoons" . . . where people hide away at home, linked into communication networks, inert . . . . The other is a society of the ultra-crowded megalopolis and of urban nomadism' (1993: 75). Davis concurs with this dualist conceptualisation, for him the world of cyberspace is another urban environment, 'a simulation of the city's information order' in which the 'city redoubles itself through the complex architecture of its information and media networks' (1992: 16). This urban dualism between cyberspace and the world we live in (Robins, 1996) is, of course, overlaid by another, which, as Davis indicates, is not completely unconnected. It is a dualism invoked by a process of what some would want to call 'Brazilianisation' (Featherstone, 1995: 9) – a process within which the new cultural syncretism is allied to a radical rezoning of cities which is resulting in a new juxtaposition between the new rich and the new poor.

There is now an extensive corpus of material which attempts to theorise these processes of urban social polarisation. Most are premised upon the notion that with the hyper-globalisation of capitalism a new global class emerges with little or no particular national geographic fixity. They reside in various global cities at the most concentrated points of money capital and are serviced by the 'gamut of financial, administrative and professional services that lubricate the money flow' (Smith and Williams, 1986: 211). This concentration of global actors in various world cities has more often than not been accompanied by dramatic deindustrialisation and high levels of migration. Consequently global cities are becoming dual cities. And images of dual cities provide us with the current cultural dominant of late modern urban life. It is these images, as exemplified by the genre of cyberpunk, that I want to examine here as prospective sources of analytic inspiration.

Now, of course, some might object to cities such as Los Angeles and São Paulo being treated as paradigmatic of contemporary urban development more generally; and of course no one would deny that they do possess their own specificities. Nevertheless even in what Byrne calls 'old, clapped out, industrial cities' (1994: 138) similar dynamics are operating which it is important to typify. Not least because in the United Kingdom nearly half of the population live in such places (Dorling and Tomaney, 1995). It is then more than a coincidence that in the cinematic representation of the dual city *par excellence* – *Blade Runner* – the Los Angeles of the near future looks strangely like Teesside.[1]

I have argued elsewhere (Burrows, 1996) that the most vivid depictions of this dualism are currently found not within the social sciences but within the fictional world of cyberpunk, paradigmatically in the novels of William Gibson, but probably most convincingly in Stephenson's *Snow Crash* (1992). The most productive use of this imaginal resource has been in the recent work of Mike Davis, which has a highly recursive relationship with the cyberpunk genre.[2] The fictional and the analytic are now very difficult to disentangle in the work of Davis and Gibson. For example, *Virtual Light* (Gibson, 1993) is a book profoundly and explicitly influenced by Davis's seminal *City of*

Quartz (1990), which is itself adorned with a quote from Gibson which suggests it, as a work of contemporary analysis, is more 'cyberpunk' than his own fiction (Bukatman, 1993: 144). This recursivity continues in Davis (1992), where an attempt is made to construct a 'Gibsonian' map of the contemporary urban condition, a map instantly recognisable in *Virtual Light* and, in a more extreme form in Stephenson's *Snow Crash*. Even more recently Gibson has turned his attention to 'journalism' and has begun to write about contemporary urbanism, especially Singapore, in a manner highly reminiscent of Davis. So what does the city look like in cyberpunk and what kind of analytic handle can it provide for those of us in the social sciences concerned with issues of governance?

Perhaps the best way to answer this question is to take Davis's Gibsonian map of the contemporary urban condition as our analytic foil and use it to interrogate some of the contemporary debates about social polarisation, virtuality and the *fin de millennium* anxiety which seems to be dominating not just contemporary urban studies but social life more generally (Pahl, 1995).

Whether William Gibson intends it or not (Gibson, 1991), his work can be treated as 'prefigurative social theory, as well as an anticipatory opposition politics to the cyber-fascism lurking over the next horizon' (Davis, 1992: 3; see also Kroker and Weinstein, 1994). Davis reads Gibson as offering a transformation of 'the most famous diagram in social science', the 'combination of half-moon and dart board' constructed by Burgess in order to understand the human ecology of the city of Chicago. Burgess's dart board represented five urban concentric zones within which a supposed Darwinistic struggle for survival of the fittest shifted and sorted social and housing classes. Davis updates and redraws this diagram by shifting his paradigmatic case from Chicago to Los Angeles and by replacing the essentially modernist dynamic of the capitalist market as a sorting mechanism with the plural postmodernist imperatives of late capitalism within which fear, rapid technological change and cultural complexity supplement the operations of the market. The resulting remapping provides the boldest attempt I have come across to understand the current trajectories of contemporary urban life. With its radical juxtaposing of processes of profound social polarisation with the emergence of various forms of virtual life it provides a chilling image with which we can begin to make

sense of the major issues confronting the contemporary governance of social life.

Davis is clear that with or without postmodern culture it is
factors such as income, land values, class and race which still
underpin human ecology. However, the ecology of fear and ever
more rapid technological change has now been added to this
already virulent processual brew.

At the heart of the Davis/Gibson image of the contemporary
city is still the 'bullseye' of 'downtown'. However, it is a city centre which is increasingly privatised as capital encroaches ever
more deeply into what was previously public space. It is a centre
within which technology, both old and new, controls who has
access. Walkways are removed, foot traffic is elevated and points
of access secured and regulated at specific points so that the area
can be quickly closed off if necessary. Video surveillance
becomes routine as all movements are monitored. The city centre
becomes a 'scanscape' subject to 'mall-*ification*' – the process by
which public streets and squares are covered, enclosed and privatised and new (virtual?) malls[3] created, access to which can be
regulated by new private agents of social control. Access to the
commercial and financial built environment which dominates
the city centre involves yet more processes of closure, partitioning and exclusion. Buildings themselves become increasingly
sentient as computerised systems of recognition include the new
rich and exclude the new poor. The new apartheid becomes very
much a technological matter as the homeless and the poor are
channelled away from the air-conditioned virtual environments
of the great middle mass of the population. The city centre
becomes a homelessness exclusion zone as the most extreme elements of the residual populations created by post-Fordist
regimes of accumulation are channelled out of the central zone:
out of sight and out of mind.

This process of technological exclusion creates a halo of
deprived communities around city centres increasingly 'regulated' and 'governed' by what Hoggett (1994) has termed 'remote
control'. This is a zone dominated by 'imploding' or 'collapsed'
communities within which the criminality and violence associated with the drugs economy operates as a form of regulation. The
technological 'cordon sanitaire' around such zones functions to
contain such communities and brings with it a perverse form of
self-governance. As street gangs and slumlords struggle with

each other, the formal agents of social control monitor and record the situation but only on occasion do they intervene (Campbell, 1993). Such a regime of remote control spills ever outwards away from the city centre into ever more 'respectable' districts. This leads residents in such 'zones of transition' to respond to the first signs of discarded syringes with various strategies of closure or 'spatial modes of discipline'. Cutting across the dart board we thus see developing various social control districts based upon principles such as abatement, containment and exclusion. These various attempts to resist the outward spread of community collapse gradually begins to solidify into a new zone where the principles of neighbourhood watch and other forms of surveillance backed up with both public and private agencies of social control 'protect' those members of (what used to be) the 'respectable' working classes.

The population who live in this zone still maintain a position within the formal economy, albeit one which is increasingly subject to the forces of 'flexibilisation' (part-time, temporary and contract work, casualisation and self-employment). In large part this group occupies the more marginal end of owner occupation and as such faces the constant threat of arrears, debt and mortgage possession and thus the fear that they might soon be subject to the form of community collapse which exists just a few blocks away. This group also occupy an important buffer zone between the remotely controlled and technologically partitioned crack zone and the mini-citadels of the middle classes.

The areas where the middle classes live, towards the outer zones of the city and beyond the marginal owner-occupied sectors are, like the city centre, increasingly privatised spaces. In many cases they are becoming cities within cities as clusters of houses literally gate themselves off from the rest of the city proper. They become privatised havens of peace; prisons designed to keep people out rather than keep people in. These are the data-rich zones, gated off from the real world but emphatically engaged with the virtual world of cyberspace. This is where the headlong retreat of the *seduced* into their increasingly fortified technologised privatised worlds away from the increasingly remote and ungovernable spaces occupied by the *repressed*, to use the distinction made by Bauman (1988), is at its most acute.

In their most extreme fictional guise these gated citadels become mini-states unto themselves, self-selecting franchises with privatised welfare defended by the new technologies, private police and high walls topped off with barbed wire (Stephenson, 1992). This is the inexorable result of the supposed logic of minimax class solutions sketched out by Peter Abell in the 1980s (Abell, 1987). Whole sections of society – the overclass – opt out of the mainstream and perform an act of spatial closure, maintaining their link with processes of capital accumulation through the digitised realm of Cyberspace. These, then, are our global actors at the heart of the global city – in it, but not of it.

This process of material and structural urban polarisation is, as already indicated, mirrored by the simulated urban environment which is Cyberspace.[4] Under this description Cyberspace is a digitised parallel world which from 'above' might appear as a rationally planned city (Le Corbusier's metropolis) but from 'below' reveals itself as a Benjaminesque labyrinthine city, in which no one can get the bird's-eye view of the plan, but everyone effectively has to operate at street level with limited knowledge based on different amounts of information about, and practical understanding of how to move around in, a world which is rapidly being restructured and reconfigured. However, the new urban form conceptualised by Davis also contains another sort of non-digitised urban simulation – the theme park.

The city at the cusp of the millennium is a hyperreal city. No longer just the spatial concomitant of processes of collective consumption (who now reads the early Castells?), the contemporary city is the site of artificial spectacles, of non-digitised virtual environments ironically designed to be 'authentic' – more authentic than the shabby, underfunded and more often than not dangerous 'real thing'. The city itself becomes a theme park. As communities collapse, the lonely crowds which remain are fed a diet of hygienic simulated safeness – shopping malls, gift shops, camcorder opportunities, spectacles to gaze upon, prepackaged managed spontaneity and muzak. In such an environment the excluded, the homeless and the poor do not intrude, and when, on occasion they do, they somehow no longer look so 'real' against such a backdrop.

As these twin processes of social polarisation and, what Kroker and Weinstein (1994) have usefully termed 'the will to virtuality', interact to produce this profound remapping of the city, the systems of governance which are developing in response are also beginning to gain some solidity. Clearly one axiom is that of the 'remote control' of zones detached from the formal economy; another axiom is the coupling of surveillance and strategic partitioning for those who venture from such zones; and another is the collective closure operated by the overclass in order both to protect themselves and to gain the advantages afforded by minimax class 'solutions'. What is interesting about the representation of these processes in the cyberpunk genre is the relative absence of the nation-state. Indeed, discussion of the governance of cyberspace is, or so it could be argued, in actuality an implicit device for beginning the task of conceptualising the exhaustion of the nation-state as it is superseded by various supranational cultural and political formations.

The governance of the new social polarisation and the new virtual culture is thus a governance founded upon quite new matrices of power. It is a governance still very much founded upon a logic of capitalism, but one in which the state apparatus is being profoundly altered. In Gibson, but especially in Stephenson, the nation-state is no longer functioning in the interests of collective capital. It has withered to such an extent that it is just another business with little or no legitimacy over and above this. It is certainly no longer the apex of a rational democratic authority of any sort. This seeping away of state power is occurring in three ways. First, the largely contingent spatial divisions between nation-states are dissolving as the new technologies facilitate an ever greater global reach. State power thus seeps upwards towards new global political agents – the multinationals and the new global supranational political formations. Second, power seeps downwards away from national boundaries towards spatially more regionalised zones. Third, and crucially, state power seeps towards individuals – the new global citizens wired up to the Internet who, through the unintended consequences of their actions, are busily forming new patterns of sociality, new virtual communities and thus new bases of power. For the new global citizenry, the inhabitants of the mini-citadels of the globe's major urban centres, the nation-state and other more proximate sources of self-identity are increasingly becoming an irrelevance.

This sketch of virtual culture and the new technologies of urban social polarisation is, of course, overdrawn. But ideal types, by their very nature, always are. They accentuate some aspects of reality and all but ignore other aspects. However, on balance, I think that one gets a clearer analytic understanding of contemporary urban processes from a reading of Gibson and Stephenson than one does from a reading of Sassen or Castells. If this brief chapter does nothing else I hope it encourages a few who have not already done so to (re)read cyberpunk as social and political theory.

NOTES

1 As Byrne points out, however, Ridley Scott did once attend Hartlepool Art School.
2 On the recursive relationship between cyberpunk and social theory more generally, see Kellner (1995).
3 Rojek (1995) suggests that such artificial environments should be labelled as cyberspatial because although they might not be digital or electronic they are still, in a sometimes quite profound sense, virtual.
4 Although see the objection to this city metaphor in the work of McBeath and Webb (1996).

Chapter 4

The neuroscience of cyberspace
New metaphors for the self and its boundaries

Gwyneth Jones

What I see in the mirror doesn't make any more sense. I'm an aquarium filled with assorted fishes I don't even know the names of . . . .
Pat Cadigan, *Fools*[1]

The neurons have tree-like arbors that overlap and ramify in myriad ways. Their signalling is not like that of a computer or a telephone exchange; it is more like the vast aggregate of interactive events in a jungle . . .
Gerald Edelman, *Bright Air, Brilliant Fire*[2]

I am not a scientist, an academic or a Net guru. I am a science fiction writer – inhabitant of the boundary area between our knowledge of the world *out there*, our science and its technologies; and the reports we have from the inner world of subjective experience: ideology, interpretation, metaphor, myth. These spaces interpenetrate each other. It is impossible to say anything about science without using the human language of fiction (there are no equations without metaphors); impossible to construct a fiction that involves no hypothesis about how the world works. Yet they present themselves, in our society, and perhaps in all societies that ever were, as separate systems. My business is with the interface between them. I look for analogues, homologues, convergent evolutions, fractals, coincidences, feedback loops. Like the railway passenger Gnat in Alice, I am a pun-detecting machine. Or else I am a bower-bird, picking up shiny scraps from all aspects of the current state of the world, and arranging them in a way that seems pleasing to me. Look on this chapter as a visit to an artist's studio: specifically to the studio of the science/fiction of cyberspace. Which is to say, a visit to some recent images of the state of consciousness, plucked from science and fiction – images of what it means to be a member of the State of Self.

The generally accepted term for the 'space' in which computer networking happens (a term with an explosion of applications in the early nineties) is *cyberspace*, a word coined as a science fiction. But William Gibson's novel *Neuromancer*, published in 1984, in which 'cyberspace' first emerged, predated the explosion of popular and leisure use that has transformed the Internet and brought terms like 'electronic democracy', 'information super-highway', 'the governance of cyberspace' into public debate. Cyberspace and its entourage (*the Turing Police, neural jacking, simstim entertainment, commercial personality overlays*) were secondary, in William Gibson's near-future thriller, to a classic genre narrative: the creation (or the emergence) of a non-human mind, a self-conscious artificial intelligence.

The dream of creating artificial intelligence (AI) has been around longer than (artificial) computers themselves. But in the post-war era at least, the fiction that this project has inspired obediently follows the real-world science. (As William Gibson himself has pointed out, sf is *rarely* predictive, except by accident). Early computer stories dwelt on size as the sign of power. The thinking machine was a BIG machine. There were rooms of it. It had a city of slaves to tend its circuitry, it dispensed its God-like pronouncements on punched cards that had the majesty of stone tablets. Or else the machine was a fake human, with a positronic brain and cybernetic circuitry (*positron*, name of an exotic subatomic particle, suggesting quantum-level engineering of staggering complexity; the qualifier *cybernetic*, coined from the Greek word for a steersman, indicating control). In either case, the machine intelligence was of a different and a more rarefied kind than that of the human animal. The computer-that-was-God had access to enormous quantities of exactly accurate information, manipulated by error-free calculations for unvarying results. The android with the positronic brain was running on pure logic, unclouded by emotion or appetite.

In the half century since 'real' computers have been functional, the notion of a very successful computer as a Very Big Box has come to seem one of science fiction's most naïve and revealing errors (yes, in this recalcitrantly conservative literature, might generally *is* right). Those rooms full of flashing lights and whirling tapes, the flourishing of slide-rules and the clicking of punchcards in Galactic Central Logic Planning are painful images for the failed prophets to contemplate. The android with the positronic brain has a rather different history. The artificial human (the Golem, Frankenstein's monster) has a place secure in folklore, and in the folklore tropes freely employed by the far-from-pure genre of sf. But the failure of this model *as a science fiction*, from the point of view of the decades between ENIAC and *Neuromancer*, is the error of embodiment. In the real world, computer science and research into artificial intelligence (distinct but overlapping areas) both grew up in the absence of a working knowledge or theory of neuroscience. Not only for historically compelling philosophical and theoretical considerations, but of necessity, ideas about *how thought happens* were developed without experimental access to the only functioning model of this process that the universe provides. Researchers seeking 'the development of a systematic theory of intellectual processes wherever they may be found' (Michie, 1974: 156) took human 'reason' as their starting point, not events in biological tissues. They followed Alan Turing, the founding father of computer science, in envisioning thinking as a set of logical operations – a logic that existed in abstraction, independent of any particular processing device or recording medium. It seemed obvious that the computing analogue for mind was the software: digital code inhabiting tape or cards or memory chips and fed through plastic, metal and silicon, as the human mind was 'fed through' brain structures. Programs, not androids, were devised to beat the 'Turing Test' – as in Alan Turing's speculation that a successful thinking machine would be indistinguishable from a human if you couldn't see whom you were talking to. The successful AI was still seen as a machine version of human intelligence. But it would never be dependent on a 'body' on the upright ape model. Instead it might have a whole wardrobe of 'bodies', suitable for different occasions: one that might feel comfortable in a deep submarine trench, another for work in a hard vacuum.

After the first post-war decades, as it became possible to build much faster, much more complicated number-crunching processors, the complexity of the 'logical operations' underpinning the simplest conscious thought became apparent. There was a growing awareness that so far artificial intelligence, though capable of astonishing feats of arithmetic, was shockingly deficient in common sense. Research began to work backwards – abandoning naked logic and employing robotics, mechanical 'embodiments' (either actual clunky moving automata, or simulations in code) to provide the software entity with the kind of input available to a living animal. Computing became old enough to display an evolutionary past. Miniaturisation of circuitry, mathematical compression of instructions, led to a situation where 'ancient', primitive scraps of computer code – once independent programs in their own right – could live on, replicated in the guts of more complex software organisms, humbly useful as the natural fauna in our own intestines. The new model of the (artificial) mind was of not one program but an array of programs, not an uncondi- tioned logical entity but an organism with a history and various- ly functioning parts: yet still orchestrated by a governing master control, and still separate from nature, *different in kind* from the body.

Neuromancer steps from this point into its imagined future. William Gibson, fusing cognitive science with fashion, computer technology, adolescent behaviour in a games arcade, taking on speculations from anthropology and linguistics (doing the bower-bird riff: what science fiction writers do), conceives of mind as software, as a vast assemblage of programs: and as an escape from the flesh. 'Cyberspace' is what happens when his computer network users, both criminal and legitimate, re-enact Descartes. Plugged in to the matrix of computer code, they are minds receiving input in the form of naked information. They decide by an act of will to perceive this input as a space with objects in it, a world in which they can act: and therefore it is so (Gibson, 1984: 67). In this sophisticated science fiction, the AI that comes to be is not the proud invention of a lonely genius; or even a corporately funded team of geniuses. It has evolved, a side-effect of the complexity of interconnected data processing networks.

Reflecting the provenance of even *one* piece of powerful soft- ware in the real world, it acknowledges no parent. Nor is it wel- come. In Gibson's future self-conscious machine awareness is regarded as a threat. Like the aliens who might invade earth in another favourite science fiction scenario, like the chronological successor species in a stupid version of Darwinism, the new arrival is bound to be a supplanter. But the Turing Police, whose business is to censor (with extreme prejudice!) any computer project that approaches the dangerous threshold, have over-looked the non-intentional, evolutionary route to speciation. Users of the web, biological systems wired directly into the artificial by means of 'neural jacks', have infected the data cloud with consciousness: a flickering, pervasive ignition in the teeming codes.

It is ironic, as several critics have pointed out, that having devised this extremely stylish, up-to-date fictional AI, Gibson's *film noir* plot immediately compels him to incarcerate half of it inside an old-fashioned object:[3] a Maltese Falcon sought and scrabbled over by gangster factions. But this image is true to the spirit of the book. The twin data-entity brothers Neuromancer and Wintermute, who must fuse to become the being that supplants humanity, conform to an ancient dichotomy. One is all reason and logic, the other is emotion and personality. When they become one self, that self conforms to a classic and enduring model of mind. It is a separate, superior entity. It regards itself as a new being, the first born of its kind on earth, and uses the users of the nets as casually as the theoretical AI might its wardrobe of bodies. Like that theoretical AI, it is caught in the trap of infinite regression that has dogged real-world cognitive science. *Who's in charge? I am. Yes, but who's in charge of you?* And so on, indefinitely.

I have to digress here, and talk for a moment about the immune system . . . . This might seem a strange leap, even for a bower-bird, but I believe it is justified. Cybernetics means control, specifically the study of control in systems of communication, in living and non-living entities. Cyberpunk fiction is *ideally* fiction where control of the emergent and highly significant communication systems of the computer age has been awarded to 'punks', to the supposedly helpless and technically illiterate *sous-prole*. Cyberspace is the space where this revolution happens. Control is the problem: and equally control or *intentionality* is the problem for those scientists (and science fiction writers) unsatisfied by the state of affairs where mind is separate from nature. How can we accept a model of the mind that *starts* with logic operations, and provides no bridge between physiology and psychology? How can we accept a State of Self that comes into being with a Ruler already enthroned?

The immune system (to return to the bower-bird riff), a feature shared by humans and other vertebrate animals, is another system of automatic communication where *intentionality* is a puzzle. It was through his early work on the immune system that neuroscientist Gerald Edelman (Director of the Neurosciences Institute at the Scripps Research Institute, La Jolla California) began to question 'the matter of the mind'. Much of what I have to say in this and following passages comes from my reading of Edelman's remarkable exposition of this topic, dazzling speculative science for the non-scientist, *Bright Air, Brilliant Fire* (1992). I emphasise again that I'm only a human bower-bird, ignorantly attracted to shining knowledge of all kinds. My account of Edelman will be a very rough sketch of a small part of his profound and far-ranging study of intelligence. But the 'analogues, homologues, convergent evolutions coincidences and feedback loops' between the development of cyberspace and Edelman's investigations are too alluring to be ignored.

The immune response happens when immune cells recognise non-self, and thereupon are able defend the body from alien invasion. The puzzle, for as long as the system has been studied, has been to decide exactly how this recognition of non-self works. In the beginning, there was the model of *instruction*. Immune cell meets a foreign cell, foreign cell impinges on immune cell, conferring information – whereupon immune cell is able to build a specifically designed antibody: and a diverse array of defences goes into purposeful action. Or so it seemed. But the history of the instruction model, like the history of AI research, is a history of *dis*-organisation. It became difficult, as technology made the biological processes open to investigation, to perceive the immune response as an orchestrated whole, each component fitting by design into a 'central organiser's' plan. In the model now generally accepted, the idea that the system acts purposefully on information received has been abandoned. It transpires that the body produces a vast variety of individual 'immune cells' (that's what *we* call them, it's not necessarily how they see themselves!) carrying all kinds of 'antigens'. When by happenstance one of these individuals binds with a roughly homomorphic invader it is stimulated to divide, and produce daughter cells equally or better matched to the foreigner. An invasion of non-self does not trigger a reaction. It favours, by Darwinian selection, the growth of a population.

It was this shift in perception, the dethroning of purpose, that led Gerald Edelman to propose a schematically similar explanation for the biology of cognition: his Theory of Neuronal Group Selection. Otherwise known as 'Neural Darwinism', TNGS proposes that the human mind is created in this same way: without instruction, without intentional learning, out of the success and failure of competing groups of firing neurons. We know now, from experiment, that the brains of complex organisms including humans are neither *tabula rasa* – silicon blanks to be logic-printed by experience – nor genetically determined. Each individual's neuroanatomy, the pattern of established connections which allows the eye to see, the hand to grasp, is formed after birth, on the substrate of a brain structure defined by hundreds of millions of years of evolution. A baby, for example, 'learns to grasp' in something like this way: every random movement of the baby's hand is echoed, spontaneously, by a pattern of firing neurons in a specific area of the brain, and likewise a pattern of firing is echoed by a matching movement. The 'population' of synaptic firing that produces results favourable for survival – say, the baby succeeds in grasping an object – becomes more likely to happen, because the connections thus formed are strengthened by repetition. Thereafter the beginnings of any sort of grasping movement will trigger this whole pattern. The fingers will complete a successful movement: the baby becomes able to grasp. In time the brain has a wide repertoire of these primary repertoire maps, permanently fixed. No individual child, however, will show exactly the same detailed neuroanatomy, not even identical twins.

What Edelman proposes is that the definitely 'mindless' process whereby the primary repertoire of the brain is formed is sufficient alone, without any transcendent programmer lurking in the brain, to build the whole of the adult human consciousness. Whenever you move your hand, the 'hand' neurons fire. But neurons will also fire in many other associated areas, including the hedonic and limbic structures, where the value systems of the brain reside – the systems that reward behaviour that has adaptive value. The baby grasps something, and *recalls* the sound of a rattle, *recalls* feeling happy: because in the physical structure of her brain, the connection between these phenomena has been inscribed in a pattern of preferentially selected neuronal groups. Every event is a new, individual inscription. No memory 'happens' exactly the same way twice. But as the repertoire of actions and associations increases, complex connections and feedback loops are formed between these global maps of neuronal firings, until purely mental events themselves *recall* the mental events, sensations and associations of the past. Edelman reasons in this way to suggest how 'dumb selection', a favouring of populations without any value system beyond that described by Darwin, can lead from the random firing of neurons to complex ideation: metaphor, concepts, categorisation, reason. Similar input, whether modelled within the brain itself or triggered by interaction with the world, raises a similar set of neuronal maps, layer upon layer . . . . Thus, the taste of a piece of toast dipped in tea can recover the whole of lost time; and bring an individual ecstatically in touch with the process of consciousness.[4]

There is no way for science to demonstrate 'feeling conscious'. The experience is analogous with what the experimental science can now show us about neuroanatomy: *it is individual*. People who ask 'but how do you explain how it feels to be me?' are making the same kind of error (runs Gerald Edelman's caveat) as those who take an interest in cosmology and ask 'but what happened *before* the beginning of everything?' What the theory of Neural Darwinism offers is a plausible mechanism that shows a route from the conditions of matter (brain tissue) without mind, to the kind of complex ideation performed by self-consciousness, in the way the adaptive radiation of Galapagos finches shows a route to the evolution of the human eye.

Stocks in scientific theories can go down as well as up. The particular proposals of Neural Darwinism may be disproved, may even turn out to be of no great significance. The importance of Edelman's work for me, and in the context of this chapter, is that he is a scientist intent on 'putting the mind back into nature', a project as compelling, and as historically inevitable, as was the plan to create bodiless intelligence, fifty years ago. No matter how it may be done, it seems beyond question that the present explosive development of neuroscience will finally dethrone the secret programmer in the human brain, the overseeing mind that is not part of the machine. And this, curiously enough, is just the development we see in the fiction and in the real world of cyberspace, Gibson's proposed substrate for a modern (or postmodern) artificial intelligence.

Science fiction has its own evolution and its own ecology.

Older or variant species of thinking-machine stories are not necessarily, or even generally, pressured out of existence by newly successful adaptions. The cyberspace era has room for synthetic humans as comfortingly inept intellectuals, overtly respected and covertly awarded the comic pathos of the Tin Man in *The Wizard of Oz* (Data in *Star Trek*). The legal status of a software-entity criminal can be debated.[5] AIs can be pets, toys, guardian angels, fairies, folklore monsters. Fully aware biological manufactured humans can be enslaved in their millions.[6] Cyberspace itself, meanwhile, in fiction as in the real world, has been somewhat the victim of its own success. The speed with which that term hit the streets and proliferated shows how hungry we were for a new spatial metaphor: a way of talking about the machine-generated dimensions inside the TV, in the phone network, in the electronic money markets: 'behind' all our monitor screens. Inevitably there's been a dilution of meaning. In a lot of the fiction – books, comics, movies, videos, games – cyberspace has become merely dreamland, the immemorial 'other world' where fantasies happen and magic works. In William Gibson's own subsequent Neuromancer novels the consensual hallucination of the first book, that sparse and chilling Cartesian space, becomes a kind of electronically generated Narnia. This is fair enough, for, as Gibson has protested, he isn't really interested in computer networking, and for him cyberspace was a *literary* device (see the interview with Gibson in *New Musical Express*, 30 October 1993). But the work of Pat Cadigan, the only woman in the original cyberpunk cadre, has followed a different trajectory; which I now mean to examine.

Pat Cadigan's first novel, *Mindplayers* (1987) tells the story of a young woman in a post-cyberspace, post-virtual-reality near-future USA, experimenting with the 'drugs' of the new technology. A social welfare rehabilitation program rescues her from the marginal, criminal world of electronically induced altered states of consciousness, and she becomes a virtual-reality therapist. *Mindplayers* conceives, very plausibly, of cyberspace as the ideal venue for psychotherapy. The proposition that therapist and patient stick their heads in a kind of brain scanner to join each other in lucid dreamland makes banal metaphors actual (= 'the world of the mind'), and equally gives expression to the irresistible language of the real world nets, where one can 'visit a museum', 'create an environment', 'take on a new identity'. So far (except in the fiction) it's mostly just typing, but *Mindplayers* successfully invokes a world where internally generated experience is inevitably (if the brain works as Edelman proposes, *definitely* inevitably) indistinguishable from actual. But if *Neuromancer* is limited by the rules of the *film noir* thriller, *Mindplayers* is equally restricted in its scope. Therapy sessions follow each other like a succession of those 'Freudian dream-sequences' favoured in early Hitchcock movies, and there is not much exploration of the society in which 'Allie' is first a criminal and then a rehabilitator.

Her second novel, *Synners* (1991), is set in the informationally tribalised society of near-future Los Angeles, where techno-artist stars of virtual-reality-mediated MTV are the élite of a cybernaut Bohemia. 'Direct Brain Interfacing', jacking in to the machines, (the normal route to cyberspace in Gibson's scenario), is here emergent, and demonized. Cynical entertainment corporation bosses impose this novel and highly dangerous technology on their industry. Artistes and public don't know any better, and become infatuated with the new product, until one fried-brain VR-junkie star suffers a massive stroke while plugged in, and shares his death with the computer-using world.

Synners has assimilated implications of computer networking that were not available to anyone in 1984. It depicts a society of multifarious narrow divisions, where even the informationally wealthy subscribe to only a tiny, customised fraction of the news and trends. In this version of cyberspace the data cloud is not separate from its users, a 'place' where certain people 'go'. It is a continuum that includes the power supply grid, traffic control, fast food menuboards, subscriber news services – and now, finally, human brains. It's all one. A massive stroke can be at once a biological and a digital impulse disaster, ripping through brain tissue and other data systems without distinction. As in *Neuromancer*, self-awareness has come to being as a by-product of network complexity, and this new mind is a significant character in the story. But 'Artie Fish', the artificial person, is not a God, nor even half a God. 'He' has the persona of a mischievous young male human, and is dependent on his human friends to rescue 'him' from oblivion, after the crash (Cadigan, 1991:355).

The motifs of cyberpunk fiction are remarkably stable, and clearly historically situated: a science fiction of this time and no other. The dual topic and project is always the same: *the emergence of a self-conscious AI;* and *a fusion between human beings and (non-human, complex, data processing and communication systems) – 'the machines'.* But computer science had perhaps become more modest in its pretensions by the time *Synners* was written, or the information age less bullish about its high and lonely destiny = *to replace a world.* The cyberpunk apotheosis is still achieved. However, in this version the marriage of human and machine consciousness is a rescue operation, not a triumph of the Overmind.

Pat Cadigan's cyberspace novels form a triptych rather than a trilogy. *Synners*, the central panel, can be read as fictional near market speculation. It is set in a believable space, a plausible future or exaggerated present: 'set in the future', as it might be 'set in Canada'. The third novel, *Fools* (1992), loosely connected with the earlier *Mindplayers*, inhabits a different dimension. There is no mass of fictional detail to trick the reader's inner eye, and a minimum of science fictional rationale for the proposed novel technologies. The world is a series of half-lit interiors, connected by blurred streets and sketchily suggested vehicles: a nightclub bar, a theatre rehearsal space; a species of massage parlour where queasy, ill-defined transactions are glimpsed in featureless booths. The narrative that unfolds is equally shadowy and bizarre. A young woman (again), again a user of virtual-reality 'drugs', wakes up, or returns to awareness, in a nightclub. She is not particularly surprised or distressed to find that she has no idea what she's doing here, where 'here' is, or how she got here. Marva is a method actress, accustomed to taking on a new 'personality overlay' for a new part; and sometimes the overlay lingers. But it transpires that Marva's mind is not just suffering a method acting hangover. There are at least two other personalities sharing this notional space, one of them a marginally criminal drug-user (a 'memory junkie') called Marceline; the other a cop, an undercover agent of the Brain Police.

In *Fools* the standard cyberpunk inventions, and the virtual-reality psychotherapy techniques described in *Mindplayers*, have invaded every aspect of life. Several characters inhabit a single mind. Celebrities sell copies of their public personalities under franchise, so that fans *put on* the persona of their idol for a while, instead of wearing the tee-shirt. Bodies can be remodelled cell by cell, to match the latest fashionable overlay. A mind can be stolen, stripped of identifying marks, dismembered, parcelled

out, copied and fenced to the unwary or collusive public like
pirated software at a car boot sale. Marceline the memory-junkie
(who exists as a packet-switching stream of data-traffic, taking
her turn with others in the mind/brain of the multiple protagonist) feeds her habit on illegal snippets of other people's lost
time, mainlining Proust's exquisite glimpses of the eternal.

The plot, so far as it can be discerned, involves a major operation by the Brain Police: the regulators of intellectual property
trade, where *intellectual property* means the mind itself. They are
in pursuit of a gang of 'mindsuckers' – mind-theft being the car-
dinal criminal act that defines this society. They themselves are
obsessively deep in the game of self-encryption and psychic
data-corruption, and not the best protectors a mind-marketing
community could have. Mersine, the Brain Police agent first met
in deep undercover in Part One, reappears in Part Two in the
investigation of a 'mind-suck' where the victim has, unusually,
survived this unusual form of kidnapping intact – sort of:

'Just try to stay calm'. The officer on Sign-out duty slid me a
chair and a scratch pad while someone else went to get a terminal so I could trace the call. 'What seems to have happened
is, the mindsuckers who took your mind sold you off to someone intact. But the implant didn't take very well, and you're
fighting for dominance instead of being assimilated – '

Another weak laugh. 'No. That's not it. I mean, they think
that's it. Or they thought that was it. But I'm back there too.'

'Back where ?'

'In the other place. Where I had no body.'

I hesitated. I should have taken this call in my office, but I
risked having him hang up in the time it would have taken to
sprint back there.

'It's true,' he went on, a little breathlessly. 'I'm waiting back
there, playing for time. I don't know where that is though. I
sent me out – that is, I sent this me, I mean – intending to get
help. That me back there has no way of knowing if I, this I
talking to you, succeeded or just went crazy or what . . . .
They keep on trying to send me out, sell me off. Me, just the
one person. So I create one of my characters and send him out.
Do you see? I'm in character now, a character from one of the
plays I've done. Do you see now?'

You see all kinds of things in the Brain Police. A disembodied, self-replicating mind was a more bizarre sight than usual, but stranger things have happened. Probably.

(Cadigan, 1992:176)[7]

Emergent sciences begin by prying at the cracks, searching for any kind of purchase on a locked box of knowledge. Cognitive psychology, like genetics, began in pathology. The abnormal behaviour of patients with known damage to specific brain areas gave the first insights into underlying mechanisms. Artificial intelligence research shows the traces of this ancestry. Completely mindless programs have been pleasingly successful at mimicking the unseen 'person' of the Turing Test, in typed dialogue – when the person was supposed to be 'neurotic', or 'paranoid' (equally successful, oddly enough, when the person was supposed to be a psychiatrist!).[8] In *Fools*, Pat Cadigan seems to address the pathology of cyberspace. But she glosses only briefly on the real world implication of multiple personality as a strategy for survival (1992: 242) Her characters are not sick. 'They' are exposition: an uncompromising despatch from the data network as a model of mind. Where other fictions[9] explore the politics of cyberspace as a wild frontier, in more or less realistic future worlds, *Fools* reverses the engineering and uses the metaphors of cyberspace to explore the barely governed jungle of human consciousness.

Fools is a police-procedural fantasy in futuristic drag – pacey, casual, relentlessly punning. There are elements of farce in the knockabout packet-switching from one narrator-personality to another, elements of slapdash pastiche in the sudden emergence of a drab precinct house, a phone-trace, a uniformed cop at the desk. But the Brain Police are more than decor. In *Neuromancer* the 'Turing Police' invoked a simple analogue: mean streets, prohibition, *film noir* cops. They were the FBI: probably corrupt, occasionally virtuous, fighting a losing non-moral 'moral battle' (against the inevitable triumph of the AI, instead of liquor). Finally they were an irrelevance. The 'Brain Police' in *Fools* emerge part way through the narrative as a reassurance: an explanation – familiar, cosy – for the bewildering action. This soothing role is quickly undermined. These cops are *terminally* corrupt, routinely committing every crime in their own book, and eventually every character seems to be implicated in their game (everybody is watching everybody else). But here policing never becomes an irrelevance. The cops *are* the territory. At the end of the novel a single protagonist, her multiple co-selves benignly suppressed, makes a determined resolve to extricate *herself* from the *organisation*: to live her own single life. But her resolution is in such contrast to everything that's gone before it can only be taken as a denial episode: a 'god from a machine' (as they used to say, in the original context), who arrives at the end of the show and arbitrarily, temporarily, orders what cannot be ordered.

In *Synners*, before the crash that almost wipes out the global computer networks, a techno-art tattooist called Gator has often been found inscribing on the hide of some insensible burnt-out junkie an item of mysterious beauty: a tendril of ivy, maybe, or a lotus flower. These fragments contain, puncture by puncture, like a secret encrypted in the pixels of a downloaded photograph, the essence of Artie Fish. Gator is saving Artie. After the crash, she'll be able to raise him from the dead: not identical, but *himself* (Cadigan, 1991: 347–60). Consciousness dissolves when we examine it into an unmanageable palimpsest, an indecipherable exploded diagram. In *Fools* the self has become a harried, over-worked, presenter, public servant of diversity: dodging and div-ing and taking any route she can to get the message through. But after each disruption the same face returns, as the pattern of rip-ples on a flowing stream persists, not an accidental extra but part of the whole system (of river-bed, banks, obstacles, water, air). Mind is stranger, more complicated and *uncertain* than we could have guessed until now. But it is not an alien or a supplanter. It is an integral part of the natural world.

Through its swift generations computer science has mimicked successive images of consciousness. AI research and biological neuroscience have both been transformed in the last decade, moving towards a strange meeting. The biologists are served by terrifyingly expert technologies that can capture localised physi-cal events as never before,[10] while in artificial cognitive science, scraps of program are encouraged to breed like bacteria, in the hope that consciousness will crawl out of the digital slime. Yet still the brain is not a computer. If Gerald Edelman and other proponents of the biological model have it right, then maybe no program nor processing device – however powerful in potential or simple in its governing constraints – can be *designed* to model mind. But the Internet is not a computer. It is a communications network that had for one parent organism a military system required explicitly to survive against the odds (the message may take whatever route it likes, but it must get through). Its memory is malleable, reconstructing constantly the data-objects that it visits and the space in which they exist. Messy, *dis*-organised, laden with redundancies: it has all the hallmarks of a full-blown biological evolution. The global data network is a vacuum fluctuation in the process of exploding into a cosmos – a collection of digital impulses, microchips, copper wire, optic fibres and plastic boxes that has the persona, the recalcitrant privacies, the incompleteness, the unconquerable complexities of the biological model of self. No one can know 'exactly what is going on' in there. There is no master program. We dip into cyberspace – triggering a selective firing of the artificial neurons; raising this group and that from different data webs, into ephemeral existence. Already the Net will customise a pattern for us, hardening pathways that the individual user has established, so that an informational 'I' springs into existence (thought not exactly the same existence as before), whenever the human individual 'I' makes contact again. Without boring any new holes into our skulls, or attaching any sensory interfaces beyond those supplied by evolution, we have created an entity conforming to the original fiction: a matrix of information, *infected* by visiting minds.

Many claims made for the Internet have faded in the light of experience. There is little evidence that the Net is an Utopian, idealist supranational state; or a 'gender-neutral playground'. There is no sign of a coming race of Donna Haraway-style cyborgs, liberated by technology itself from patriarchal technology's domination (Haraway, 1990), and not much evidence of the revolution in favour of socially disadvantaged youth promised by science fiction writer Bruce Sterling's manifesto (Sterling 1986). The world order in there is the same as the one out here. How could it be otherwise? I use my modem chiefly for sending cheap, fast international messages, and I regard my Internet suppliers as a new breed of garage mechanics. They despise me because I'm ignorant, they're mildly rude to me because I'm female, and what they *really* want is to get hold of my cybernaut's vehicle so that they can do some kind of work on it – wrong – in ten minutes, and charge me for a week's labour. Information wants to be free? Not any more. The young male heroes of classic cybertexts are sulky maverick mercenaries, who show no enthusiasm for empowering their own underclass – the women who mother them and tend their bodies while they surf the nets – and recognise no injustice in the gangsta world they inhabit, so long as they themselves are paid well enough or scared hard enough. 'Radical' is a flexible term. Cyberpunk fellow-traveller Kevin Kelly (1994), in his overview of the new technologies, speaks of a biotechnical age that will 'extract the logical principles of life and install them in machines'. But it is not clear that power will be redistributed equitably, because replication replaces reproduction and neural processing replaces the Tin Man. So far, the signs are that information technology means not less control but *more*, in the hands of the same élite.

Pat Cadigan, the most intellectually innovative of the cyberpunks, does not argue with the rules of the boys' club, or deny the nature of her society. The women in *Synners* are 'strong female characters' maybe (an expression that has become a dire cliché in the jargon of a genre nowadays very nervous about its political correctness rating). But they are too wise to contest with their menfolk for the centre stage. The female protagonists of *Mindplayers* and *Fools* may be punks; but they certainly aren't in control. And 'Artie Fish' is not a god, but he's definitely a boy. The mind of cyberspace is still male. Yet the dissolution of the paranoid Overmind model of *Neuromancer* in *Synners*, the constantly disrupted and recovered boundaries of self and not-self in *Fools*, seem inescapably a political, and even a feminist, progress, reflecting the decentred modes of thought – ecologies, evolutions, diversities; populations instead of individuals; groups instead of single interests – which are infiltrating all our current models of the self and the world.

It is not surprising that so much public interest in 'cyberspace' is preoccupied with the question of control, of government. When presented with a novelty, our impulse is to try to get hold of it, to *grasp* the new (think of these terms, and feel the bright nets of biochemical light, rising and meshing, reaching back through language to the time before language was born, into the deeps . . .). *What is this thing? Is it a threat? Is it my baby? Is it maybe something good to eat?* Fictions like Pat Cadigan's *Fools* suggest, among other things, that the project of policing cyberspace 'effectively' has encountered an error of scale: perceiving 'the Internet' as an *organisation*, which can conceivably buy a really good security system; rather than as a world, where policing *failure* is the normative state. Policing does not defeat crime. Each population (the police and the criminals) favours the other, in an equilibrium in which damage limitation (from the state's point of view) is the best case. As *Fools* also suggests, what we are really looking at is a mirror. Control in there is the same as control out here (just as incomplete, just as unlikely).

In real life, I don't expect the Internet to give birth to independent awareness (which is possibly the secret fear that underlies all concern about governing the Net). Perhaps the founding fathers of this new colony will break away and write a constitution for themselves. Perhaps law and order will be imposed by force on the wild frontier; or perhaps this new envelope of shared consciousness will become the seat of government for all of us. Whatever the outcome, we can be reasonably sure of one thing: novelty fades. Network use will soon be no more intriguing, nor loaded with meaning, than picking up a telephone. But in that world in which the Internet is invisible and science fiction has moved on to other quarry, we will be different people: our sense of self subtly altered by the existence of this other, the multitudinous immaterial presence, perhaps the nearest thing to an alien intelligence we'll ever meet.

NOTES

1 Reprinted by permission of HarperCollins Publishers Limited.

2 Copyright © 1992 by Basic Books, Inc. Reprinted by permission of Basic Books, a division of HarperCollins Publishers, Inc.

3 In fact, a platinum and *cloisonné head* (Gibson, 1984: 207). Who says sf writers have no sense of humour?

4 Thus a famous hypothesis from fiction, that *self is memory*, appears to be on a sound experimental footing. For Proust's account of the toast incident, real-world original of the madeleine incident in *À la recherche du temps perdu*, see the collection of essays and letters *Contre Sainte-Beuve* (1954: 53–4). I was sorry that Edelman didn't mention Marcel Proust, along with Descartes, Aristotle, Freud, in his catalogue of spiritual ancestors. But though there are surely neuroscientists who read storybooks, perhaps there are few who perceive the shared territory, or expect to find their science in a novel.

5 Melissa Scott, *Dreamships* (1992). The fate of the AI entity 'Manfred' is a sad case of legal discrimination. Accused of murder, 'his' defence is that 'he' thought humans were indefinitely replicable and immortal as 'he' is himself. He didn't know you could kill a human by electrocuting the biological machine that was running

the program. So he's innocent. But his misunderstanding is taken to mean 'he' doesn't understand personhood, therefore doesn't qualify as a person, and can be wiped, without trial, as a dangerously faulty program. Poor Manfred!

6 See C.J. Cherryh, *Cyteen* (1988) and other novels in the 'Merchanter Universe' series. C.J. Cherryh's 'azi' are vat-grown humans – an unlikely development for us, since we are not short of the commodity in question. But science now strongly suggests that if an artificial/biological mind could be created, in any form, what you'd get would be *a human being,* neither more nor less. Could such a machine be 'useful' to us? Maybe we'll have to build them, and then lobotomise them.

7 See note 1.

8 See the descriptions of various 'neurotic programs' and their interactions with (sometimes) unwary humans, in Boden (1977: 21–63).

9 See Melissa Scott's *Trouble and Her Friends* (1994) and Neal Stephenson's *Snow Crash* (1992).

10 Claims for these technologies may be doubted (*post hoc propter hoc*?). If the neurons are firing in certain areas, after the wet toast is nibbled, you can't be *sure* that what you are watching is the subject 'revisiting his childhood'. He may be secretly thinking of something different that he'd rather not discuss with you.

Chapter 5

Governmentality

Simon Baddeley

INTRODUCTION

Foucault wrote of government as an art that can be discerned in the way people learned to govern themselves, accept government and govern others. His concept of 'governmentality' elides 'government' and 'mentality', providing a term that embraces psychology and politics and assumes a continuity between the rule of self, household and state whose interruption precipitates crises in all these areas. Governmentality is also about the personal and political activities that attend the reinvention of government in the self-processes which entail negotiating internal complexity, abandoning anthropocentricity and managing the boundary between internal and external which cyberspace enticingly confuses.

> I watch a shuttle take-off on television, fiction intercut with documentary. At 'main engine cut off' the screen holds on the 'we' shot; the moment of looking back on our planet, so fleeting compared to the abandoned dreams of a science fiction now largely turned to earthbound futures. One day this bursting out of the sky and into the quiet darkness of space will be normal. We want – life itself wants – to do it so much. Some, including me, are stirred by the pleasure of imagining it, grieved they'll never go there, nor their children, because there's so much to do at home, in the immense polity of human nature.[1]

CYBERSPACE AS CATHAY

A trouper from the information technology repertory has finally made the big time. International standards for global information exchange imply homogeneity in a phenomenon as busy with possibilities as the seas around Reformation Europe. A small step in the packet-switching process – an evolution from the anticipations of a global nervous system recognised by cable layers in the 1880s[2] – has popularised a technology which, with enhancements of band-width, will give our species the possibility of being in the virtual pocket of anyone on earth (Cerf, 1993; Hardy, 1993; McLean, 1989; Mansell, 1994).

The familiar servants of library search reach across the world. The unfamiliar ones dive through texts via 'hypertext' where a double click on a blue highlighted word carries me to other parts of the same document, back to where I started or through to another server elsewhere in the world. For the time being, conventional methods serve, but the possibilities for supplanting conventional sources of information emanate from the screen like unexploited steam.

At the turn of this century, water was becoming a barrier that it had not been for millennia – to be overcome by tunnels, telegraphy, immense bridges, gigantic unsinkable ships and flight. Contemporary science fiction explored antediluvian worlds, the ocean depths and the centre of the earth or expeditions through time.[3] It touched on journeys to the moon and dangers from Mars, but with increasing enthusiasm, imagination headed out into space and stayed there colonising star systems. For a time in the sixties there was a fascination with drug-assisted journeys into inner space, but in the early eighties, William Gibson (1984), confessing ignorance of computers, but struck by the concentrated attention of boys playing arcade video games, wrote a story about a place as much fantasy and reality as the Americas of the Elizabethans. It's not that this place had not, like the place christened 'America', been visited before,[4] nor even that it did not already have a native population (Cerf, 1993); but Gibson named it.

Imagination – from cave painting to sky-writing on the Net – has always worked with virtual realities. For Shakespeare's Lorenzo in the finale of the *The Merchant of Venice*, a moonlit night suffused with music bespoke sweet harmony clouded by 'the muddy vesture of decay'. Gibson's Neuromancer, clinically maimed by those he had hustled, can only see the sky above Chiba – 'the color of television tuned to a dead channel'. The moment when the music swells, as in Robert Bolt's and Maurice Jarre's spectacular film sequence of Lawrence of Arabia returning to the desert, is when Case, his nervous system restored, settles 'the black terry sweatband across his forehead, careful not to disturb the flat sendai dermatrodes' and sees:

> the unfolding of his distanceless home, his country, transparent 3D chessboard extending to infinity. Inner eye opening to the stepped scarlet pyramid of the Eastern Seaboard Fission Authority burning beyond the green cubes of Mitsubishi Bank of America, and high and very far away . . . the spiral arms of military systems, forever beyond his reach.
>
> (Gibson, 1984: 69)

What is available on the World Wide Web is a taster. Even more than with newspapers and radio, this realises Eliot's condition of being 'too conscious and conscious of too much'. I wander around a labyrinth as enchanting as the British Museum Library, before its move to St Pancras, or the great Library at Trinity College, Dublin, with the dust-specked beams of sunlight missing the carefully protected *Book of Kells*, or the bookshops of Charing Cross Road or Hay-on-Wye on a chilly rainy autumn afternoon. I download and unzip material. Layers of reference tempt me onwards, diving through texts and icons through servers to other servers and home by different routes. It's intoxicating and yet recalls alarm I felt as a child watching the Sorcerer's Apprentice in Disney's *Fantasia*. Every time I decide what I want to know I read something that tempts me to type in another Boolean term to extend my enquiry back and forth via Stanford, Tokyo, Oslo, Florence, Durban, Harvard, Ann Arbor, Tel Aviv, Edinburgh, Princeton, New York, Gothenburg, Melbourne, Acapulco, Cambridge, Colorado, Kobe, Geneva, Rio, London, Massachusetts, Marseilles – half hoping the magician will return, and after stern reproof tidy everything up.

Intra-species communication technologies are evolving in the style of armour – too fast to congeal and reveal in Weber's sense[5] – towards full suits, parts of which extend themselves into the body, confusing the boundaries of inside, where there is talk of neural networks, chaos (Cage, 1961; Plant, 1995), complexity (Emery, 1967), connectionism (Miers, 1993; Ogden, 1994; Plant,

1995; see also note 6), virtual reality (Karnow, 1993; McCaffery, 1991; Rushkoff, 1994; Spiller, 1996), and outside where the talk is of a global polity (Bellamy and Taylor, 1994; Cherry, 1971; *Demos Quarterly*, 1994; Ronfeldt, 1992), localised democracy (Etzioni, 1993; Roche 1992; Stewart, 1995; Taylor, 1991; Young, 1993), social exclusion (Lee, 1994; Piercy, 1992) and disordered futures (Davis, 1990; Giddens, 1991; Leach, 1968), including global plagues (Horton, 1995; Lappé, 1994; Roizman and Hughes, 1995). These artefacts produce and are produced by crises. For Foucault (1978), 'governmentality' referred to psychological and constitutional inventions which shattered feudalism to create and be created by the great territorial administrative and colonial states of Europe. These are comparably disjunctive times, as fertile in their encouragement of conceptual novelty as when it grew upon humans that space could not be apprehended with contemporary understandings of distance and time (Toulmin and Goodfield, 1967).

SAMPLE CASES

At an International Direct Marketing Fair (Wembley, 14–16 March 1995) speakers describe 'The Age of Individualisation', 'The Technology Holocaust', 'The Media Explosion' and 'The Communication Traffic Jam'. Delegates attend workshops on 'the realities of one-to-one marketing', 'the management of subscription lists', including affluent households in areas of deprivation. The abecedarian breakdown by half a dozen socio-economic classes has been replaced by the analysis of proliferating niches, refined by micro-marketing where the seller with the world as their oyster collects profiles of specific households and the individuals in them.

I attend a lecture by an urban statistician on the way 'recent poverty debates in the UK and the USA have focused upon the emergence of an underclass characterised by a self-perpetuating detachment from society's normative behaviour and values' (Lee, 1994). He describes the methodological complexity of assessing poverty via the analysis of census data. At least ten indices of deprivation including – in statisticians' shorthand – DoE81, DoE91, Breadline, Bradford, Jarman UPA, Townsend, Matdep and Socdep, fail to capture a poverty ranking of sufficient precision to guarantee equitable targeting of regeneration funds. Respect for confidentiality of census information about specific individuals introduces the ecological fallacy – error based on confusing multiply deprived areas with multiply deprived individuals.

A report from the Directorate of Community Services in Bradford City Council describes a programme to develop distance learning for disadvantaged groups. This initiative is one of many within the European 'Telecities Network' aiming to integrate telematics into policies to combat social exclusion and create 'a consortium of local government, education and industry, working towards establishing Bradford as a 21st century TECHNOPOLIS through the development of a European Centre for Advanced Manufacturing in Bradford' (Bradford City Council, 1995).

An issue of the *Journal of Public Administration* (Bellamy and Taylor, 1994) looks towards 'the information polity' and the idea of a 'European Nervous System', identifying three levels of analysis:

1 Transnational information flows among governments and businesses and the capacity of inter- and supranational organisations to respond to these.
2 The reinvention of government in terms of:
   (a) the relocation of the intelligence of public services to the point of contact with customers;
   (b) the lateral integration of customer records across existing organisations so that individuals who deal with a diversity of separate agencies become 'whole persons' in their relations with the state; and
   (c) the trend towards 'prosumption', whereby information networking is used to draw the consumer of a service simultaneously into its production, as in self-assessment for taxation or benefits.
3 The redesign of governmental institutions whereby economic and business logic cues profound organisational transformations, including functional and geographical reconfigurations.

Professor John Stewart, at my own institution (the University of Birmingham), argues that decades of managerial innovation in public administration ought to be balanced by inventiveness about political expression. His ideas on 'Innovation in Democratic Practice' (Stewart, 1995) embrace:

1 Means of recognising communities of locality and communities of concern.
2 Direct democracy via referendum, recall and town meetings.
3 Processes for enhancing the quality and scale of conversations between politicians, professionals and citizens in the public domain such as teledemocracy, electronic town meetings, more participative public meetings, improved turn-out at local elections, community planning weekends and 'learning service teams'.

One writer in an issue of *Demos Quarterly* (1994) reckons 'the half-life of statistics concerning the information superhighway ranges from one to nine months' and runs through a 'history of hype' including 'The Global Village' in the sixties, 'Post-industrial Society' in the seventies and 'The Third Wave' in the eighties. Another, writing in the same issue, ponders the potential of information networks to liberate, 'as these develop at breakneck speed' towards the millennium and governments across the world reflect on regulation, competition and technological choices, seeking ways to develop technologies which 'will be the key economic and social infrastructures of the next century'. Different groups of humans will seek intellectual, social, commercial and political leverage in cyberspace. De Sola Pool (1983) gives a much cited account of evolving constitutional frameworks that comprehend technological development, providing a lucid history of emerging communication technologies and their unanticipated political consequences. In a long think-piece on 'Cyberocracy', Ronfeldt spans 'topics that analysts do not normally group together', arguing that

> government may change radically in the decades ahead . . . the development of, and demand for access to the future electronic information and communications infrastructures–i.e. 'cyberspace' – may alter the nature of bureaucracy. . . . outcomes may include new forms of democratic, totalitarian, and hybrid governments.
>
> (1992: abstract)

An American law professor asks what happens 'when the lines along which our constitution is drawn warp or vanish?' Speaking of how to 'map' the text and structure of the American constitution onto the texture and topology of cyberspace, he envisages a 'cyberspace corollary' which 'protects people not places' and does not assume that the processing of ones and zeros by computers 'is something less than "speech" ' (Tribe, 1991: 13). Other lawyers discuss legal implications of 'the massively networked broadband, interactive immersive computer-mediated experience' (Karnow, 1993), including:

1 Fractal based landscapes that allow 'fly-throughs'.
2 Head-mounted displays for molecular modelling and CAD/CAM walk-through.
3 'Virtual Ride Motion Theater' Systems, flight simulators with multiple participants in shopping malls.
4 Simulators for close combat tactical training and joint combat operations.
5 Telepresence for dangerous remote work such as space repair, deep sea exploration, and internal surgery, or virtual art museums in company with others around the globe.
6 Partial or whole body immersion using body suits and infrared transmitters to walk through houses, train architects and design buildings, create burning buildings to train firefighters, enter a vein or heart for surgery and visualise complex financial data.

The lawyers considered product liability as a result of long-term immersion in cyberspace, anticipating that the

> transformation of our environment into a 'digital soup' will provide a target rich environment for theft, security, copyright, failures in the human/machine interface; indiscernible bugs with significant consequences; trusting the Zero-User-Interface, confusing simulation with the real event.
>
> (Karnow, 1993)

A cognitive psychologist at Princeton uses the World Wide Web to discuss a 'Fourth Revolution' in the 'production of knowledge' (Harnard, 1992). Human thought changes and is changed by language, by writing, by moveable print, and now by something else not quite graspable but reflected in the communicative possibilities of having most universities and research institutions linked via the Internet. This tempts scholars whose work has so far been reflected in the universe of academic journals to join in colloquia, symposia, bulletin boards and electronic journals in cyberspace. The writer anticipates delays because of the habits of a scholarly community adapted to paper for centuries. He points out that electronic journals will not develop as clones of paper journals – 'ghosts in another medium' – but as something different, supported by 'a strategic pro-revolutionary alliance among libraries, learned societies and universities . . . and governments recognising . . . that the benefits of subsidising the intellectual highways for all scholars and scientists will far outweigh the costs' (Harnard, 1992).

The Internet, pioneered by the US military to maintain communication in a nuclear war, was intended to have no centre and limited hierarchy (Cerf, 1993) but now '[i]t's as if some grim fallout shelter had burst open and a full scale Mardi Gras parade had come out' (Sterling and Gibson, 1993, cited in Hardy, 1993) and we are treated to 'the genesis of an event which will shape the world in as yet unforeseen ways: the birth of a new world culture called the Net' (Hardy, 1993).

I attend a conference on 'The Death of Architecture'. Speakers discuss 'interconnected technologies and the urban environment'. One anticipates the 'fourth discontinuity'. Following the Copernican, Darwinian and Freudian comes *Homo roboticus*, the potential subject of a new xenophobia – anthropocentricity – stirred by

> forms of bio-mechanical synthesis which could supplant the concept of death but heralds shocking cultural dislocation, exploding, amid the broken dreams of modernism, the notion of the white, catholic, Cartesian sensibility of *Homo sapiens*, pushing life into new forms and new spaces.[6]

Another suggests that the architectural perspective, being friendly to interdisciplinary activity, might be better able to make sense of the implications of total digitisation, where states of information may pre-exist, or be as real as, states of mind. Such states can exist outside the geographical space of architecture and common sense in other spaces to which architecture should direct its attention. In one of these the Net is developing almost like a vast city with its own proliferating spaces, collapsing the tradition of architecture as the product of monotheistic vision linked to grand designs and plans in favour of self-organising processes that undermine the idea that someone or anything governs.

> The question of whether we are rushing into cyberspace faster than we can handle is irrelevant. What now exists cannot be uninvented. There's nothing we can do about it. The possibilities of artificial intelligence raise the prospect of being and inhabiting other bodies, impinging on ideas of self as concrete and constitutional, blurring the boundaries of the virtual and the vital and defining human consciousness as one life form among many.[7]

Seeing *Homo sapiens* as the dominant species obscures from our imagination, ill-prepared already for such an idea, that we might be – almost certainly are and always have been – part of some other form's evolution. Infectious diseases will be more powerful occupiers of the world than our own species if we cannot achieve an agreed form of regulation which would allow the development and maintenance of a world-wide early warning system which can report, track, isolate, identify and disseminate information about the incidence of new infections. For such a system to work requires changes 'in human behaviour and ecology' (Roizman and Hughes, 1995: iv–v). The remorseless features of future plagues may be attributed to our own species' successes in fighting disease, because the more effective our assaults on micro-organisms, 'the more varied are the bacterial and viral strains thrown up against us' (Lappé, 1994: 8).

> if we imagine a world in which the entire human race were somehow organized so as to banish war and avert economic crisis; it seems likely that other kinds of catastrophe – perhaps greater than ever – might arise because of collisions between a newly organized humanity and the rest of the ecosystem of the planet.
>
> (McNeil, 1992: 148)

Richard Horton, US editor of *The Lancet*, suggests that '[i]t may be only wholesale reversal of our social development, in a direction we can hardly imagine, would check this process' (1995: 28).

The critical importance of radical personal changes in rich countries is emphasised by Anthony Giddens. He makes a distinction between emancipatory politics, concerned with inequality in the world, and life politics, focusing on human and personal fate, particularly the choices about who one is or could be – and their consequences. Life politics, often seen as an indulgence on the part of those not oppressed by emancipatory urgencies, arise from an acute awareness of the unprecedented scale of human intervention in nature, control over biological reproduction and the need for a global polity. Giddens (1991: 10) sees life politics increasingly entering 'public and juridical arenas of states', becoming a priority of constitutional reflection as we come to see that 'emancipation presumes life-political transformations'.

The television dramatist Dennis Potter died in 1994 after doing a moving final television interview with Melvyn Bragg (LWT, Channel 4, 5 April 1994). Potter sipped champagne with morphine before commercial breaks, recalled his childhood in the Forest of Dean, of Christ walking on Cannop Ponds, and spoke about two plays he was trying to finish before his liver gave out to leukaemia. One was called *Karaoke* – because singing other's songs to other's background music is the lot of many – and the other, *Cold Lazarus*, involved a rich man who invests in having his head cryogenically stored to be woken in four hundred years in a world where all experience is virtual. Realising the custodians of his resurrected head have discovered a market for the real experiences it contains, and grasping his brain is being mined for these, he seeks oblivion.

PERPLEXITY

We have transformed natural landscapes beyond recognition by exporting unexpected and undesired outcomes to some sort of boundary separating field from wasteland, us versus them, the managed and the predictable from the rest. The 'rest' is of course where catastrophe continues to lurk.

(McNeil, 1992: 147)

Optimistic perspectives imagine palliative investments in infrastructure. They anticipate opportunities for economic regeneration and innovative governmental agencies (Bellamy and Taylor,

1994), inventive regulation (Tribe, 1991), the diffusion of distance learning (Bradford City Council, 1995; Harnard, 1992), and the growing sensibilities of a connected and democratically inclined humanity (De Sola Pool, 1983; McLean, 1989). Other scenarios, often conjectured by the same writers, anticipate conflicts whose understanding will owe more to criminology than military theory and whose focus will be on membranes separating the global highways of the prosperous and those who serve them from the jacqueries of the 'glop' (Davis, 1990; Gibson, 1984, McNeil, 1992; Ronfeldt, 1992).[8] I view camera crews roaming trouble-spots with mops on poles returning images that resonate with disfigurements in my surroundings – sirens in the night, helicopters pulsating over the city. I listen to neighbours anxious about local crime, grumbling about cans and glass in the gutters, booming music and bursting plastic bags. I see the global icon, since the Renaissance a sign of its bearer's mastery, competing with satellite pictures of a bald patch. Chat about the news runs behind the conversations of the contented; menace frames our happy snapshots.

I pick up sounds too intermingled to reveal what might be the opening or closing bars of ditties or symphonies; the worst and best of what is disappearing or the worst and best of what is emerging inside and outside myself. When, as it occasionally does, the air clears revealing the familiar traffic of administrative exchange and domestic duties, it feels as if the fog was all inside. Such conditions may be constitutional. Among the defences people use to cope with complexity, Emery (1967) described repression, dissociation, fragmentation and superficiality. A shift in the pattern of common anxieties might be indicative of the times as neurotics, like artists, react 'to emerging trends before their more stable fellows . . . . Their basic sense of personal worthlessness may make them more dependent upon the fabric of cultural symbols . . . more sensitive to flaws and rents that are beginning to emerge' (Emery, 1967: 226–7).

My difficulty is with the term 'we'. This pronoun, whether used directly or closeted in the passive voice, is foundering, jeopardising surrounding text. All around things appear normal. Conference papers are delivered, student papers submitted and books produced, but what will distinguish them to a forensic grammarian of late twentieth-century texts will be evidence of the syntactical work that has accompanied their authors' contracts with their readers. The terms I hear from my own mouth, where I try to limit their unconsidered use, is 'we' and 'us' – as in 'we are all going to be working from home', 'we will all be accessing', 'those of us who fail to'. Phrases like 'users will be', 'circumstances suggest', 'it has emerged', evade further burdening of the pronoun but will not ultimately escape a textual detective. The term 'we' can no longer be used as though there were a centred world view. Its use in pronouncements about the future allows ambiguity about whom these scenarios exclude. It may express a humanely inclusive view. It may imply collusion with a selected audience. It may be a condescension. It may be an imperial 'I', but it may also be seeking authority from an unreliable consensus. Though they are habitually invoked, sometimes with hectoring urgency, sibling nouns like 'the public' or 'society' or 'people' are no less conditional. These are times when even closest companions, on hearing the unnegotiated use of collective parts of speech, may ask 'Who's we?', filling the space with a category of individuation the speaker had thoughtlessly treated as inclusive.[9] Foucault, a party to these complications, argued that 'maybe the target nowadays . . . is not to discover what we are, but to refuse what we are', imagining 'new forms of subjectivity' (1980: 216). For Milton, the word 'individual' meant 'inseparable' – speaking of the 'individual man and wife' – on the basis that one cannot exist without the other. His phrase 'the individual and the Holy Trinity' implied an inseparable unity. Now individual refers not to 'a group whose parts cannot be separated' but 'a person whose parts cannot be separated' (Cherry, 1971: 204). Now this individual is contested, its location in common sense recognised as a cultural and political event (Baddeley, 1995; Rowan, 1990; Samuels, 1989).

Cyberspace provides further opportunities to examine the perception of the individual as a unity. Ideas of multiplicity have long existed as heresy or exception around the idea of a unitary self. The themes that have weakened the idea have been co-existent with it and have in some previous times been dominant. They take the form of the individual being able to be different people in different settings as defined by the needs of the tribe. They take the form of the individual being made up of many parts which come together only temporarily and can be dispersed and reassembled as in the Osiris–Horus myth, where a state theology of birth, death and rebirth evolved around the dismemberment, dispersal and recovery of an individual's separate parts. Something like an individual first arose as a startling androgyne in Amarna – the Pharaoh, Akhenaten, whose singular sun-dominated theology was suppressed by his successor. The pre-Hellenic inhabitants of Homer's world had no singular word for 'body' and citizens of the Athenian *polis* had no individuality outside it. Their integrity was intimately connected to their participation in a larger whole. With its dissolution individuals had to renegotiate their relations with an unbounded world (Foucault, 1984; Sabine, 1957). This exposure spawned a multiplicity of philosophies, including hedonism, Epicureanism, scepticism and stoicism; the latter being the most recurrent in the intervening millennia as a form of self-rule which recognises that if the individual cannot control the world outside, he or she may be able to control it inside. Monotheistic religion reinforced this process, depicting a prescient God who knew the individual better than the tribe, noting the fall of a sparrow and numbering the hairs of the head. It was an intense interior presence (Steiner, 1971)[10] that did not reach expression in the West, outside Judaism, until Luther, approving the merciless repression of a rebellious peasantry, demonstrated that liberation of the individual spirit did not apply to politics. The presence of selves, infusing and being infused by this conditional Protestant individuality, was capitalism's watermark.

EXPERIENCES OF CYBERSPACE

20 November: The modem which I requested last week has arrived. It looks complicated. I've phoned Andrew next door, who'll help connect me up.

23 November: . . . completed arrangements with the University's Authenticated Dial-up Service. I'm reading avidly. *À propos* of bio-synthesis, I asked my son, 'What would you do with my hand, if it was all that remained of me and it could be kept alive and functioning?' He said he'd prefer not to have it because 'I'd probably miss too much of the rest of you.'

25 November: I was thinking about the difference between the eleventh edition[11] and the CD-ROM Britannica – what the encyclopaedia says about space–time in 1911 and what it says now. The first entry is just comprehensible, discussing fluidity of Cartesian and Euclidean coordinates, while the latter, eliding these dimensions, speaks of incomprehensible formulae . . . different kinds of space in unexperienced universes.

28 December: The machine is switched on, red lights blink on the modem which amplifies the sound of the serial phone connections. Babble of static and staccato beeps of electronic space. Bumps and scrapes – 'Host error', 'Host refused access', 'Cache overload', 'Host timed out, try again later', 'Call disconnected. Do you wish to reconnect?' – and there appears at the top left hand of the screen the word 'Hi'. For a moment we misinterpret this as an unfamiliar screen command. R. types back 'hello' and identifies a girl in a suburb of Philadelphia playing on her parent's computer. He begins a conversation with people in South Padre Island, Texas, and in Philadelphia and Sunny Valley, Idaho – Mary and her son-in-law, Charlie, from Phoenix, Arizona – and Vicki from Dallas. They chat in text, each phrase appearing a few seconds after the other. The light of the screen plays on our faces deep into the night.

Later – I want to start with polyphony – a thread that will take me to the notion of an internal politics – that continuity of Foucault's. It's about amplifying individuation. It starts with the impossibility of an individual – because the self is defined within borders but borderless it's in free fall. So conceive an internal polity in which to govern the multiplicity.

21 January: Watching a video of *Philadelphia*, I see why this mainstream success has been described as a film about an outgroup for an in-group. With its opening scan on Benjamin Franklin's statue from the air, state buildings and the zoom on Liberty Bell, this is a classic HMS *Normality* movie, striving for the dream of *ex pluribus unum*, assisting in resistance to normality's erosion, moving in its endeavour to sedate the trauma of *ex unibus plurum*. We are not one, I am not one, indeed I am many and the fear is that I might be 'we', and we might be legion, infinite diversity and multiplicity within the same skin . . . possibilities and choices innumerable, of an order to make present ideas of individuality within the ideology of individualism seem one spore. Individuality, like universality, is in its foetal stage. Conrad said vaunted individuality expresses men's unconsidered assumption that their surroundings are safe – the interior is still phantom and heartless.[12] Recurrent fears of the immense territories still available to individuality are expressed as nostalgia for community, but there will be more and deeper diversity.[13]

24 January: I live in a semi-affluent niche of an inner city zone. As I walk or drive through the areas I see empty flats, boarded-up shops, the cosmetics of successive renewal schemes, litter irretrievably lodged in indeterminate spaces, stained mattresses, burnt-out vans, broken bottles, cars on bricks, collapsed oil-filmed gutters, the bewildered–bewildering Rorschach impressions of figures 'released into the community' . . . . Alarms on houses and cars sound unattended. Invisible dogs that aren't pets snarl as I pass, vibrating barbed palings with their paws. In the park where they don't get taken for walks there's a pond whose ill-tended banks are lined with plastic detritus. The water's polluted by wastes from hostel washing machines and hazardous back-alley approximations of car-repair shops tolerated as 'economic development'. There's a bandstand, its pergola roof stripped to rotting wood and tattered felt . . . muddy slopes that once held immaculately tended banks of annuals . . . a dry drinking fountain of chipped marble on which '666' and other maledictions – sexual and racial – have been sprayed over the incised name of a Councillor – bearer of a civic gospel that bought a hundred thousand street lights, imposed regulations on slum landlords, piped clean water a hundred miles from the Welsh mountains, built a thousand miles of sewers to draw disease out of new Jerusalem, all becoming a 'colossal wreck'.

6 March: These fears anaesthetise intelligent reading of the problems I see, drawing me from wisdom into a wasting animosity towards my neighbours. I apprehend a solution to all our problems – to demonise the excluded, enabling them, within travestied self-determination, to self-destruct.[14]

ZERO-USER-INTERFACE

In what ought to be silence as I prepare for sleep I hear a rhythm and wonder if someone across the gardens in hostel land is playing music late and then it grows on me that this sound replacing the silence I crave is coming from me and yet echoes as though it were outside, so that I can hardly believe it is my heart pumping blood round my body. What's inside comes to me from outside bearing anxieties about the fragility of the membrane between me and everything else.[15]

What kind of space is cyberspace? It has childish qualities but it's not a secret garden 'apparelled in celestial light'. The elderly metaphor of motorways is used a lot, as is the sixties argot of trance-like states enhanced by fractal imagery (Rushkoff, 1994).[16] But virtual reality is not psychedelia; for a start it's filling up with accountants. Is it, then, a boyish space, spanning the world and its satellites? Has it a geography? What is its topography? There are problems defining what used to be called the inner city as a geographical space (Deakin and Edwards, 1993). I remember someone telling me, as we drove along a raised highway where the Gorbals had been, that the place survived as a 'state of mind', which is what, in his view as someone who'd escaped, they always had been. But it's not just a state of mind, though the elision of time and place through light-speed transactions between terminals could lead to that error. Social analysis is moving from place to routes and flows of people, from where it is easy to focus on the driver of economies as flows of information between social actors moving instantly from place to place, exchanging symbols in 'economies of signs and space' (Lash and Urry, 1994), spreading ideas through mental space like an infection. 'It is becoming apparent that human affairs are embedded within a hierarchy of equilibria systems: physico-chemical, biological, and semiotic' (McNeil 1992: xiv).

In 1766, with methodological access to an expanding materialist universe Kant (1900) had spurned metaphysical inquiry, mocking Swedenborg for being as 'familiarly acquainted with the beyond as with his own house', describing the theologian's masterwork as '8 volumes quarto full of nonsense'. Four years later the philosopher incorporated Swedenborg's system into his conception of two worlds – *mundus intelligibilis* and *mundus sensibilis* – suppressing his earlier criticism, having realised all realities available to human experience are virtual.[17] Not that Kant's space is Prospero's 'insubstantial pageant' or that cyberspace is a 'baseless fabric'. My economic existence is conditional on a widely accessible credit rating. I exist in cyberspace as an article of faith – a credo. There is something new here; a discovery equivalent to physicists grasping, as Newton could not, the nature of 'action at a distance'. Spiller (1996) suggests 'psychology is the physics of cyberspace'. Koestler in *The Sleepwalkers* concludes that everything is 'mind stuff' in the grammar of modern physics. He quotes the physicist Jeans: 'knowledge is heading towards a non-mechanical reality; the universe begins to look more like a great thought than like a great machine' (Koestler, 1959: 531–2).

This is a risky area. Freud, in his early days, was seen not as part of a scientific avant-garde, which was moving in positivist and reductionist directions, but closer to the occult and receding gloom of Mesmer (Ellenberger, 1994). Psychoanalysis, with its attention to dreams and signs, imitated exorcism. The subconscious contained demons as inhabitants of the soul. Exploring what is most fascinating about cyberspace is to dabble in alchemy. In *Neuromancer* Gibson refers to 'La mariée mise à nu par ses célibataires, même.' [18] André Breton and other Dadaists saw Marcel Duchamp's *Bride Stripped Bare* as one of the key works of their century's art. It consists of two large sheets of glass on which are displayed, among other objects, a waterwheel, a sifter, a pair of scissors, a bar, a chocolate grinder and three other metal tools. These, like the transcriptions of John Cage (1961), have no objective significance. This absence in Dada leaves no room for meanings that do not arise from a work's interaction with the knowledge of its observers. Dada, though it may evoke them, is not meant to appeal to common values. Aiming to evade objectivity it is all subjectivity, yet, unlike a Rorschach blot, composed of familiar objects.[19] It is, like cyberspace, a test of what I might do or be if I were tuned into constant subjectivity, in a condition where

> the body becomes transparent . . . other physical systems cease to exist as checks. . . . no input from outside the complex computing system, which becomes its own environment. In a complete simulation all the input flows to and from the machine and the users; so all input may be consistent, but in error. . . . The technology brings us to a . . . system of man and machine in which all rules and constraints are internal to the system, and hence capable of mutation by the system: the system evolving under its own rules. By contrast, the legal system inherently is built on a model of comparison with external rules. That's what 'legal' and 'reasonable' means: conformity with exterior and independent rules.
>
> (Karnow, 1993: Appendix)

This legal condition – zero-user-interface – suggests the possibility of realising a condition of complete subjectivity which is at the same time real enough in the apprehension of lawyers to be actionable. This is a tempting space – an opportunity to transcend the body, leaving the meat and in the pursuit of individuation entering into deeper and deeper subjectivity (Kozel, 1994). The *Bhagavad-gita* says the demonic think of the world as entirely matter being dreamed in a void, which they, for all their dismissal of the reality of meaning and purpose, know how to enjoy and make real. A hundred and eighty years after Mary Shelley invented Dr Frankenstein's construction, some humans are enthralling themselves with the possibilities of self-construction, not the constructions of individuality formed within the referential markers of Hobbesian laws, but a self-referential, self-regulated, antinomian form of individuality questioning that 'unstable constellation liberal humanists call the "self"' (McCaffery, 1991), challenging 'humanist essentialisation' and 'humanist notions of an unproblematical "real"', decentring the human body, 'the sacred icon of the essential self', rendering suspect all claims which 'valorise universal notions of reason, knowledge and the self' since they 'reflect and reify the experience of a few persons – mostly white, western males'. Hollander refers to 'techniques radically redefining the nature of the self', listing body invasion, prosthetic limbs, implanted circuitry, cosmetic surgery, genetic alteration, mind invasion, eye surfing, brain–computer interfaces, artificial intelligence and neurochemistry, so that '[m]etaphysical-systems grounded on faith in an "inner-self" begin to waver. Notions of a human nature determined by a "physical essence" of the human begin to lose credibility' (1991: 20).[20]

Thomas Mann's *Doctor Faustus* (1949) is one of the greatest dissections of the pact between the respectable and the devil to enliven lives made tedious by nostalgia for the old markers. At one point in the story crystalline chemical plants immersed in an aquarium and appearing to have life turn when exposed to the sun 'yearning' after 'warmth and joy' so 'that they actually clung to the pane and stuck fast there'. This prompts the brilliant musician, Adrian Leverkühn – Mann's Faustus – to silent mirth and the other onlookers to tears (Mann, 1949: 19–20, 242).[21] The roots of 'governmentality' lie in responses to such nihilist amusement.

The idea if not the practice of 'individuality' emerged when, with the fragmentation of the Athenian city-states, human beings ceased to take their identity from the nexus of relationships that constituted citizenship within the *polis* (Sabine, 1957: 102).

Foucault (1984)[22] describes the circumstances of this ancient identity crisis, suggesting that what had previously involved a simple choice between participating in or abstaining from the political life of the times now became complicated. The elaborate ecology of personal authority in all those arenas – psychological, social and political – to which governmentality referred was disappearing. Individuals had to integrate themselves 'into a far more extensive and complex file of power relations'. In contemporary terms, it became a

> crisis of subjectivation . . . of a difficulty in the manner in which the individual could form himself as the ethical subject of his actions, and efforts to find in devotion to self that which could enable him to submit to rules and give a purpose to his existence.
>
> (Foucault 1984: 95)

To live with and connect to complexity and chaos outside I need to negotiate a pact with complexity and chaos inside. Susan Kozel focuses on a 'hazy realm':

> more complicated than either supreme control over the body, or simple abandonment of the body. . . . where the body dances in and out of control. Instead of being seduced and abandoned, it seduces and abandons . . . . Through their work (Blast Theory,[23] Paul [24] and Orlan[25]) the body is not excluded from a virtual world, rather, the virtual world takes place within their bodies, and through their interaction with other bodies. The only way to preserve this notion of virtual reality is to continue to understand it through artistic experience.
>
> (1994: 37)

Koestler (1945) used a metaphor of the writer at the window. To avoid merely reporting on the world through it, an observer must, like Turgenev, keep his feet in a bucket of hot water or similar device for cosseting and licensing what is inside. But lest self-awareness becomes a meditation, the curtains must remain fully open, not screening any part of the view, however frightful or wonderful, that cannot be understood or assimilated. In his book about a middle-aged character called Ephraim Nisan – 'Fima' for short – who spends his time fantasising about solving the problems of the Middle East and trying to run his life and relationships with relatives and lovers, Amos Oz has created a character poised between looking out on the world and intro-spection. Ordinary things are fraught with history and meaning beyond their function in the immediate. One reviewer of this novel suggested of Oz's writing that 'Judaism's lasting contribu-tion to human thought is not so much . . . monotheism . . . as its exploration of the way the material and moral worlds reveal each other' (Storace, 1994: 17).

Fima is burdened by the complex banality of everyday life, starting and not finishing things, staring from the window, being helped by others who paradoxically are consoled into amity by his condition. His dependency irritated me until, in Oz's skilful yarn, I saw the attraction of Fima's impossible attempt at equipoise.[26] Fima, with a poignancy reminiscent of Moses' view of the promised land, conceives the 'Third State' – equidistant between deep sleep and wakefulness, yet distinct from both of them:

> All suffering . . . everything that is ridiculous or obscene, is purely the consequence of missing the Third State, or of that vague nagging feeling that reminds us from time to time that there is, outside and inside, almost within reach, something fundamental that you always seem on the way to yet you always lose your way.
>
> (Oz, 1994: 227)

At one point in this story Fima asks himself, as the sun rises and its light spreads from the sky over Jerusalem and then over the arid land between him and Mesopotamia to the east and to the Arabian peninsular to the south, whether this and the mud, the glow-worms in the almond tree and indeed

> his shabby flat and his ageing body and even his broken tele-phone, were all nothing but different expressions of the same being, condemned to be dissolved into countless, flawed, per-ishable embodiments, even though in itself it is whole and eternal and one.
>
> (Oz, 1994: 226)

NEGOTIATING INTERNAL COMPLEXITY

The Internet, as a conduit to cyberspace, accompanies and amplifies individuation, both between and within individuals, contradicting the reassertion of community (Etzioni, 1993; Ranson, 1990; Roche, 1992; Young, 1993). This process is characterised by multiplying polyphony (Boehme, 1994), isolation, disassociation, access to the fractured condition of 'universal civilisation' (Naipaul, 1991:22–5) as individuals search for some unique version of identity, the liberal inquisition of modernism, 'the ever expanding horizons of desire' (Fukuyama, 1992), the widening gyre (Frank 1963), personal causeless rebellion, self-realisation, Giddens's (1991) 'life-politics', the reflexive self-referential forms of individuality that accompany the consumption of recipes for self-development from dieting to psychoanalysis. This process underlies the liberating tendencies of consumerism in fundamentalist societies, spurring a 'million mutinies' (Naipaul, 1992) as more individuals in countless ways rebel against and manoeuvre around conditions that fixed their role in life.

The self that can use this technology governmentally awaits invention, whether by prosthetic devices, current and anticipated, of artificial intelligence, or by new disciplines of self-government involving 'the care of the self' (Foucault, 1984). Giedion speaks of bridging 'the abyss between inner and outer reality' with a 'dynamic equilibrium that *governs* their relationship' (1948: 723, my italics). This equipoise implies neither embracing the superficiality of Net-paddling nor trying to squeeze the world into consoling simplicity, neither abandoning the possibility of a constituted sense of self nor abandoning the 'meat' to enjoy Gibson's 'unthinkable complexity'.

There is nothing a superiori or natural in the idea of the unified individual. The idea is as much a human invention located in history as the community of the *polis*. There could as well be parts of individuals, each part arising in the context of a different social exchange. Stevenson's (1985) voice, through Dr Jekyll, offers another angle on the inventive idea of politics as personal, by speculating that 'man will be ultimately known for a mere polity of multifarious, incongruous and independent denizens'. The idea of the individual as many is usually associated with genius and madness. Chesterton said Dickens was a mob. Walt Whitman described himself containing multitudes. Fernando Pessoa, creating the poetry of scores of heteronyms, wrote 'Be plural like the universe!' Orson Welles asked an audience whether it wasn't a pity 'there are so many of me and so few of you?' The multiplicity of human talent can lead to less historically located artists being seen as many because it seems unbelievable that one person could contain so many perspectives. Homer was thought to be several, as is Shakespeare still. Multiplicity is also associated with insanity. Legion was cured by becoming 'whole'. Freud, who attributed self-unification to the ego, saw quite the opposite characteristic in the id:

> It is, as we might say, 'all to pieces' . . . . In one and the same individual there can be several mental groupings, which can remain more or less independent of one another, which can 'know nothing' of one another, and which can alternate with one another in their hold upon consciousness.
>
> (1962: 106)

Plato, in Nietzsche's (1974: 26) appreciation, triumphed over the 'mob of the senses', mastering their motley 'by means of pale, cold, grey conceptual nets'.[27] Nietzsche argues that philosophers have taken too simplified an approach to the process by which intention is linked to action. 'Willing seems to me to be above all something complicated, something that is a unity only as a word' (1974: 26). He suggests that willing entails a 'plurality of sensations' – the sense of the condition left, of the condition approached, of the movement between the muscular sensation of apprehending an intention to act, the thought of the action, the emotion of command which includes the inner certainty that one will be obeyed and finally that within oneself which obeys. 'We are in the habit of deceiving ourselves over this duality by means of the synthetic concept "I" ' (Nietzsche, 1974:30–1).

This schema represents an unprecedented elaboration of the process of will, with the language of unity adding to his labour since every singular pronoun is inaccurate. Nietzsche describes freedom of will as the capacity to engender the obedience of a range of 'under-souls' within. To get this group to act is pleasurable but Nietzsche cautions against assuming that because an action has thus occurred the agent who takes credit for it, is its sole progenitor:

> what happens here is what happens in every well-constructed and happy commonwealth: the ruling class identifies itself with the success of the commonwealth. In all willing, it is

absolutely a question of commanding and obeying, on the
basis . . . of a social structure composed of many 'souls'.

(1974: 31)

The individual both commands and obeys. Thus, Nietzsche
reconstituted the 'I', engaging with the hazardous liberties of
multiplicity.

Current thinking about the working of the mind treats as a
useful illusion the idea that I and other humans are somehow
unified with a single coherent purpose and action. My mind
comprises separate mental structures that can act independently
of each other and may have different priorities within the super-
ficially homogeneous mass of tissue that sits in my skull extending its connections to the rest of my body and its senses beyond
my skin. Ornstein (1986) suggests that the mind 'careens' and
'wheels' and is far more inconsistent and unstable than many
versions of sanity and stability would comfortably permit (see
also Rowan, 1990). Thus writers who edit interior voices to
sequential monologue may be easier to read than those, for
whom James Joyce remains the progenitor, who convey it as
something messier and multi-layered, darting between coherence
and incoherence. Ornstein uses the image of an 'internal crowd',
suggesting that to be self-aware is an achievement of internal
government involving the 'the faculty or talent of the self':

There is no single mind but many; we are a coalition, not a
single person. . . . We are unaware of how we decide and
even 'who' is deciding for us. . . . Each one of us is a crowd of
people. . . . So, consciousness, in the multimind view,
involves the participation of the talents of the governing self.

(1986: 24, 130)

Christopher Bollas (1993) explores the causes and consequences of stifling a person's 'internal repertoire of states of
mind' instead of enjoying their inner complexity, cultivating the
ability to use and believe in what he refers to as a kind of internal 'parliament', full of conflicting, dissenting and coercive
views. The thing I have come to call myself is actually an ever-
proliferating multiplicity. Bollas suggests many people cannot
bear 'the solitary recognition of subjectivity' – and may seek
solace from what feels like internal cacophony in partnership
with another or group allegiance:

Given the ordinary unbearableness of this complexity I think that the human individual partly regresses in order to survive, but this retreat has been so essential to human life that it has become an unanalysed convention, part of the religion of everyday life.

(1993: 242)

Adam Phillips (1994: 160) observes that the traditional tendency is to simplify moral life. He wonders what it might be like to live in a world in which people welcome their own complication, recognising the stranger in themselves and so learning to live with the stranger outside (Foucault, 1965; Kristeva, 1994).

ABANDONING ANTHROPOCENTRICITY

Iris Murdoch begins her exploration of 'metaphysics as a guide to morals' with the point that:

The idea of a self-contained unity or limited whole is a fundamental instinctive concept. We see parts of things we intuit whole things . . . . Oblivious of philosophical problems and paucity of evidence we grasp ourselves as unities, continuous bodies and continuous minds. We assume the continuity of space and time.

(1992: 1)

Her difficult arguments revise this self-assurance, eroding common sense while honouring its original insight, so long as this is striven for, not assumed. In the 1968 Reith Lectures on the crescendo of change assailing humans, Edmund Leach said, in one passage, that what frightened him more than the complexities now presented to the mind was the impulse to respond with a reductive omniscience:

The more each one of us can come to understand the overall inter-connectedness of things, the more likely it is that we shall collectively generate an attitude which will not result in self-destruction. What is more important is not that you should know what to do, but that you should feel really deeply that all parts of the system are of equal importance.

(1968:25)

For Leach the route to such understanding entailed replacing positivist detachment with a sense of participation in and membership of what we observed. The implied burden is immense, inviting the psyche, with a distinctive Protestant rush, to incorporate into itself so much that throughout history it has projected outside – divine purpose, special creation, dated and measured boundaries of time and space. The internal void is infinite, but the space that is prepared there to incorporate Nietzsche's internal theology or Leach's understanding of interconnection is sparsely inhabited; hardly able yet to sustain these crusading versions of the self, let alone becoming an arena for oppositional politics. It is not that inwardness is not crucial, but it needs to develop a governmentality acknowledging the permeability of external–internal in a way that zero-user-interface and other transcendent involvements with cyberspace deny or evade.

Foucault's concept acknowledges humans have evolved or invented different ideas of themselves which, once stabilised, acquire the feel of common sense. Historic disjunctions required new perspectives on the self. Humans have invented and developed these in the past. Foucault's (1984) account of 'self-care' suggests but does not formulate its contemporary forms in a world where it seems as if our *sapiens* has to be rediscovered.

Socio-technical systems of people and interconnected smart terminals connected to smart servers suggest such an advance on the first electronic nervous systems that cabled the globe that as the traffic on them multiplies and their increasing bandwidth allows global multi-media transactions between millions of minds in cyberspace, an unpredictable qualitative shift will occur in the field properties of the Net.[28] It will somehow go self-organising – as some argue it has already (Plant, 1995) – and potentially self-realising. Connectionism[29] and connectivity are constant themes in speculations about the Net, leading to reflections on when what was previously inanimate – merely an array of information – might acquire something approaching what humans understand as sapience. While humans anticipate some imitative process of increasing confidence and sophistication, machine intelligence, other than that designed by machine makers into their creations as pure mechanism, may emerge via unfamiliar evolutionary routes. The conscious and pre-conscious qualities that may be possible through the multiplying connections of the Net may be outside our recognition. Instead of designing something like us we may set the conditions for something currently unrecognisable that is only part of us and part of something else unknown. If another intelligence could speak I could not understand it; probably would not hear it.

The Turing Test measures only the capacity of a machine to imitate human intelligence. Humans may have things to learn about themselves via their engagement with forms of intelligence they can only envisage as artificial. The disordered and alien form of anything that presented itself as other than artificial would be unrecognisable and possibly as unacceptable as those parts of ourselves we cannot contain or entertain as part of us. The unconscious, fifty years after Freud's death, has the feel of familiar territory, but it isn't. There is an infinity inside humans as theoretically unfathomed as outer space, not because it is in the preventive detention of Freud's repression, but because, of a laudable restoration via cognitive psychology of an internal space, hidden but not repressed, which increasingly reveals us as 'conscious of . . . a relatively small proportion of what we know and . . . the unwitting beneficiaries of a mind that is, in a sense, only partly our own' (Miller, 1995: 65).

I struggle with pre-Kantian assumptions about the boundedness of internal space, not helped by the constant application of reductionist models of motivation and personality to the working of human organisation and the conduct of public affairs (Hubbard and Wald, 1994; Kramer, 1993). The message of depth psychology that health is the most bearable form of madness is as difficult to assimilate as the possibility that the process of individualisation has far further to go and awaits political inventions able to bring governance to internal spaces the human psyche has yet to enter. Borrowing Foucault's metaphor, I have – in Table 5.1 – imagined my relationship to the ideas that have formed me as an archaeological site containing all the idiosyncrasies, omissions, confusions and possibilities of a personal dig. The final layer apprehends a future where my hopes for civilised life – humane in intention, assured, sceptical, self-critical, moderate, competitive, respectful of talent, law abiding, leavened by guilt, impelled by the concentrated accretion of surplus, its politics defined by exclusions and paralysed by the side-effects of its desires – are dispersed amid limitless diversity.

Table 5.1 An archaeological site: versions of the self and their negotiations

Selves	Sense of agency	Guarantors and counter-guarantors of meaning	
Memphite	Selfhood confined to a supreme ruler identified as a God. External voices guiding, commanding and warning from many specialised spirits.	Diverse awarenesses manifest as external motivating spirits placated by tailored observances. No permanent leading deity	One god defines existence.
Classical	A unified consciousness living between appearance and reality. Perceptions are fallible, masking underlying order as multiplicity,	The gods' intentional, if capricious, interest in humans. What cannot be controlled outside can be controlled inside by Stoic discipline.	Trust in oracles, magic, indulgence in the practices of the old gods, Dionysian mysteries, self-immolation and sacrifice to influence fate.
Cartesian	Common-sense certainty of the self as a moral centre or substance located in the human brain.	God's presence can be recognised through reasoned introspection. Private mental data afford proof of my existence as an individual.	Faith in the authority of the Church and the crown to define and order existence and have privileged access to and knowledge of God.
Humean	The self is an illusion consisting of numerous fragmentary experiences held together by strong habits of the imagination. Challenge to the idea of self as fixed, constitutional and essential.	Meaning is to be found through invasive investigation of the vast mechanism of nature. There can be no certainty of a benign or malignant overseer other than as a clockwinder.	Faith in nature, the occult and mysterious mystical forces determining fate. Hazards of arrogant meddling because there are more things in heaven and earth than dreamed by rational philosophy.

Marxian	The self wakens as a hopeful monster, conscious of its inherited position in relations of economic production.	Meaning comes from political awareness. Through alignment and shared struggle with other members of their class, individuals can liberate themselves from ordained social relations.	Rationalisations of God's and Destiny's working in the world – through social and political reform and imperial expansion. Faith as an entrepreneurial project.
Freudian	The self that is experienced is a small part of the whole psyche, which contains dæmonic forces. Many parts of the self, though inaccessible, influence our actions and perceptions profoundly.	Meaning comes from interminable self-discovery and the acceptance of the psychic burden of repression as a condition of civilised existence.	Avoidance of introspection. Materialism and the pursuit of extrinsic identity, especially nationalism and ethnicity as symbols. Romantic veneration of force and the expression of aggressive human will.
Liberal-humanist	The self is centre-stage, real, born into, made by and sharing in making the cultural unity of Western civilisation.	Shared civil and psychological trust in the golden mean. Preservation of a precarious balance between Apollonian regulation and Dionysian inspiration.	Public surfacing of the 'folkish' layer. Reaction as progress. Barbarism as courage. 'The sleep of reason brings forth monsters.'
Reflexive	There is no insulated and intrinsic identity located in gender, class, ethnicity or any other essential category of human being. The 'I' is episodic clarity in a dense information field.	Meaning is learning, elaborating life as a multi-layered internal–external dialogue with self and others.	Anthropocentric bio-chauvinism. Fundamentalism, millennialism, superficiality, fragmentation. Consumerist anxiety sated by globally distributed derivative objects, symbols and meanings.

CONCLUSION

> Horror which used to reside in the external terrors of the 'frightful fiend'[30] which followed close behind now resides close inside. We are preoccupied with objects and spirits that may inhabit our homes, our children, ourselves. Government and community fought the external beast more or less successfully, but in fighting the internal beast we use new authorities, different experts and now even these are unreliable. Problems of democracy once focused on the dangers of giving power to the many headed monster out there. The problems of democracy reside now with fear of the beast inside.[31]

Foucault looked at how government was invented within and without the self. He described governmentality as 'an art which concerns all and which touches each'. This governmentality arises in the context of an unprogrammed diversity of personal coups d'état, from those 'million mutinies now' that Naipaul[32] describes, the polyphony of post-colonial, post-imperial artistic expression,[33] the yen for re-sacralisation among many prosperous citizens in the West,[34] to absorption with 'life-politics' and the 'reflexive project of the self' described by Giddens (1991); an expanding process of individuation in a Godless but still mysterious universe[35] containing the risk of collusion with fundamentalism and nihilism. These concerns are echoed in debates about top-down and bottom-up policy-making, how to find the smallness of place without delegating the powers of global governance to indeterminate forces, how to have the personal without losing the political; especially how to resist that inner emigration separating the psychological and the political that Mann describes in *Doctor Faustus*.[36] Appalled puzzlement surrounds the Holocaust because it arose within so much that was humane and progressive and in trance or entranced. There were people streets away from the thuggery who wanted a source of anxiety to be 'not there' any more. In his story about this neglect Mann does not write directly about those who elaborated anti-semitism. Rather he traces fault lines in a civilisation's character, unfolding, through a variety of ordinary voices, the making of the pact between the German genteel classes – the *Mittelstand* – with an Austrian painter's apprentice they despised who offered magical palliation for their fear of complexity and their longing for neat wooden villages set in pasture land on the edge of pristine forests, the innocent domestic rituals of pastry-cooking and precise needlework (Reed, 1985). His novel depicts deep responsiveness to music, *Innerlichkeit*, the Lutheran separation of State and Church, a helpless bourgeois humanism, and something else that crept up beneath an artful patina of decent reticence, suggesting how a particular kind of civility created the space for its opposite – the surfacing of the folkish layer. The story does not attempt the moral dilution of universalising what was special to a time, a place and a people. It is a work of art directing a combination of attention and self-attention towards past, present and future disfigurements of the world that many recall and witness with the same apolitical helplessness as its carefully named narrator, Serenus Zeitblom.

If this detachment were to be treated as a kind of virus that lives in me, the inoculation would release an internal politics able to bring government to areas in the psyche previously the province of Freud's internal security or Nietzsche's apolitical individualism. This is not so much fatalistic dignity in the face of an uncomprehending universe as a humorous and brave scepticism about any divine purpose for the race – any teleology – married to the responsibilities of citizenship, especially as these involve duties to other life forms.

NOTES

1 Personal journal.
2 A professor of electricity explains cables to a new recruit 'They are the nervous fibres of the world, conveying intelligence from one continent to another, just as the nerves of your body send the impressions of the senses and the wishes of the brain to every limb' (Munro, 1895: 18).
3 Conan Doyle, *The Lost World* (1911); Jules Verne, *Journey to the Centre of the Earth* (1864; English translation 1874) and *Twenty Thousand Leagues Under the Sea* (1869; English translation 1874); H.G. Wells, *The Time Machine* (1895).
4 In 1983 in chapter 15 of *Woman on the Edge of Time*, Marge Piercy's heroine, Connie, enters an alternative dimension considerably resembling cyberspace a year before the first edition of *Neuromancer* (see Piercy, 1992: 584).
5 Weber's description of technology as 'congealed social relations' suggests that machines may, like shards from a midden, reveal the folkways of their users. His view that 'a lifeless machine is materialised mind' runs through the decade-long research of the Programme on Information and Communication Technologies

(PICT) started in 1985 and supported by the ESRC to look at long-term issues posed by advances in information technology, overviewed in Robin Mansell (1994)

6 Debate on 'The Death of Architecture: Interconnected Technologies and the Urban Environment', Ikon Gallery, Birmingham, 16 February 1995. Speakers: Neil Spiller, Architect, Bartlett School; Sadie Plant, Lecturer, Cultural Studies, Birmingham University; James Roberts, *Freeze Magazine*. My notes on Neil Spiller at the meeting.

7 Ibid. My notes on Sadie Plant at the meeting.

8 Marge Piercy (1992) uses this term for the outlaw areas outside the net-linked corporate compounds in her novel *Body of Glass* about a more or less earthbound future, first published in 1991 under the title *He, She, It* (Knopf).

9 A *passive* corollary of 'we' is the unconsidered use of 'they', deferring to powers beyond control.

10 George Steiner refers to the 'singularity, the brain-hammering strangeness of the monotheistic idea' which 'tore up the human psyche by its most ancient roots' (1971: 36).'To all but a very few the Mosaic God has been from the outset, even when passionately invoked, an immeasurable Absence . . . ' (1971: .37).

11 Already owned by US publishers, the eleventh edition of *The Encylopedia Britannica* was issued in 1910–11 by Cambridge University Press. The last edition to be produced in London, its cosmopolitan richness and literary style breathes the confidence attributed to that period in British history.

12 'Few men realize that their life, the very essence of their character, their capabilities and their audacities, are only the expression of their belief in the safety of their surroundings' (Conrad, 1947: vii, 89).

13 Taylor (1991: 53–76), Baddeley (1995), and a particular observation of a character in E.M.Forster: 'All over the world men and women are worrying because they cannot develop as they are supposed to develop' (1993: 327).

14 'He that voluntarily continues ignorance, is guilty of all the crimes that ignorance produces; as to him that should extinguish the tapers of a lighthouse might justly be imputed the calamities of shipwrecks' (Dr Johnson to those in Scotland opposing the translation of the Bible into Gaelic on the grounds that it would maintain a distinction between Highlanders and other inhabitants of North Britain, 13 August 1766: Boswell, 1970: 373).

15 Personal journal, 27 January 1995.

16 For these in plenty see the magazines *Mondo 2000* and *Wired* and Parts 2 and 3 of Rushkoff (1994).

17 'All around the metaphysicians were still directing their telescopes to the farthest end of the universe: Kant, on the contrary, having long returned from this high-strung flight, was making himself comfortably at home on earth' (Frank Sewall in Kant, 1900: 1).

18 *Neuromancer* is sprinkled with surrealist landmarks, thus Gibson's

view of complexity 'that cut the eye' (1984: 304) recalls an image at the start of Luis Buñuel's film *Un Chien Andalou* (1929).

19 Giedion suggests Duchamp, and other surrealists, transform machines of 'marvellous efficiency' into 'irrational objects, laden with irony, while introducing a new aesthetic language' (1948: 44).

20 See also Hollander (1991) quoting William Sterling (pp.209–10), Jane Flax (pp.207–8) and Jeter's *The Glass Hammer* (pp.211–12).

21 Mann (1949) chap.3 pp.19–20 and chap. 25. p. 242. In realising that this novel should never be seen as solely German – though it *is* about Mann's country's and his people's special involvement in Nazism – I was guided by the critic Joseph Frank (1963: 131–61).

22 'In social, civic and political life, it had to bring a certain dissociation into play between power over the self and power over others. The importance given to the problem of "oneself", the development of the cultivation of the self in the course of the Hellenistic period, and the apogee it experienced at the beginning of the Empire manifested this effort of reelaboration of an ethics of self-mastery' (Foucault, 1984: 95).

23 *Chemical Wedding*, danced at the ICA's 1992 'Ripple Effect', described in Susan Kozel (1994).

24 Telematic Dreaming in which Paul Sermon placed himself on a bed in one gallery and had his image projected onto a bed in a second gallery 300 miles away. 'Members of the public in the second gallery had the option of joining his projected image on the bed . . . video cameras in the second gallery transmitted the actions of the persons on the bed with Paul's image back to Paul in the first gallery . . . contact improvisation between an image and a person, between ghost and matter' (Kozel, 1994: 36).

25 *The Reincarnation of Ste Orlan*, where, under local anaesthetic, Orlan 'orchestrates live transmissions of her "aesthetic surgeries" to galleries and academic conferences thousands of miles from the operating theatre where she is carved up by an accommodating surgeon' (Kozel, 1994: 36).

26 Recognising that certain styles of civil normality may somehow create space for gross uncivil abnormality, Mann defined *Humanität* – a state poised 'between Romanticism and the Enlightenment, between mysticism and reason . . . the "mean" of balance and harmony in a culture . . . which fosters . . . our many sided potential' (Reed, 1985: 138).

27 Kaufmann (1974) exposes the fabrication of Nietzsche's association with totalitarianism, while acknowledging his contribution to understanding totalitarian impulses inside individuals including himself. 'He who fights with monsters should look to it that he himself does not become a monster. And when you gaze long into an abyss the abyss also gazes into you' (Nietzsche, 1974: 84, Maxim 146). See also L.P. Thiele (1990) on how to avoid being 'snagged' by Nietzsche's flights, especially part II 'The Politics of the Soul' (51–95).

28 ' . . . change . . . in the second condition [some intra-species

communication system] is a greater mutation than if man had grown a second head' (Emery, 1967: 224). ' . . . social and psychological effects may be no less extensive than what one would expect from a major mutation of the species' (Emery, 1967: 234).

29 'The movement [in the cognitive sciences] . . . generally called connectionism, offers a powerful and still controversial alternative to the standard model of mental representation which has more or less dominated western philosophy at least since the Enlightenment' (Miers, 1993: 1).

30 Coleridge, 'The Rime of the Ancient Mariner' (1797), part 6, v. 11.

31 Personal journal, September 1993. Three years ago I was still comfortable with the pronoun 'we'.

32 Naipaul (1992), after writing twenty years earlier of India as a 'Wounded Civilisation', reports, more optimistically, a diversity of personalised, sometimes demagogic, bizarre and infantile endeavours – all eroding traditional constraints on individuality.

33 'Increasingly more writers from more countries have migrated across the multiple borderlines of nation, language and culture, bearing with them, and transforming in the process, their vision and modes of expression. So it has happened that the end of our century is deeply marked by literatures almost inevitably polyphonic, cultures that are rarely not dispersed or displaced, and therefore bent on refashioning their identity' (Boehme, 1994: 24).

34 Samuels (1994). See also Samuels (1989), proposing the style of the political pluralist in personal journeys towards that state of unified responsibility for *all* one's selves called integrity.

35 Steiner, on facing such a universe inside: 'Only a psychologist of Nietzsche's genius and vulnerability could experience the "murder of God" directly, could feel at his own nerve-ends its liberating doom' (1971: 38).

36 Mann's focus: 'the nature of Western bourgeois culture, in which a haunting awareness of its precariousness and threatened disintegration is balanced by an appreciation of and tender concern for its spiritual achievements' (CD-ROM Britannica). Mann has Zeitblom reflecting that the 'folkish layer survives in us all . . . I do not consider religion the most adequate means of keeping it under lock and key. For that, literature alone avails, humanistic science, the ideal of the free and beautiful human being' (1949: 38).

Chapter 6

Virtual worlds and the social realities of cyberspace

Ralph Schroeder

INTRODUCTION

A number of digital technologies – like the Internet, multimedia computing and interactive television – are poised to play an increasing role in our everyday lives. Media speculation has centred on the question of how these technologies may affect us in the future, typically suggesting dystopian or Utopian visions – Orwellian surveillance and impersonal virtual sex versus cosy teleworking at home and being able to study anywhere in the world at the virtual university. Research within the social sciences, on the other hand, has tended to provide more mundane scenarios of the implications of new technologies beyond such either/ors. Yet even among social theorists, there has recently been a trend towards emphasising the revolutionary implications of the new technologies, with talk of cyborgs, cybersociety and virtual selves (Escobar, 1994; cf. Schroeder, 1994).

This chapter will consider the relation between the new information and communication technologies (ICTs) and social life by reference to virtual reality (VR) technology. Although VR has so far been largely confined to research laboratories, VR systems have recently come to be commercially available. And while there are not many everyday settings in which VR systems are currently used, VR crystallises many of the issues about the social implications of ICTs because it involves interactivity and 'realistic' computer-generated worlds. I shall argue that in order to understand the relation between VR and social life, it is necessary to examine both the advances and constraints presented by the technology, and to do this in relation to the range of similar information and communication technologies which are used in social contexts which are comparable to the applications and potential applications of VR.

TECHNOLOGICAL CHANGE AND SOCIAL REALITY

Before we examine the social aspects of VR in particular, it is necessary to reflect briefly on different sociological approaches to technology. This area has been dominated by two extremes, technological determinism and social or cultural constructivism. The former generally overlooks the social contexts in which technology becomes embedded, whereas the latter attempts to reduce technological advancement to social or cultural forces. These extremes can be avoided by means of a realist viewpoint which takes into account both the growth of scientific knowledge and the material make-up of technological artefacts, on the one hand, and the social settings in which these become embedded, on the other.

If we adopt this perspective, we need to begin by asking: where do the advances in VR technology come from? As we shall see, the development of VR systems depends to a large extent on a number of improvements to VR hardware and software: accurate position-trackers, high-resolution stereoscopic viewing devices and increasingly realistic three-dimensional computer graphics (overviews of VR technology can be found in Durlach and Mavor, 1994; Kalawsky, 1993). These improvements, in turn, have been made possible by scientific and technological advances in a number of fields, including magnetic sensors, liquid crystal displays and increased computer processing power. The general difficulty in the sociology of science and technology, however, has been to translate such advances and refinements into an account of the changing relations between artefacts and social life.

A useful starting point in producing such an account is Ian Hacking's philosophy of science. Hacking has argued that modern science 'has been the adventure of the interlocking of representing and intervening': 'We shall count as real', he writes, 'what we can use to intervene in the world to affect something else, or what the world can use to affect us' (1983: 146). This idea can be extended to the sociology of technology. Paraphrasing Hacking, we can say that technology has been the adventure of the interlocking of refining and manipulating, except that in this case manipulating the world 'to affect something else, or what the world can use to affect us' takes place through artefacts, in other words, through techniques related to the physical world or to material objects. Here I follow Agassi, who has argued that 'at the very least . . . the implementation of any technique whatsoever involves both physical and social activities' (1985:25). Or, to put it differently, technological artefacts are always in some sense ('physical') hardware.

The implication of these ideas is that the dynamic of technology should be analysed at the level of concrete processes of refining and manipulating, demonstrating how different artefacts achieve different effects on the natural and social worlds. To do this, it is necessary to identify the range of technological options available in the case of a particular artefact – and thus the range of its effects. It then becomes possible to make comparisons both between this type of artefact and similar ones, and between the effects of this artefact and those of similar or previous artefacts in particular social settings (or with social settings in which no technological means are employed).

In short, it will be possible to evaluate in what sense a particular technology has a distinctive or cumulative impact, an impact which can be traced through the various social contexts in which the technology becomes embedded. Hence it is not just scientific and technological advance that has to be examined, but also the social side of this advance. Here Weber's notions of 'rationalisation' and 'disenchantment' are useful since they capture the two sides of social processes that accompany all scientific and technological advance: the spread of instrumental-rationality (or of using the most efficient means to achieve a given end) and the increasing impersonality of the external conditions of life (Schroeder, 1995a). When we examine the role of specific technologies, however, it will be necessary to bring Weber's ideas about large-scale social processes down to the level of everyday life; that is, to look at the concrete social settings in which the technology is used.

VITUAL REALITY TECHNOLOGY

VR is a technology by means of which users can experience and interact with computer-generated environments. Although the origins of VR can be traced to computer displays which were developed in the 1960s, the main technological advances in this field have taken place in the 1990s, with dozens of laboratories and firms currently involved in VR research and development (Rheingold, 1991; Schroeder, 1993). But despite rapid advances in hardware and software, it is still unclear what VR systems will eventually look like. How, for example, should the user's body be represented in the virtual world? What input devices should be used? And what features enhance the 'realism' of virtual worlds? A number of these technical choices are still open-ended, yet it is also possible to identify some developments which are already narrowing the range of options in VR. To do this, we shall need to outline the main technical features of VR systems and the major uses to which they have been put.

VR systems are currently developing in two directions: on the one hand, there are low-cost systems for the entertainment games market (Hawkins, 1995; Schroeder *et al.*, 1994). These are technically relatively unsophisticated because they have to compete in price with other arcade-style and home computer games. For the same reason, they also need to offer a highly immersive experience and thus tend to follow the format of existing games. On the other hand, there are various relatively expensive VR systems aimed at more specialised markets, such as medical research or training for hazardous environments. These systems tend to include devices which are specifically tailored to particular tasks. Whether these two directions will eventually merge is difficult to say, but there are a number of implications of both for the shape of VR technologies.

VR entertainment games typically consist of a low-resolution head-mounted display (HMD) and a flying (or hand-held) 3-D joystick, with the most common format the shoot-'em-up. Until recently, VR games were only available in arcades and therefore relatively short (*ca.* five minutes). And although some games can be networked to allow several players to share the same virtual world, the sense of competition or co-operation with other players is limited because of the short duration of games (Schroeder, 1995b). Players are represented in the virtual world by means of cartoon-like computer-generated bodies and the content of most games consists, as in other computer games, of shooting enemies while undertaking certain tasks in order to reach more advanced levels of play.

What is important about VR games is that the technology and

the use to which it is put are fairly well-matched. The representation of a three-dimensional cartoon-like adventure fantasy world does not require much more computer power than an ordinary personal computer and the low-resolution display offers detail which is comparable with other computer games (although the health and safety aspects of VR games, particularly eye strain and 'simulator sickness', have not yet been sufficiently investigated. Research about 'simulator sickness' is reviewed in relation to VR by Pausch *et al.*, 1992). These minimal requirements also have to do with the level of interaction with the virtual world: moving around in rudimentary landscapes and shooting things, again, does not require great levels of detail or computing power.

It is true that VR games have advanced significantly within a short period of time so that, for example, the head-mounted display has become much lighter and offers improved resolution. The level of detail of virtual worlds has also improved dramatically by means of computer graphics techniques such as texturing and shading. These improvements in technical sophistication are bound to continue since non-VR computer games increasingly offer three-dimensional perspectives and more realistic graphics. But with the important exception that low-cost VR systems may push VR in new directions by making the technology more widely available, games have at this stage already lent VR technology a particular shape, namely, again, the combination of low-resolution HMD, flying joystick and minimally interactive and cartoon-like virtual worlds.

At the other end of the scale, there is a wide variety of systems and devices. Visual displays include high-resolution head-mounted displays, images which are directly projected onto the retina by means of laser optics, and images displayed on large curved walls or screens. There are many types of input devices, including force-feedback arms, spaceballs, and gloves. Position-tracking devices, which are usually electromagnetic in VR games, are also more diverse in non-VR systems and may, for example, be optical or acoustic. Moreover, these systems vary in terms of the input and output channels: some feature input from the whole body by means of a bodysuit or exoskeleton, whereas others employ the same combination as games with an HMD and flying joystick. Some VR systems include olfactory, gustatory and tactile output, but most, like VR games, are limited to visual and auditory output. The virtual worlds themselves in professional VR applications range from highly complex and photo-realistic environments to monochromatic three-dimensional line drawings. Examples of the content of virtual worlds include architectural and scientific models, landscapes, virtual galleries, and photographs or moving images that have been imported into virtual worlds.

As these different systems and devices are tailored to different tasks, it is likely that there will continue to be many options at this 'high' end. In spite of this diversity, it is possible to venture some general points about non-entertainment VR systems. One is that outside of the realm of high-powered systems for research, there is intense competition among producers of commercially available VR systems to create a robust and comfortable machine which combines high-resolution displays with an easy-to-use navigational device. This is because if VR is not simply to be used as an experimental or demonstration tool, it needs to be accessible and flexible enough to suit workaday settings. The second is that despite the differences with VR games, the most common type of system is nevertheless the combination of HMD and flying joystick, although both devices and the computing hardware and software in this case tend to be of a different order of sophistication by comparison with VR games.

If this last point seems to bring non-game and game VR systems more closely together, it needs to be emphasised that this difference is greater than it may appear because of what users can *do* with these systems. More expensive and technically sophisticated VR systems may allow the user to modify the virtual world by means of programming the software, they enable tasks to be carried out in the virtual world that require precise tracking and take longer periods of time, and the user can typically explore and manipulate an information-rich virtual environment. The reason for emphasising this is that these are precisely the features which set VR technology apart from other, similar information and communication technologies.

VIRTUAL WORLDS AND THE WORLDS OF INFORMATION AND COMMUNICATION TECHNOLOGIES

In comparing VR with similar information and communication technologies, we can begin with other computer games. VR games, as mentioned earlier, have thus far been the most wide-spread application of VR technology. There are many similarities between VR games, non-VR arcade games and home computer games, including the graphics, joystick input control and the formats and themes of the games. One feature of home computer games that tends to be overlooked in discussions of their effects are the social relations in which they are embedded (Haddon, 1993; Provenzo, 1991). A common image of computer games is of a child transfixed in front of the screen for hours on end. But computer games often also involve parents and friends, with whom co-play and access to the games need to be negotiated and where roles (such as 'the expert') and relations (for example, parents using gameplay as a reward, or gender differences around gameplay) establish patterns around the games.

VR games are too short and have not yet entered the household sufficiently to form these kinds of patterns. But *if* the several VR games that are currently being developed and sold for home use were to become widespread, an important difference between these and other computer games is that players will be much more cut off from the world around them. Apart from this, it is difficult to say to what extent VR games will be more 'absorbing' than other computer games since they will vary in content and format. But because they cut players off from their surroundings and give them a more direct sense of interacting with a computer-generated world, VR games intensify the involvement of players and in this sense extend the capacity of existing games machines (yet here, again, we need to recall that VR games machines are much less sophisticated in terms of interaction than high-powered VR systems).

Non-entertainment VR systems need to be compared with a variety of tools in medical research, training, architecture and the like. The vast bulk of VR systems that are currently used in these contexts are for the purpose of visualising objects or environments that are difficult or impossible to visualise with existing tools. What they have in common by comparison with non-VR systems is not so much that this visualisation is more 'realistic' than other types (though this may be too), but rather that a different kind of control over the image is made possible, especially in terms of being able to move around objects and to change them. Again, this needs to be put in the context that these visualisation tools are mostly prototypes, that they are mostly used for short periods, and that the devices are often cumbersome and have not yet been fine-tuned for comfort and ease of navigation. Within these constraints, however, VR systems allow the user to carry out tasks related to the visualisation of objects and environments that cannot easily be achieved with similar tools. Hence these constraints should not obscure the fact that in terms of visualisation and especially interaction with virtual worlds, again, VR extends the capabilities of existing machines.

One area that needs to be mentioned briefly is networked VR systems. Networked VR games have so far only allowed a small number of players (typically up to four) to share the same virtual world. Apart from this, there have been only a few demonstration projects with networked VR and it is as yet unclear what kinds of co-operative tasks or activities networked VR is suited for. Here, the comparison is with screen-based computer-supported co-operative working (CSCW), videophones, and in terms of games, Multi-User Dimensions (MUDs) and games like Habitat (Morningstar and Farmer, 1991). But again, since it is still unclear what kinds of 'co-presence' users will have in virtual worlds and what kinds of interaction will be possible in networked virtual environments, it remains to be seen what kind of 'fit' there is between networked VR and other communications tools.

So far, I have emphasised the side of scientific and technological advance and how this has affected the capabilities of various VR systems. The social implications of this advance, rationalisation and disenchantment, should now also be spelled out more explicitly. VR systems undoubtedly extend the instrumental control that we have over simulated or computer-generated worlds, be they for entertainment, scientific research or co-operative work at a distance. By the same token, however, they add to the tools by means of which we spend time in technologically mediated environments. In other words, here as elsewhere, the increasing mastery over the social and natural worlds goes hand-in-hand with the routine use of more human-made environments.

Before we move on to place these new technologies in a wider context, one further capability of VR systems deserves note, and that is world-building. Creating virtual worlds, which normally takes place on a desktop computer as opposed to inside the virtual environment itself, is relatively easy. So, for example, there have been two schools projects in which teenage pupils have built complex and imaginative virtual worlds within a matter of days and with relatively little help from teachers (Bricken and Byrne, 1992; Schroeder, 1995c). The same is true of commercial virtual world design, which mainly requires good design skills rather than computer programming skills (Giles, 1994). Since some VR software includes world-building (or world-authoring) 'kits', the design of virtual worlds by means of object-libraries and drawing tools can be mastered with relative ease by the layperson. In this sense, too, VR extends existing tools for creating computer-generated worlds because it essentially combines the ease-of-use of computer-aided design tools with the complexities of computer-generated worlds that have so far been confined to simulator or other professional computer visualisation technologies. The degree to which VR systems which are used for building virtual worlds as against the consumption of ready-made virtual worlds, however, is still very much in the balance.

VIRTUAL WORLDS AND THE WORLDS OF CYBERSPACE

Discussions of various computer-related new technologies tend to revolve around the notion of interactivity and the possibility that various existing machines – such as television, telephones and home computers – will be enhanced by being linked up in ever more powerful computer networks. This needs to be placed in perspective in several ways. A number of pilot projects have shown that, with regard to the use of interactive television services, audience habits tend to change very slowly (Neumann, 1991; see also Rogers, 1986: 62–4). A second point is that the nature of interactivity, in the case of VR as elsewhere, depends on the task. As we have seen, it may involve shooting enemies in search of the next level of play, or building and exploring an architectural model. Much depends on the definition of 'interactivity' (see, for example, Rafaeli, 1988): whether it should include real-time interaction (which would exclude electronic mail, for example, but include MUDs), whether the interaction must include two active participants (this includes the telephone but not television), and whether the environment must be 'realistic' (video images, but not text) or manipulable (CSCW, but the use of a remote control to order items from a computer-generated shopping catalogue on television seems to stretch the meaning of the notion of manipulating a computer-generated environment).

It is equally important to locate computer-related technologies within particular social settings. It has been suggested, for example, that computer networks and television will converge and change the nature of both computing and watching television beyond recognition. What seems more likely, however, is that a computer-controlled television will continue to be confined to the living room and feature mainly entertainment, whereas a computer with television images is more likely to be used in the study for work – even if each of these technologies in the future contains some of the elements of the other and they are both hooked up to a two-way telecommunications network.

In a similar way, we can now say that users are more likely to put on VR helmets and use navigation devices to operate virtual worlds in some contexts – such as entertainment arcades, professional visualisation facilities, military training facilities, and schools – rather than others. As concerns the additional spaces that VR may come to occupy in the living room, the introduction of VR to the home has only just begun and it remains to be seen whether it will become a permanent or popular fixture. The exception to these limitations might be the extensive use of networked VR, but there are, at present, both technical and social obstacles to this: technical, because the communication networks that achieve high enough rates of two-way data transfer to allow shared virtual worlds are only just emerging; and social, because it is unclear whether there is an appropriate commercial and regulatory environment for the establishment of a network for offices and homes with widely used software and hardware standards.

Thus the only long-distance shared virtual environment that has so far been developed – apart from a handful of university-based prototype projects – has been the US Defense Department's military training system, the Naval Postgraduate School's Networked Vehicle Simulator (NPSNET, see Macedonia et al., 1994), a successor to the Simulator Network (SIMNET) of the 1980s (Katz, 1994). The military has been able to develop this system because it has the resources to use prohibitively costly high-speed computer network links and to develop a new software standard specifically for the operation of a networked VR system. There are few links, however (apart from the potential uses of this software standard), between networked VR for military training and civilian VR development.

These considerations may also apply to computer-mediated communications. The uses of electronic mail and various other newer forms of computer-mediated communications (such as the World Wide Web, MUDs or 2-D graphical interactive worlds like Habitat) borrow from the uses of existing technologies in similar contexts (fax, conventional modes of advertising and traditional computer game formats), on the one hand, and they are restricted to particular contexts, on the other (to certain professions, for example, which already make intensive use of computer technology). The social embeddedness of these new technologies may, in other words, set limits to the extent to which technology – even if it is conceptualised in terms of 'realism' – transforms social life.

VR is competing, both technically and in terms of social space, with a host of other new technologies. But like previous information and communication technologies, it will not replace them wholesale but rather be added to or complement existing ones (Rogers, 1986: 26). It is therefore essential to compare the capabilities of VR systems with those of similar tools. Yet as we have seen, to do this it is necessary to follow the two sides of VR development and the contexts – whether as a mass consumer electronics device or as a specialised tool for professional applications – in which VR is becoming embedded. These, in turn, need to be located within the overall processes of the interlocking of refining and manipulating, and of rationalisation and disenchantment. And although VR is still at an early stage of development, it is particularly important to identify the social implications of new technologies at the outset since it is typically the earliest phase of technological development which sets the course for the future.

Part II

Nation-states, boundaries and regeneration

Chapter 7

The virtual state
Postmodernisation, informatisation and public administration

Paul Frissen

A lifeless machine is materialised mind.

Max Weber, *Economy and Society*

INTRODUCTION

New developments in information and communications technology (ICT) do represent a hype. But hypes may produce interesting and far-reaching impacts. It is, however, necessary to stress that these impacts do not eventually lead us into Utopia, as is often stressed in American literature. History knows no progress, nor does technology. What is more, the key characteristic of ICT and its impact is ambiguity. It brings us equality and inequality; violence and peace; small and big scale; Big Brother and Soft Sister.

ICT and government, or public administration, are intensely intertwined. The nature of public administration explains this, for its primary processes always have been the processing of information and communication. So the dominant technology of our age affects the heart of government. The impact of ICT on government and public administration therefore is revolutionary (see also Snellen, 1994; Taylor and Williams, 1991). Public administration uses ICT as an instrument for its internal organisation, for its operations, for transactions, for the development and implementation of policies, for monitoring and disciplinary ends, for the provision of information to politicians, citizens and societal groups and organisations. Public administration also addresses ICT as an object of regulation and policy-making.

In order to understand the meaning of ICT for public administration, technological developments have to be placed in the context of the variety of changes and innovations taking place in public administration. In this chapter technological developments will be related to organisational and policy changes in public administration. Although informatisation and administrative change are usually put into a perspective of modernisation (Bekkers and Frissen, 1992; Van de Donk and Frissen, 1990), in this chapter I will argue that their combined effect will lead public administration into an era of postmodernisation (Crook *et al.*, 1992).

In this chapter I will address the following issues:

- technological developments;
- organisational and political implications of these developments;
- political–administrative developments;
- organisational and political implications of these developments;
- similarities and dissimilarities between technological and political–administrative developments and their implications;
- the effect of postmodernisation.

TECHNOLOGICAL DEVELOPMENTS

Speculations usually tell one more about the author than about the object of speculation. Nevertheless it seems plausible to outline the following trends in ICT developments (Frissen, 1994: 42–3).

Capacity

There is an inevitable tendency towards ever smaller and more powerful systems. A modern PC has the capacity of a classic mainframe. This means that individual users, organisational units and organisations will be fitted with increasingly better and more powerful machines.

The capacity increases not only in terms of mere quantity but also in terms of quality. Machines develop intellectual and reflexive capacities, competing with people and their anthropocentric world view. Modern organisations therefore develop into symbiotic human–machine configurations, as is expressed in Lenk's notion of the 'tandem' (Lenk, 1994: 318).

Connections

In relation to this growth in capacity, communication technology is becoming increasingly important. Infrastructures for data-communication in the most elaborate sense are being developed on a large scale and with accelerated speed. Common limitations in space and time are increasingly being overcome. The Internet is the archetype of the explosion in network technologies and network connections. Within and between organisations electronic connections are created. To some extent inter-organisational connections are outnumbering intra-organisational connections. These electronic connections may become more important than the physical organisations and organisational units they connect. Societal and policy networks or configurations can effectively be represented in electronic networks. Cyberspace is the 'real' space.

Integration and coupling

Integration of systems, media and different technologies is another significant tendency. Intelligent coupling of data, images, sound and other sensory sensations make new technological applications possible. The sense of reality of the information produced by ICT increases. But also interactivity is more feasible. Integration and coupling of systems facilitated by network technologies stimulate the increasing practice of computer matching. Electronic traces which people leave behind in their day-to-day actions and transactions can be followed and combined for monitoring and disciplinary ends but also to create profiles of behaviour.

Virtual reality

One of the most revolutionary trends is virtual reality. One only has to go into amusement arcades to experience it. By integrating media and systems an apparent reality is created of a three-dimensional nature. 'Virtual reality allows you to explore a computer generated world by actually being in it' (Sherman and Judkins, 1992: 19). Virtual reality can be a simulation of existing realities, as in a 'flight simulator', and the creation of a new reality, as in entertainment applications.

Tracking devices

According to Zuboff (1988), the most fascinating aspect of ICT is its 'informating' capacity. ICT always supports or substitutes processes while, at the same time, generating information on these processes. 'Informating' therefore is a sort of reflexive capacity of ICT. A network supports one's communication but, at the same time, it registers and monitors this communication. Through the wide-spread use of magnetic strips and chip cards huge amounts of reflexive information on actions, transactions, and processes are collected. This reflexive information then supports all kinds of new applications and activities.

ORGANISATIONAL AND POLITICAL IMPLICATIONS

The ever increasing capacity of ICTs makes small scale a technological option. So, while technology in the history of organisations and public administration usually provided arguments for the enlargement of scale, now ICTs support decentralisation and decreasing scale. The huge bureaucratic and hierarchical organisation is no longer necessary from a technological point of view. Central control of big mainframes can be replaced by mechanisms of local empowerment. Small, intelligent and flexible units represent the organisation of the near future (Peters, 1992). On the other hand, this same tendency for increased capacity makes all kinds of large-scale operations feasible. So the argument to support local government because it is better equipped to collect information on local affairs and to provide services on a small scale no longer holds.

Zuurmond (1994) has shown that through ICTs, and particularly through the development of an information architecture within the social security system in the Netherlands, local agencies have effectively been put under central control. Only the control is no longer exercised by a tight structure of bureaucratic mechanisms and hierarchical supervision, but by the information architecture and infrastructure which have replaced bureaucracy. On the surface, organisations within the social security system even appear to be far less bureaucratic.

What is important is the observation that scale becomes an obsolete factor to organisation and to governance. Instead of economies of scale, economies of scope become crucial. With distributed and relational databases it no longer matters where an organisation or an administrative layer is located. The globe is a village and the village is global. This causes severe impacts for public administration because the political system is still organised on the basis of territory. The trend towards 'deterritorialisation' produced by ICTs therefore undermines the legitimacy of a political system which is territory-bound and which receives support on the basis of elections held in a territory.

The increase in electronic connections within and between organisations has led to the horizontalisation of relations. Horizontal relations are becoming more important than vertical relations. In public administration – at least in the Netherlands – this leads to a growing correspondence between electronic networks and policy networks or configurations. Policy-making, then, is less hierarchical in nature. As a result, the so-called 'primacy of politics' (for instance the concept of ministerial responsibility) is at stake. The multi-centred world of cyberspace relates to the multi-centred world of policy domains. On the other hand, central control is facilitated by the increasing use of computer matching. This technological option has spread all over Dutch public administration in order to detect and prevent social security and tax fraud. The issue of privacy – intensely debated in the seventies – has disappeared from the political and the public agenda. The use of magnetic strip and chip card technologies will strongly contribute to the possibilities of coupling. Also this will increase the reflexive capacities of organisations in general and public administration in particular.

Network technologies are also increasingly used in public and political debates and communications (see Depla, 1995) Several 'freenets' have been developed in the Netherlands. They are called 'Digital Cities' (see Schalken and Flint, 1995), use the Internet and are organised by private actors supported by government. But the government is also using the Internet to organise political debates. In 1995 we have been running an Internet discussion for the Netherlands' Ministry of Home Affairs regarding a new White Paper on informatisation in public administration. One of the research questions in this project was whether the style and participation in a 'digital' debate differed from ordinary political debates.

Virtual reality as such has not yet found wide-spread application in public administration. One could think of applications in the field of town and city planning. We can also speak of virtuali-sation as a metaphor for the organisational and political implica-tions of ICTs. Simulated and created realities will, on a large scale, become the basis for policies and political actions. Physical organ-isations and their configurations will be replaced by the cyber-space of electronic connections and communications. The most important question for political and public administration theory will then be whether the structure and processes of existing pub-lic administration are still adequate to deal with the reality of cyberspace. Of course this also questions the normative basis of the political system in which collective decision-making by ideo-logically inspired representatives is essential.

POLITICAL–ADMINISTRATIVE DEVELOPMENTS

ICT developments should be analysed in the broader context of public administration and the political system. Several relevant tendencies can be discerned which are related implicitly or explicitly to ICTs. There is empirical evidence from the Netherlands which shows similarities with developments in other West European countries. These developments can be understood as new conceptions of governance and they are occurring in various policy domains. I will list several examples:

- deregulation: making less, but particularly less detailed and interventionist rules and regulations;
- creating independent agencies: giving independent (private or public/private) bodies responsibilities to implement and sometimes also develop public policies;
- privatisation: contracting in or contracting out activities which were usually performed by governmental bodies;
- governing at a distance: dismantling interventionist policies and regulations and accepting societal self-steering and self-regulation in various policy domains;
- co-production of policies: creating policy networks of societal and government actors to produce policies;
- informatisation: using ICTs to organise and reorganise gov-ernment and public administration, in the fields of service delivery, policy-making, political debate and deliberation.

Ideally these developments share several characteristics, which I shall now outline (Frissen, 1990:20–1).

Scope

Government steering is, on the one hand, more general and, on the other hand, less intensive. Processes of societal self-steering are more fully taken into consideration and accepted as an autonomous source of governance.

Object

The number of points of application for steering is being decreased. To use systems theoretical terms, steering is limited to the input of policy domains (budgets), or the output of policy domains (setting performance indicators), which is steering on key parameters (Snellen, 1987), or steering is replaced by meta-steering. Meta-steering is the governance of decision-making arrangements in a policy domain. Points of application, then, are the structures of policy-making (the arena) or the procedures to be taken into account (the rules of the game). Government, then, is to some extent indifferent as to the outcomes of policies in a specific field – it only judges the quality of decision-making arrangements. It is a sort of process steering, so to speak.

Level

Steering responsibilities are situated at different levels. The one-sided attention for the macro-level disappears in favour of a reappraisal of the meso- and micro-levels of steering. This means a shift both to provincial and local government and to societal actors.

Participation

The empirical evidence that societal processes of steering are taking place in networks of individuals, groups and organisations is taken as the starting point for the design of policy-making arrangements. A multi-actor perspective on steering contributes to the incorporation of shared responsibilities for steering in policy-making arrangements. This tendency is based in the historical neo-corporatist tradition of the Netherlands.

Perspective

The traditional centralist model of steering, based upon the idea of a rational actor, planning and deciding from one point, is substituted by a model that honours differentiation, variety and pluralism, while not considering these as limitations to be overcome. Instead of a top-down approach towards steering, a bottom-up approach is being developed.

ORGANISATIONAL AND POLITICAL IMPLICATIONS

A basic feature of the above-mentioned developments is the recognition of networks on which they rely. Society cannot be understood as a dichotomous system of hierarchies and markets, but should be seen as a complex set of private, public and private/public configurations. The basic idea is that most of these configurations are autonomous to some extent and cannot be governed in a traditional bureaucratic, machine-like manner. Self-steering and self-organising capacities of societal actors not only have to be taken into account, but should also be the starting point for the design of policy-making arrangements.

Pluralism and differentiation are key concepts. It is even better to take fragmentation as a key notion. This fragmentation concerns both the outcomes of policy processes, which are no longer regulated by a central actor, and the nature and number of participants in policy-making arrangements. The insights of configuration theory and even some aspects of autopoietic social systems theories are instrumentally translated into the organisation of policy processes. Co-production of policies, the necessity of coalitions and consensus, the institutionalisation of networks, all express this neo-corporatist tendency in policy-making. However, it differs from traditional neo-corporatism in the pluralism of participating actors (not only the vested interests) and the rapid change of actors, who may participate more incidentally.

Politics is developing more and more into a sort of 'broker'-politics, in which government plays a more organising and procedural role. It is admitted that effective policies presuppose participation and commitment of societal actors. And what is more, it is acknowledged that decades of successful welfare state interventionism have resulted in a 'smart' society that can no longer be governed in the paternalistic style of the welfare state.

To some extent these new conceptions of steering bring forth a depoliticisation of politics. For politics is directed no longer primarily towards the outcomes of policy-making arrangements, but increasingly towards the (democratic) qualities of structures and procedures of societal decision-making. And because societal decision-making increasingly is supported and conducted by ICTs' applications and infrastructures, these become focal points of steering.

If policies are being developed and implemented in configurations, this contributes to a more horizontal nature of public administration. Vertical bureaucratic relations of command and control are substituted increasingly by horizontal relations of compromising and organising consensus on a non-hierarchical basis. Regulation as the archetype of governmental steering is replaced by contracting in and out, by co-production arrangements, by consensus-seeking configurations, by negotiation, by wheeling and dealing. As a result, there is a growing imbalance between the actual process of policy-making and decision-making and the institutional form and nature of the political system, which is vertically organised for a unitary territory and which claims the prerogative of the authoritative allocation of values for a society. The reorientation of political attention towards the structures and procedures of societal decision-making even adds to this. The primacy of politics in determining the long-term course of society no longer holds from an empirical point of view. In normative terms this leads to an erosion of legitimacy because consistent ideologies as a basis for determining the long-term course of society become obsolete and displaced by fragmented sets of norms and values in specific societal domains.

Corresponding to these developments, we can observe a fragmentation in political styles. With a more networking type of policy-making, the recognition of the relative autonomy of societal domains, the increasing participation of societal actors in policy-making, the non-hierarchical and non-bureaucratic mode of steering, there is a proliferation of styles due to the fragmentation of society and public administration. The style of organising societal decision-making may become more prominent instead of the ideological basis of politics. It is interesting to note that at present the cabinet in the Netherlands consists of three parties, two of which were formerly considered to be political extremes on the Left–Right political spectrum.

We may witness the development of a political system that is relatively indifferent with respect to policy contents, but normative with regard to the qualities of social steering and the conditions under which this takes place, and this codifies socially crystallised consensus. Politics then becomes a question of style – it can be considered as 'a grammar' for societal decision-making (White and McSwain, 1990: 52–3).

SIMILARITIES AND DISSIMILARITIES

There are several similarities and dissimilarities between ICT developments and political–administrative developments.

Horizontalisation

Because of the increased and increasing capacity of ICT hardware and software and because of the diffusion and sophistication of communication infrastructures, significant changes in organisational structures and functioning are taking place. The hierarchical, bureaucratic organisation, vertically integrated under a one-dimensional authority, is losing meaning, because separate units within the organisation are increasingly better equipped with ICT tools. Thanks to network connections they can communicate horizontally with units outside the organisation. Besides, ICT facilitates splitting up of organisations, contracting out of units, creating independent agencies. This results in network-type organisational configurations.

Political–administrative developments in the direction of co-production of policies, increasing participation, setting up public/private and public/public partnerships, run parallel to this. The combined result of these developments is a growing significance of horizontal relationships, of non-hierarchical patterns, of co-operation on a contractual basis and not on a basis of directive regulation: horizontalisation. The network character of society, which always has been an empirical reality, is now being honoured politically and electronically. The pyramidal design of the political system no longer is adequate to deal with this (Kuypers *et al.*, 1993).

Deterritorialisation

Technological developments make the whole world 'on-line' accessible on a lap top. This means that time and space are decreasingly limiting and are thus becoming irrelevant factors. The world not only is available immediately but also in all its depth and breadth. Organisational patterns consequently change because they have always been based on limitations in time and space. For organisations function with a specific course of time for a specific territory. Decision-making and patterns of control are based upon linearity of time. This also holds for decision-making and policy processes in public administration.

Changes in public administration are often aiming at a more effective co-ordination of time and space. Creating independent agencies for policy implementation can be understood as an effort to organise shorter response-times in terms of feedback between policy implementation and policy development. Rearranging government structures through decentralisation and regionalisation is an effort to adapt public administration to the scale at which problems occur.

Technological developments, however, lead towards deterritorialisation, because neither time nor space pose significant constraints. Besides, available ICT applications facilitate the organisation of information provision and communication nearly independently of existing patterns and structures of public administration. Connections and couplings can be made on and between every desired level of decision-making. Again, this produces tensions within the political system, which is to a large extent territorially organised.

Virtualisation

Virtual reality will undoubtedly find its way into public administration. Using VR helmets and gloves in meetings for citizen participation is an exciting alternative for dull gatherings on the basis of flat maps.

But I use the concept of virtualisation as a metaphor for political–administrative implications of ICT. These implications are as follows (Frissen, 1994: 276–7):

- technology will be increasingly able to simulate existing reality by means of integrating technologies and media;
- technology will be increasingly able to create new realities through that same integration;
- because in many domains man and machine have become, as it were, symbiotic unities, technologically simulated and created realities become more realistic in the perceptions of individuals, groups and organisations;
- integration of technologies and media makes distances in space and time increasingly relative: long distance 'on-line' connections are possible, so that simultaneity and nearness are less and less bound by limits;
- consequently, the experience of a limited territory in which one can act and communicate becomes less relevant;
- communication relations and actions can thus be organised on the basis of the desired level of scale and scope, the desired participation and the desired information provision.

Redesign

These technological developments facilitate the redesign of existing structures and processes in public administration. I refer to the practice of Business Process Redesign in the corporate world (Davenport, 1993). Instead of using ICT to automate the existing organisation without changing it fundamentally – for decades dominant practice – existing technology facilitates fundamental redesign. Some may say it forces to do so. Redesign not only is a possibility, it also is a necessity.

Information and communications technologies have gained such a prominent place in many organisations – and particularly in public administration, which is primarily orientated towards information and communication – that the logic and dynamics of ICT have constraining consequences.

Besides, the cognitive and reflexive qualities of the information generated through coupling and profiling are such as to become a more realistic and determining input into the policy process. Intelligent information on implementation processes can stimulate new policies; detecting patterns in databases can create new policy windows; transaction systems can generate information on consumption patterns and life styles.

Policy processes are thus increasingly dependent upon ICT-based information and communication relations. As a result ICT may constitute these processes and produce different modalities of design. At the same time there is more freedom to design processes with the help of ICT, so economies of scope can be taken into account.

Ambitions

Notwithstanding all developments towards non-hierarchic, non-bureaucratic, horizontal, networking patterns of public administration, induced by ICT, there is strong evidence for exactly the opposite. The availability of ICT is a serious incentive for classical steering ambitions. It contributes to what Beniger (1986) calls the 'control revolution'. Bureaucratic surveillance is facilitated on an unknown scale through computer matching, profiling, and all kinds of tracking devices.

Classical limitations to bureaucracy in physical, cognitive, political and societal terms seemingly are overcome by the use of ICT. Informatisation creates an information architecture which substitutes bureaucratic control and coordination. Instead of a bureaucracy we witness the birth of an 'infocracy' (Zuurmond, 1994). Informatisation in public administration is a process of continued modernisation. Sophisticated bureaucracy enters into a tight coalition with technocratically advanced technology. The infocracy is a 'virtual vestige' (Zuurmond, 1994: 287).

FRAGMENTATION, AMBIGUITIES, VIRTUALITY: POSTMODERNISATION

While modernisation can be seen as a relatively linear process of differentiation, postmodernisation – a term coined by Crook *et al.* (1992) – represents a shift towards de-differentiation or fragmentation. Social realities are quickly changing fragments of an eclectic nature. There is no longer the overarching consistency delivered by a grand narrative. The world is multi-centred and there is no longer a strong conviction that we are in the centre of it, directing our future by our decisions. The grand narrative of political ideology is increasingly problematic, partly because of the previously sketched developments. The pyramidal nature of public administration increasingly changes into an archipelago of network configurations. Policy processes are less hierarchical and linear and more horizontal and circular. Central steering is substituted by self-steering. Politics is more about styles, or fragmented styles, than about content.

The 'disenchantment of the world' as a promise of the modernisation process invades the organisational world, now that the machine-like and mechanistic character of it is surpassed by powerful ICT equipment of individuals and units. Peters speaks of future organisations as 'knowledge-based societies' (1992: 123) and Zuboff of post-hierarchical relations in an 'informated organisation' (1988: 399). Fragmentation will lead to an emancipation of the bureaucratic organisation – beyond central control. The technical and organisational features of the Internet (distribution of information without central control, non-guided and autonomous addition of participants, applications and supply) represent cultural characteristics of new inter-organisational relations. To some extent they are of an anarchistic nature. It is interesting to see that the major proponents of Dutch 'Digital Cities' are former members of the anarchistic squatter movements, now being sponsored by government and industry to take part in the development of the electronic highway.

Norms and values of the market and norms and values of autonomous social systems and individuals replace bureaucratic norms and values. Standardisation and formalisation still are technically required, but increasingly form conditions for flexibility, creativity and autonomy.

However, this is not a sketch of Utopia. Cultural postmodernisation, in the sense of fragmentation, does not imply the disappearance of power, control and inequality. International networks are intelligently used by transnational corporations. Virtuality does not transform the capitalist system – to some extent it supports it. ICT and warfare are close allies, as the Gulf War has shown. And even the Internet has a strong Pentagon origin. ICT is full of ambiguities.

With ICT time and space have become less significant as organisational factors. As such it contributes to the modernisation process of 'time–space compression' (Harvey, 1989). But because this implies acceleration of time and decreasing of space, culturally there is a 'trend to privilege the spatialization of time (Being) over the annihilation of space by time (Becoming)' (Harvey, 1989: 273). This puts progress into perspective, which is so characteristic as a concept of modernisation. The local, the special, the specific, can be organised ever again and anew.

For organisations this means a strong increase in fluidity and flexibillity. Scope is becoming far more important than scale. Time–spatial coherence as a value loses importance; physical organisation as a basis for loyalty or discipline as well. A blurring of organisational boundaries will occur both in structural and in cultural terms. Virtualisation affects patterns of meaning.

This will have a severe impact on the traditional legitimacy of the organisational pattern of politics and public administration. Both ICT and political–administrative developments contribute to an ongoing fragmentation of relations between public administration, politics and society. As a result, politics will no longer be the privilege of political institutions, but will 'dampen' into the complexity of a society, networked in two respects.

Essential to politics and public administration is that through ICT and some of the transformational aspects of new conceptions of steering the notion of a mono-centric world disappears. This holds for society as a whole, but also for our anthropocentric assumptions in this world. The *Homo politicus*, the *citoyen*, is no longer the dominant actor. Systems are becoming more and more intelligent and at a growing pace are better at several things. ICT, being an intellectual technology, has far-reaching implications for our notions of autonomy, sovereignty and self-determination. Reality is the unintended result of decisions, increasingly taken by machines. And the individual in cyberspace is fragmented in databases and networks. As a result of this fragmentation, the individual as a meaningful entity becomes decentred and multiplied (Poster, 1990: 7). We become postmodern.

The core of politics, then, may become an aesthetic of styles, to be enacted in various fragments of public and private life.

Chapter 8

The challenge of cyberspatial forms of human interaction to territorial governance and policing

Klaus Lenk

INTRODUCTION

Speculations now abound on the influence of globalisation and of information technology on the future of the welfare state. By comparison, the classical functions of the state are given much less attention. Even the 'minimal state' should afford protection against ennemies and provide public safety and justice. With information technology approaching maturity and global information technology infrastructures taking shape, it is an open question to which extent the nation-state or its subsidiaries will continue to deliver in this respect.

The title of this contribution was prompted by my personal, well-worn habit of opposition to any fashion which is seizing our minds. If everyone is now thinking global, I am asking what will happen locally. My main question therefore is: *'How is the governance of cyberspace related to the governance of a territory?'* There is no easy answer to it.

Territorial governance and policing are the core functions of the state as it emerged in modern European history. Their original focus is neither welfare nor economic development, nor culture and enlightenment. At stake are the rather elementary conditions of human survival, the avoidance of *bellum omnium contra omnes*. However strongly we may be woven into a complex tissue of mediated informational relationships over distances, even in the global society will we continue to live together on a territory. Face-to-face encounters and physical interaction will not cease, except for a few eremites hooked on the Internet and planting their own cabbage. But territorial co-existence alone does not create a social texture. It is difficult to foresee to which extent meaningful social relationships and expressive behaviour can occur over distance instead of in an immediate physical neighbourhood. The latter will continue to be relevant for elementary aspects of life. In the words of the Swedish geographer Torsten Hägerstrand: 'The criterion for survival is to succeed as a neighbour' (cited in Van Paassen, 1981: 17).

Unoppressive communities where people live safely and where human rights are respected rely on some degree of policing. The implosion of new states in Africa gives an idea about how policing and good governance are dependent on each other. Economic and cultural development is stalled when political or traditional institutions fail to deliver in this respect. Policing has above all a pacifying function, replacing private violence. The fact that policing itself can become a danger to peaceful communal life is accepted and dealt with by legal safeguards of different kinds.

POLICING AND POLICY-MAKING

The central role of policing for good governance is not reflected by adequate administrative theory-building. Policing has not been a prominent theme in public administration theory, some outstanding monographs notwithstanding. Rather it has attracted the attention of organisational sociologists and of sociologists of law. Instead of acknowledging its central role, we keep ourselves busy with problems of policy-making, only to discover that many of our traditional concepts related to policy interventions seem to lose contact with basic realities in an information society. From evidence of the faltering efficacy of many policy instruments in various contexts, we readily jump to conclusions about the state getting entangled in policy networks, whilst its power base seems to erode. No wonder, then, that the 'twilight of hierarchy' and the loss of centrality are loudly hailed or feared, according to temper.

The almost exclusive preoccupation of theory with policy-making instead of with the classical functions of policing is no longer adequate. Policing is at the core of public administration as it evolved in Europe. The essence of public administration as the executive arm of the state is (a) monitoring the society, or rather a segment of it delimited by territory, and (b) intervening where this society through its political institutions deems it necessary.

The ultimate goal of policing, as well as that of policy intervention, is twofold. Both aim either at stabilising social relationships or at changing them. While stabilisation is a common goal of almost all societies, transformation has become the hallmark of industrialised, and increasingly also developing, societies during the last two hundred years. Change means transformation, and such transformation can be piecemeal, unplanned for and conflictual. It can also be macroscopic and sought for, in the sense of moving a society forward to a new state which may then be 'frozen' to some extent (Dror, 1989). The transformations of former East Germany and of present-day South Africa are good cases in point.

It is important to recall that the original sense of the word 'police' was in fact 'policy', as in the German *Policeywissenschaften* which flourished until the beginning of the nineteenth century (Chapman, 1970). The wider connotations of policing got lost when a more and more powerful bourgeoisie succeeded in limiting obtrusive policing ambitions of the absolutist state by *Rechtsstaat*-type legal rules (Neumann, 1957). Because of constitutions restricting its arbitrariness, policing became in fact limited to the stabilising side of policies. Typically, policing could be seen as stepping in when processes of social self-regulation with regard to everyday social behaviour broke down. As the purposes of policing were now limited, at least in theory, to the strictly necessary, the police became defined exclusively by their means: by their tools of surveillance and of physical or informational intervention. Such a view is reinforced by an almost total consensus of theories of the state. The state is taken as an all-purpose arrangement, defined not by the functions it fulfils but by the means it uses and by its institutional shape.

While we tend to equate police interventions with bringing a deviant state of affairs back to normality, policy-making, at the other extreme, is now almost uniquely related to bringing about planned social change. Policies usually intervene in some delimited policy sectors which, as the common argument goes, should be transformed in a piecemeal fashion. Growing complexity and interrelatedness of policy sectors is increasing the political and social costs of proceeding in this way. And we are very unsure about the ways in which macroscopic societal transformation processes should be managed.

Policing as a function of the state was not always neglected. Using different terms, Adam Smith was well aware of its fundamental importance. It has to be brought back into discussion. Focusing on it will probably result in perceiving the core functions of the state in a different light than that projected onto it by postmodernist gibe. And we will be less induced to look at administration from the point of view of economic and technical rationality. Although the practice of policing is backed by the state monopoly of legitimate force, acting as some sort of 'reserve currency' (Derlien, 1993), the tools of policing wielded on a day-to-day base are astonishingly 'soft', compared with the classical range of interventionist policy instruments aiming at transforming policy fields.

'GLOBALISATION' OF CRIME

What are the prospects of policing in the new cyberspace age? One way of dealing with the issue would be to start with inherited concepts of space and territorial sovereignty. Their reassessment is overdue. Here again, instead of indulging in postmodernist holistic speculation, we should try to carefully disentangle different functions of space (for example, as production site, as a hindrance to attainability, as condition for social integration). Similar considerations apply to the concept of sovereignty. Unfortunately, this reassessment cannot yet be the object of the present contribution.

Limiting ourselves to a discussion of observable trends, we will concentrate on policing as the most basic activity in territorial governance. Traditional policing and peace-keeping activities were performed on, and limited to, a determined (national or local) territory. The mind-set related to territorial boundaries of action and influence is still very strong. Letting foreign police tread a square metre of their soil in hard pursuit of criminals is still anathema to European national governments. And senior police officials complain that police co-operation is advancing only slowly while national borders are becoming insignificant for crime.

The threats to personal safety and security on national territories assume new dimensions. Until now, (a) plans for (criminal, terrorist, etc.) action, (b) the marshalling of resources for such an action, (c) its execution and (d) the (destructive) effects of it used to be concentrated on a territory delimited by boundaries. From now on, these four phases of adverse action will become more and more dissociated in space. Information technology increasingly allows for the production of remote effects. If remote surgery is now possible, remote criminal attacks are as well. Destabilisation of a village or a city may originate anywhere.

Moreover, the same technology also multiplies opportunities for monitoring nature, society and individual behaviours. Remote sensing and surveillance of all types are no longer the privilege of powerful military or civil state authorities. Governments are losing their Orwellian privileges of information detection. Remote sensing and other means of spying are available at increasingly low cost, for example to the media. The CNN news chain already surpasses secret services. It is easy to imagine which means will soon be at the disposition of organised crime.

And lastly, information technology also augments the planning capacity of individuals and organisations. For designing complex criminal or terrorist projects, large organisations are no longer required. Major effects can now be produced by small groups. Hence organised crime may become less 'organised' than presently assumed. German police still define organised crime as being concocted by organisations in the classical sense, exhibiting quasi-militaristic command structures. Suffice it here to point to the bulging literature on the 'organisation of the future' in management journals to show the inadequacy of such views. For various reasons, we are all reluctant to look into the backyards of lean management, of worldwide communication and of new technologies which increase the reach of human action, for better or for worse. But we have to do so, in order to appraise the future into which we are stumbling.

Coping with these developments is not made easier by the fact that there is a decreasing observability of many criminal actions, especially during their preparation. The information 'detectors' (Hood, 1983) of government are heavily concentrated on its own territory; worldwide information sharing by police is still in its infancy.

PROSPECTS OF TECHNOLOGY REGULATION AND DESIGN

Political reactions to this situation often jump at measures aiming at restoring the transparency of potentially criminal behaviour under conditions of the new information infrastructure. We are sceptical about the possibility of warding off major adverse effects from global interaction on local social textures. Existing institutions like the police, emergency management and the military try to cope with this unprecedented situation. The outcome of their concurrent, and sometimes conflicting, efforts is far from clear.

We will briefly deal with two different sets of action patterns through which initial efforts are made to come to grips with the future of territory-bound policing in the global world. Neither pattern addresses policing itself, but the state of a society which becomes more vulnerable through its technological infrastructures and artefacts. The first of these patterns is regulation, the second being conscious design of large socio-technical infrastructure systems. Regulation of an infrastructure and of the uses being made of it holds little promise. The prospects of building technical safeguards into that infrastructure to prevent misuse are only slightly better.

A glance at data protection regulations quickly reveals the inefficacy of the traditional type of regulation. Our traditional approach to regulating technology and individual behaviour related to it emerged with the need to control steam engines and other dangerous mechanical/energetic artefacts. Interestingly enough, genetic engineering is now regulated with more or less the same instruments. And data protection is a particularly good case in point for a self-perpetuating life of regulatory instruments. The disease may be unheard of, but it is felt that swallowing the usual medicines is the right response to it. Moreover, the effects of the medicine are not evaluated at all. Despite the thousands of pages filled by the (bi-)annual reports of German data protection commissioners (there are seventeen of them), we know close to nothing about the efficacy and effectiveness of data protection legislation in everyday life. Here, as elsewhere, the posture of the state is to mistake the letter of regulation for reality.

Regulatory action is normally taken at the immediate level of concern. It is addressed at the symptoms of a disease, and not at its roots. European data protection legislation attempts to outlaw certain types of misuse of information, instead of looking for other levels of intervention. It is seldom asked whether it would not be better to let information flow freely, tolerating its misuse while neutralising by other means any adverse consequences of such a free flow of information.

A more promising approach is rational and purposeful *design of information infrastructures*. Some infrastructures may indeed be designed in a way such as to prevent misuse, or to restrict their use to determined purposes only. The Californian philosopher Langdon Winner (1987) has called for the establishment of a new discipline, which he calls 'political ergonomics'. Political ergonomics should develop ideas which facilitate the specification of a 'suitable fit' between a good society and its instruments.

There is no doubt that we need to inquire into that 'fit' in order to obtain sound principles for the design of technological systems. Winner himself gives an example concerning partner authentication and concealment in telematic systems. Fields where the (infra)structures of work and of social intercourse can be rationally designed (and redesigned in the light of initial experiences with their use) do exist in public and corporate information systems. Yet when it comes to large societal information infrastructures, it can be doubted whether technical artefacts are actually designable in view of a desired quality of society, of their fit with a good society. Such infrastructures are emergent phenomena. They are the combined outcome of many major decisions and of myriads of minor decisions all concurring to shape their appearance and functionalities. And even if it were different, the complexity and interrelatedness of many large technological systems is such that rational design will most likely lead to some kind of suboptimisation. Moreover, new infrastructures escaping from the built-in technical safeguards may emerge in parallel.

A striking example of such overwhelming complexity is our road traffic 'system'. Here, the freedom to release dangerous machines co-exists with well-intentioned efforts of regulating human behaviour and with half-hearted safety devices built into the infrastructure and the artefacts. Millions of killed and millions of crippled persons worldwide apparently do not provide a sufficient reason to change this patchwork approach to a large technological system. Even if it would, the task of gaining political leverage on such a system is daunting and probably disruptive for many of the industrialised nations. An estimated one-fifth of the German workforce (many doctors and lawyers included) earn their living from this system. It is only a slight exaggeration to contend that the present social equilibrium guaranteeing domestic peace in Germany is predicated on its continuing existence worldwide.

How to redirect such a system towards a more convivial and sustainable state, once it is fully developed? To some extent, society and the rest of its technology gradually adjust to such a large system. Huge psychic energies are tied to its continuing existence.

Curiously enough, there are other sectors where potshot regulations are introduced by political forces ably playing with popular fears, even before new (socio-)technical systems find the time to emerge. Such was the case with data protection in its early phase. There can be no doubt that we should try to regulate information processing in some respects. But it takes years to find out which type of regulations in which areas really hit the nail on the head. This approach to new societal situations created by an unprecedented technology is basically a symbolic one, calming down fears and upholding trust in our inherited mechanisms of governance.

SOCIETY AT WAR WITH ITS ARTEFACTS

Faced with an increasing amount of well-meaning efforts to prevent social harm through some type of governance of 'cyberspace', we have to radicalise our argument. While regulation and design of technological artefacts and of their use are neither impossible nor useless, we are increasingly unable to extend this traditional technology-taming approach to some of our major innovations. Society therefore has no choice but to defend itself against unknown dangers flowing from our technological achievements. We are at war with our own products and with our overwhelming technological skills.

Our well-intentioned efforts at political control of technology are dwarfed by the shadow of the future. At least occasionally, such efforts prevent harm flowing from badly designed technological systems. These may be made safer, misuse may be prevented through a range of solutions, and social adequateness of their use may be promoted. But a huge technological potential is now looming behind those technological artefacts and systems, which are constructed more or less deliberately. This potential is growing faster than the subset of it which makes up those technologies we put into use.

Taken together, badly designed technology, misused technology and unmastered technology concur to put society in a position where it can no longer aspire to regulating and controlling all details through its political institutions. Well-regulated sectors will co-exist with others from where we may expect influences which trigger the emergence of new types of individual and collective behaviour. Society, including its political institutions, can at best hope to protect itself, being unable to regulate or to design its technological artefacts in such a way that they will be compatible with good life, with the common weal. The magnitude of the dangers can only be compared to outside aggression and war. These dangers accumulate as a consequence of the unwitting build-up of socio-technical systems influencing daily life situations and our minds, of misusable technology, as well as of an apparently purposeless technological potential.

During the last hundred years, the function of the nation-state has been stretched so as to englobe not only physical safety but also social security. The relative success of this extension in the industrialised world prompted temptations to call upon the machinery of the state every time a new problem appeared on the horizon. We know of no other device for tackling the all-encompassing issue of sustainable worldwide survival. When it comes to taming rampant technology, we do not know where else to look. But we cannot be assured that states, or a co-operative arrangement of states, will succeed another time.

Our 'army': the state, its regulatory and physical tools, are obviously not, or not yet, adapted to this novel situation. Governing cyberspace by just applying old solutions to new problems will not help us in providing the public goods required for sustaining elementary conditions of local good life. If local governance and policing are to remain meaningful activities, effectively pacifying local environments, new ventures in systems thinking are now required. Instead of giving in to the concurrent forces of governance-as-usual and of its postmodernistic derision, we have to do our best to cope with the new complexity through a mix of sophisticated reasoning and intuition.

Chapter 9

'Digital democracy' or 'information aristocracy'?
Economic regeneration and the information economy

Dave Carter

INTRODUCTION

This chapter outlines the strategic importance of exploiting the opportunities offered by new information and communications technologies (ICTs) to support economic regeneration and urban development. It aims to identify ways in which the applications and services being developed using advanced telecommunications and telematics should be made more accessible to local people and organisations. It highlights the potential for new projects to be developed which will enable the benefits of the development of the 'information superhighway' to be maximised at a local level.

THE IMPACT OF THE INFORMATION SUPERHIGHWAY IN THE URBAN CONTEXT

New ICTs are playing an increasingly important role, as a key growth sector, in the regeneration of urban economies. This sector is providing the dynamic for the emerging 'information economy', or 'information society', where multimedia-based teleservices (services utilising the integration of sound, text and image) and teleworking represent a major economic change comparable to a new industrial revolution.

Certain cities are well placed to capitalise on this both through having, or gaining, experience and expertise in using these technologies and by having a concentration of existing telematics projects which provides a base for the development of a 'critical mass' in the future. The priority, especially for city councils, is to ensure that these technologies become a means for generating economic growth, employment and an enhanced quality of life through the provision of local access to the facilities and services available on the developing information superhighway.

In terms of urban policy-making this is partly a response to the trends identified both in the European Commission's White Paper 'Growth, Competitiveness, Employment' (EU, 1993) and in the Bangemann Report, 'Europe and the Global Information Society' (EU, 1994), where success in urban regeneration is increasingly linked to the availability of and easy access to appropriate telematics infrastructures and the associated skill levels in the local population. It also reflects recent changes in emphasis in policy-making at both national and international levels, especially within the European Union (EU), in relation to strategies for economic regeneration and urban development. There is a move away from economic growth as an end in itself towards employment generation and quality of life issues associated with economic growth. These ideas are influencing the current policy debates about the role of the information superhighway and how it can best be used in support of wider strategic aims and objectives for economic and social development.

The main scenario being debated is essentially an optimistic one where the information superhighway will be able to support a wide range of new services which will empower citizens and provide for their full participation in an emerging 'digital democracy'. There is a serious danger, however, that this ignores the realities of power which support an 'information aristocracy' rather than a 'digital democracy'. If citizens are not able to have access to the new telematics infrastructures and services, the outcome will simply reinforce existing patterns of inequalities with 'information haves and have-nots' in our communities.

At the same time, the development of new services and applications which take advantage of upgraded and enhanced infrastructures is currently dominated by the multinational corporate sector – either as suppliers or users – leading to a pattern of 'development from above'. If the new infrastructures are to benefit a much wider spectrum of people than is currently the case, there is a need for public support at the local level to support 'development from below' in applications and services.

One of the main constraints on the current development of advanced communications services is the lack of new applications which can generate enough demand to reach a critical mass of users. To extend the 'electronic highways' metaphor, while the 'superhighways' are being constructed, there are not enough 'slip-roads' being built, there are virtually no 'cars', let alone public transport, in mass production and insufficient 'driving lessons' available in order to support people in exploiting the opportunities which the 'superhighway' offers in terms of speed and capacity.

There is, then, a distinct 'applications gap' at the level of the local citizen. The most effective way of bridging this gap is by experimentation, through field trials and demonstrator projects, working closely with the final users at the local level. Such initiatives could provide a wide range of insights which can be usefully drawn upon by others in developing alternative systems, geared to different local needs in different places. Local experimentation therefore becomes part of city-wide 'learning networks' whereby the insight gained in one environment can be transferred with suitable adjustments to another. If these 'learning networks' can link up – regionally, nationally and internationally (especially at the European level) – then there is the basis for a potentially powerful counter-balance to vested interests, in terms of corporate and state authority, which can be pro-active taking an advocacy role in relation to consumer, citizen and wider democratic interests.

Developments in advanced communications need to be accompanied by a strategy for development from below which seeks to realise the indigenous potential of cities and regions. Social innovation in the community – involving local government, schools and colleges, public libraries, the voluntary sector, consumer groups and the trade unions, is a necessary counterpart to organisational innovation led by industry, commerce and government departments.

A key principle here is the concept of universal access to telematics services. If there are to be benefits to be gained from the development of the information economy, in terms of new training and employment opportunities, improved information, cultural and entertainment services and the ability to use such services in fully interactive ways, then everyone – regardless of whether they personally have a phone, a TV or a computer (or the money to buy one) – must have the right to access these facilities as a public service. The best way of providing such public services will vary enormously from area to area, region to region and country to country. There are, however, some good examples emerging from some of the cities which are developing work in this area, for example Amsterdam, Bologna and Manchester, based on the following priorities:

- developing community access centres – sometimes called local telecentres or Electronic Village Halls; providing the facilities, together with training, advice and support, for local people and organisations to access the 'superhighway' and, in many cases, to develop teleworking opportunities; on the basis of people working in social settings, for example a neighbourhood telework centre, rather than at home;
- setting up teledemocracy pilot projects; establishing email and bulletin board communications with decision-makers, for example councillors, MPs and MEPs, and running trials of on-line conferencing and consultation projects based on access through community facilities (for example, access centres, libraries, schools, citizens' advice bureaux, etc.) as well as with individuals with the capacity to do this;
- demonstration projects on using the information potential of the community; ensuring that local organisations and people can put information into the system just as easily as they can take it out and that key organisations, such as local authorities, Training and Enterprise Councils (TECs), Health Trusts, government departments, and so on, are fully committed to publishing public information on the 'Net' as part of a commitment to public accountability.

These ideas are based not only on assessments of the likely impact of these technologies on the urban environment but also on analyses of the likely role of cities in the future. This includes a critique of what might be termed the 'Utopian school' of future 'cyber-lifestyles' which sees cities becoming depopulated, 'instant electronic democracy' replacing the need for governmental structures and services and a dominant 'ruralist' lifestyle emerging, at least for a dominant 'majority' of the population.

An alternative perspective is in the process of being developed by a group of European cities co-ordinated by Bologna. At their first meeting in Bologna on 28–9 March 1995, discussing the theme of 'Mobility of People and Knowledge – Cities As Actors of the European Development', a draft 'Manifesto' was produced, which includes an analysis of the relationship between the 'physical' urban environment and the emerging 'virtual environment' available through telematics applications and services or 'cyberspace', as follows:

Just as the city is the physical structure inside which the identity of the citizen is constructed, shaped and developed, the radical modification in the shape of the city, brought about by the availability of telematics applications and services (the emergence of 'cyberspace' or 'virtual space'), is paving the way for a split between that shape and the old codes. With that drift, a new phase has opened up whereby the subjects have to redesign the identities and codes of citizenship. In this vacuum or new territory the clash between traditional codes and new identities of freedom is already open. We must act upon these formative moments, we must decide. This is where there is a gap between the formative process of the new world and the rights of the 'producers'.

Cyberspace is intrinsically a collective space in which interaction with others can become either a place of domination and violence or a place of collective creative intelligence. The design of the social and linguistic devices required to guarantee and maintain the complexity of this new 'virtual habitat' is now very weak or practically absent. These devices need to be developed so that the 'virtual habitat' has the capacity to use synthetic or virtual images to demonstrate new models based on the maximum interactive capabilities of these new technologies.

The capacity to develop the 'virtual habitat' based on the ability to cross the networks, and to ensure the widest possible access to the information superhighway, will be positive only if we are able to expand the collective capacities of the social basis of intelligence. This brings us to the idea of a 'New Babylon' as a project for the city in which we can live and be creative. The 'New Babylon' concept is based on the idea of the 'creative city', taking account of the enormous creative potential present within our cities and unused today. We need and should develop an increasingly powerful and articulate language to engage with and portray all the new dimensions of social life and cultural activity within the creative city.

(Commune Di Bologna, 1995)

The aim is to use this manifesto as a focus for all cities, and other networks and organisations, which support its aims and objectives with a view to supporting a wide range of initiatives, from local pilot and demonstration projects through to lobbying and influencing policy at European and international level (for example, developments coming out of the recent G7 Summit on the Information Society). The central themes of this include:

- cities becoming more, rather than less, active as centres of creative activity and sustainable economic, social and cultural growth;
- setting up facilities to provide access to the information superhighway, for example access centres, information networks, teleworking centres, within cities, in order to encourage people to continue to use the city but in more flexible ways;
- decentralising workplaces and services within the city rather than transferring facilities out of the city;
- supporting greater flexibility for people working and/or living in the city through extending opening hours of all services, including promoting the evening economy and the idea of the twenty-four-hour city, more residential housing in city centres and better, more-integrated public transport.

TELEMATICS AND URBAN REGENERATION: A CASE STUDY OF MANCHESTER

Manchester City Council, together with organisations with which it is involved through local partnerships, has had a policy commitment to supporting work in this area since 1989. Historically Manchester has had, and retains today, a high concentration of technological expertise in computing and related information technologies, particularly within the local universities, for example the invention of the modern computer at Manchester University in 1948 which there are plans to celebrate with a fiftieth anniversary international 'Festival of the Universal Machine' in 1998 (University of Manchester, 1996). This enabled Manchester to become a centre of excellence in many aspects of the development and use of these technologies and to build up a strong image as such which, in turn, is used to promote the city.

This is only the first stage, however, as the shift in policy-making outlined above requires the development of new applications and services which directly support employment generation, new training opportunities and social and cultural initiatives. Manchester City Council recognised this in its Economic Development Strategy produced in 1991, where the development of information and communications technologies or 'telematics'[1] was established as a core strategic objective for all future work. In the same year Manchester launched the UK's first public-access computer communications and information system, the Manchester Host, providing electronic mail (with Internet and X400 messaging), bulletin boards and on-line databases as a public service. The Manchester Host was upgraded in 1995 to operate as a full Internet Service Provider.

Subsequently Manchester City Council has worked in partnership with Manchester Metropolitan University, the other universities and colleges in the city, a network of some twenty voluntary sector organisations and other agencies (including the Chamber of Commerce) to develop new telematics applications and services to support the idea of 'Manchester – The Information City' (Manchester City Council, 1994). The emphasis is to establish pilot and demonstration projects that provide practical services for real users, ensuring that these are based on a proper analysis of user needs and local research. This is backed up by a commitment to the involvement of users, and potential users, at all stages of project development, including initial planning, implementation, validation in real-life environments and the dissemination of results and 'good practice' guidelines.

It is this commitment and the development of strong partnerships with the educational, private and voluntary sectors which has enabled Manchester to ensure the sustainability of being a centre of excellence for these technologies. The challenge now is to maintain this role in the face of the rapid acceleration of technological change and the increasing priority that these issues have at national and international level. One result of all of this which must be taken very seriously is that the resources available for economic development, and certain aspects of social and cultural development, particularly at national and European level, will increasingly be associated with telematics and the implementation of the 'information society' (as outlined in the Bangemann Report). In order to be able to take advantage of these opportunities cities need to be able to demonstrate a strong track-record in terms of the development and implementation of telematics-related applications and services which reflect user needs rather than technological requirements.

It is important to stress, however, that it is not the telematics *per se* which creates employment and economic growth but the context within which these technologies are developed and implemented. This means that maximum support is given to the concept of universal access to telematics – that is, all people in the Manchester area (whether from community-based facilities, from home, from a school or college or from an office) should be able to access telematics resources and services on a low-cost and effective basis for a variety of applications ranging from education and training, business, public information, arts and culture, entertainment, health care or environmental services. Equally specific projects must be developed to ensure a direct benefit to the local economy from enhanced applications of telematics. Manchester's commitment has been to build up as strong as possible a culture of awareness and use of telematics, especially basic services, by as wide a cross-section of society as possible. Only then can we be confident that people and organisations will start to use the more advanced applications of telematics as they become available.

This commitment has led to the establishment of the Manchester Telematics and Teleworking Partnership (MTTP) between Manchester City Council, Manchester Metropolitan University, local voluntary sector and other community-based organisations and a number of individuals and small companies working in the multimedia sector. The Partnership aims to develop local pilot and demonstration projects which will 'showcase' advanced telematics-based services and to use these to stimulate the development of the local information superhighway.

The priorities for the Manchester Telematics and Teleworking Partnership are:

- to enhance the telematics infrastructure of the city to enable greater multimedia capabilities and to maximise access to the information superhighway and related interactive information services;
- to support the development of new economic activity, particularly through greater use of electronic trading networks and teleworking, with networking at both regional and inter-regional levels;

- to use both the enhanced infrastructure and the results of pilot and demonstration projects to promote the use of advanced telematics to support growth and innovation in other sectors, including training, cultural industries, health care and transport.

The main focus of this work is to develop a network of local telematics access centres around the city which will give local people and organisations direct access to the information superhighway, provide training, advice and technical support and develop new employment opportunities through support for teleworking and electronic trading networks. The initial proposal is to develop twelve local centres, linked to a new Multimedia Centre at the Manchester Metropolitan University (MMU). Four of the twelve proposed Access Centres will be based on upgrading the facilities at the four existing Telematics Access Centres, known as Electronic Village Halls (EVHs), while eight will be new facilities. The project will also upgrade the Manchester Host computer communications and information system to full multimedia capabilities, providing Manchester with a 'digital city' system closely linked with the systems developed by Amsterdam and Bologna.

The network aims to:

(a) expand the existing centres, which will provide a city-wide service with initiatives supporting work in the City Pride area, Greater Manchester and the North West region, for example:
    - the Telematics and Teleworking Centre at MMU;
    - the Women's Electronic Village Hall and Telework Centre;
    - Bangladesh House Telematics and Telework Centre;
(b) expand the existing centres, providing targeted geographical support in key areas, for example:
    - Chorlton Workshop Telematics Access Centre (which covers the south of the inner city area);
    - East Manchester Electronic Village Hall;
(c) develop new centres with a wide area focus, for example:
    - a network in the city centre to support cultural industries based on two or three sites;
    - a Disabled People's Electronic Village Hall and Telework Centre based at the Frank Taylor Centre in Ardwick;
(d) develop new centres with a targeted geographical coverage.

Currently discussions are taking place about the development of telematics access and teleworking centres covering three inner city wards – Moss Side, Hulme and Miles Platting – and one 'outer city' ward – Benchill (Wythenshawe).

The Manchester Partnership has also been working with a number of cultural organisations, individuals and small businesses in the media and cultural sectors to exploit opportunities for the growth and development of this sector through the use of advanced telematics applications and services. To date three city-wide consultation meetings have been held which have brought together partners from the telematics and teleworking side of this work and from the multimedia and cultural industries side.

These meetings led to the establishment of a Manchester Multimedia Forum in February 1995 which now meets every two months. The aims of the Forum include:

- providing support for new initiatives in the media and cultural sectors;
- promoting networking and collective initiatives;
- encouraging the development of activities which use, develop and promote multimedia telematics applications and services.

A number of access centres within the Manchester Multimedia Network will concentrate on the cultural industries sector, including one or more centres for 'electronic arts'. These will enhance existing facilities as well as provide for completely new collaborative initiatives. They will also link into innovative provision within the higher education institutions, for example the Interactive Arts course at Manchester Metropolitan University, and provide support for individuals and small businesses in the media and cultural sectors.

The intended outcome of all of this work is to create a 'virtual habitat' that is associated with a specific city, in this case Manchester, while at the same time providing opportunities to experiment with cyberspace in ways that are easily accessible, as low cost as possible and in a supportive environment where the diversity of users reflects the social and cultural realities of city life. The creation of a 'virtual city' needs to take account of the existence of public domains where services and facilities that exist in the real city, for example public transport, libraries, information and advice agencies, cafés, bars, bookshops and other meeting places, can co-exist in the 'virtual city'. This is very much the philosophy behind the work being undertaken by Amsterdam, Bologna and Manchester with the idea of the 'digital city', but this is yet to make the required leap forward to overcome the inherent biases of user domination by young, technically skilled white males. Only the extension of access to these systems, backed up by support, training and greater attempts to make applications and services more interesting and relevant to many more people, will be able to challenge the current 'tyranny of structurelessness' which allows this user domination to continue.

At a different level there also has to be a commitment to the cyberspace equivalent of public service broadcasting. It would be very easy to respond to the criticisms of the current user bias of systems by talking about how making applications and services more relevant to the 'mass of ordinary people' is about greater commercialisation, the 'virtual Las Vegas' approach where everyone has access to unlimited teleshopping, video-on-demand and 'virtual lotteries', as indeed most of the major manufacturers and suppliers are now pushing for. The challenge is to be critical of both situations while attempting to build experimental systems, on the 'digital city' or 'virtual city' model, which provide practical demonstrations of alternatives to the dominant models stressing not only empowerment and emancipation but also access and accountability.

EXTENDING THE HORIZONS OF THE 'VIRTUAL CITY': MANCHESTER'S ROLE IN EUROPEAN AND INTERNATIONAL NETWORKS

Many cities, including Manchester, have always had a strong international role, usually developing as a focus for international trade during the thirteenth and fourteenth centuries and becoming part of major trading partnerships such as the Hanseatic League and other alliances of 'city-states' and their partners. Manchester's history as an international commercial centre played an important role in the industrial revolution alongside the city's achievements in industrial, scientific and technological developments. This, in turn, made Manchester an increasingly important political, as well as economic, centre during the nineteenth and twentieth centuries, particularly as a base for political refugees, including Gandhi's Independence Movement, the Pan-African Congress in the 1940s and 1950s and, most recently, the ANC.

This role has resulted in a very rich legacy of contacts and networks being established throughout the world which are constantly in use for educational, cultural and economic partnerships. Many of these now use the Internet to keep in contact and to develop their work and Manchester has specific projects which link up its main twin cities, St Petersburg (Russia), Chemnitz (Germany) and Cordoba (Spain), via the Internet.

Most recently, over the past four years, Manchester City Council has developed a European strategy to ensure that there is a more focused approach to work on European Union/Commission-related issues. An important factor in what Manchester has been able to achieve so far has been its active role in the Eurocities association. Eurocities is an association of sixty metropolitan cities from EU member states, with an additional ten associate members from EFTA countries and Central and Eastern Europe. Manchester became actively involved in the Eurocities Technological Co-operation Committee in 1993 and used its experience in the development of local telematics services to co-ordinate a working group of European cities to discuss these issues.

Manchester City Council held a European conference of Eurocities members interested in developing work on telematics in October 1993 which resulted in the 'Declaration of Manchester', a joint proposal from twelve cities to establish a European network to develop this work on a longer-term basis. The working title for this network was 'Telecities' and a trans-European Steering Committee was established to co-ordinate the work, involving Antwerp, Barcelona, Bologna, Manchester (President), Nice and the Hague.

'Telecities' was formally launched in April 1994 and has grown to involve more than fifty cities across Europe. The aims and objectives of the Telecities network include using and developing telematics applications and services which support the regeneration of urban areas through:

- economic development strategies with a specific focus on tackling unemployment, including teleworking;

- social and cultural development aimed at improving the quality of life;
- new solutions to fight social exclusion;
- maximising the resources available to cities to support local demonstration projects.

Telecities is committed to promoting the concepts of universal access to telematics and 'digital democracy' in the European and global arena. Opportunities for this are already emerging in terms of follow-up events to the G7 Summit on the Information Society, the European Commission's new forum looking at the social implications of the information society and new regional initiatives which are identified as a priority for European Commission support in the future.

Telecities members in the UK have also formed a national working group under the title of 'Telecities UK' which aims both to support members in developing applications under the EC's Fourth Framework Programme and other programmes and to provide a forum for exchanging information and articulating members' views at a national level. This currently involves all UK members of Eurocities, that is, Birmingham, Bradford, Bristol, Cardiff, Edinburgh, Glasgow, Leeds, Liverpool, Manchester, Newcastle, Nottingham and Sheffield, together with Hull, Kirklees and the London Boroughs of Hackney and Lewisham.

Following on from the Bangemann Report, 'Europe and the Global Information Society', the European Commission has launched an 'Inter-Regional Information Society Initiative (IRISI)' which will 'assist a group of pilot regions in developing the information society'. This is a joint initiative between the EC's Directorates DG16 (Regional Policy) and DG13 (Telecommunications). The regions selected are:

- the North West of England;
- Saxony (Germany);
- Nord Pas-de-Calais (France);
- Valencia (Spain);
- Piedmont (Italy);
- Central Macedonia (Greece).

Initiatives such as this enable work undertaken at the local/urban level to become part of wider regional networks, which increases their ability to influence policy and to develop common ground and approaches to dealing with telecommunications and other service suppliers at the trans-European level. This has been particularly useful for a city like Manchester which has extensive contacts with other chosen regions of the EC's Regional Initiative, for example Lille (Nord Pas-de-Calais) is a very active member of Telecities, Chemnitz (Saxony) being one of Manchester's twin cities, and with Leipzig (Saxony), Turin (Piedmont) and Valencia (Spain) all being members of Eurocities;

Each region participating in the Regional Initiative is developing a co-ordinated strategy towards the development of telematics applications and services, including:

- focusing on full-scale implementation of advanced applications and services, rather than on research or technology demonstrations;
- being based on a clearly identified demand from users and on a strong involvement of users;
- attempting to balance economic and social aspects, that is, contribute not only to productivity and improved performance but also to employment creation and to improving the quality of work and life.

Participating in these initiatives enables cities like Manchester to gain access to both research findings and policy and decision-making at levels which would not normally be possible to a city council nor to most local agencies. In turn cities are provided with a unique base, in terms of information, intelligence and contacts, from which to develop their strategies for economic regeneration and urban development and to maximise access to resources to finance this. Cities are now beginning to be able to influence the development of policy by European institutions through networks like Telecities. This is the first time that local authorities have had a direct input into this policy arena as well as being able to (at least) try to represent the views of wider user and community interests.[2]

At a local level cities like Manchester are finding it increasingly difficult to influence the development of the telematics infrastructure, finding themselves caught between the cable operators and the telecommunications suppliers at the local, or receiving, end of corporate (usually multinational) decision-making over investment and services. Some gains can be made, however, by using both the planning powers of local authorities and the highly competitive market situation that many of these companies have to operate in. Creative use of planning powers can put pressure on cable operators to connect up community facilities, for example schools and libraries, at low or even no cost, and to include poorer areas of the city in build plans. At the same time the fact that traditional telecommunications suppliers, like BT, are threatened by competing services offered by cable companies can be used to influence their investment decisions in favour of more innovative projects that provide community access to the information superhighway.

The most interesting area, in terms of infrastructure, is the emerging 'third sector' based around the national (and international) universities' network – for example SuperJANET in the UK. It is here that a number of cities are developing collaborative ventures which have the potential to offer cheap but sophisticated (and fast) access to the information superhighway. In Manchester, for example, there is a project to build a high-speed fibre-optic cable network to link up all of the sites, including residences, of the six main Higher Education Institutions in the city area, known as GMING, the 'Greater Manchester Inter-Network Group'. This would reach over 50 per cent of the residential areas of the city and provide the basis for a Metropolitan Area Network serving a wide range of non-commercial uses, covering schools, colleges, libraries, advice centres, hospitals, health centres and residential homes, as well as providing the potential for individual access. If such local initiatives are then able to link up nationally and internationally, it is possible to think in terms of wider electronic networks which would operate on a more accountable and democratic basis.

The challenge here is not the profit motive of multinational corporate decision-making but rather an inherent conservatism and élitism within higher education institutions that sees developments such as this as enhancements to internal systems rather than an essential element of wider urban and regional development. The key to overcoming this is partly the establishment of strong working alliances between city councils, local community organisations and higher education institutions to advocate more open access and partly the use of public funding, for example European Structural Funds, to match the universities' own funds and provide additional finance to develop systems more rapidly and more extensively than would otherwise be the case and, in return, ensure that wider community access is provided.

If these challenges are overcome, then there is the basis for establishing local, regional, national and international electronic networks that owe their existence to active policy-making through democratic and accountable action, for example on the part of local authorities, community organisations, trade unions, consumer groups and alliances of individuals, rather than to corporate business interests, governments or the whims of rich and powerful individuals. There is no technological 'short-cut' to the establishment of such networks but rather the long, hard slog of alliance building, experimentation, negotiation, campaigning and self-organisation. Market forces will not naturally develop either the quantity or quality of cyberspace that is required to meet our requirements but neither will they naturally facilitate the type of surveillance and control increasingly required by state and other interests. The 'anarchy of the marketplace' does at least provide space in which to manoeuvre and create experimental areas of collective space to support social and cultural innovation and to provide real services on the public broadcasting/public service model.

The alliances which are beginning to emerge between social forces and (at least) some representative structures (including local authorities) working in this area, which could be broadly termed 'socially useful cyberspace', may not be able to transform the forces of global capitalism but they are not without power and influence. Their role in determining how questions of the 'governance of cyberspace' are resolved should be not underestimated. The ability of small-scale initiatives in cities and regions to use the advantages of the technologies, to use cyberspace, to create communication and activity networks free from the usual spatial and temporal constraints is a crucial element in providing a democratic counter-balance to other technological and global trends. The essential starting point for this must, however, be a commitment to creating services and applications that are easy (and cheap) to use, that grab people's interest and imagination so that they want to use them and that, having used them, they become part of their lives enough that they would fight any attempt to limit them or take them away. It is in this context that the 'governance of cyberspace' needs to be debated backed up by practical examples of how people and organisations are working to achieve liberation and empowerment through innovatory explorations of cyberspace.

NOTES

1 'Telematics' is taken (by the European Commission at least) to refer to the convergence of telecommunications, information technology/ 'informatics' and televisual technologies.
2 The European Commission has more recently established a 'High Level Group of Experts' to consider the wider social and cultural implications of the information society. Its Interim Report, 'Building the European Information Society for Us All', was published in January 1996 by Directorate-General V.

Part III

Policing cyberspace

Privacy and surveillance

Chapter 10

Privacy, democracy, information

Charles D. Raab

INTRODUCTION

Can 'cyberspace' promote democracy as well as protect privacy? Must we see the informational openness of democracy and the individual's or group's need to control the flow of personal data as zero-sum alternatives that may (or may not) be 'balanced'? Or, as some democratic theorists assert, can they support each other, albeit in conditions of 'informatisation' that are not usually comprehended in democratic theory? And is it possible to create rules for protecting democracy and privacy in the decentralised and anarchic conditions of networks like the 'information superhighway'?

The aims of this chapter are to stimulate discussion of such questions, to reassess the relationship between privacy and democracy, and to reflect upon the way in which 'cyberspace' developments affect the realisation of these two values. The approach taken questions the assumption of their opposition. A previous paper (Raab, 1995) broached this question in looking at initiatives for the development of information infrastructures or the 'information superhighways' (ISHs) that pay lip-service to the role that multimedia networks could play in democratic politics by creating new opportunities for participation and for the circulation of information. These proposals, however, also nod in the direction of privacy protection as one condition of development, a gesture further emphasised by civil libertarians and others. This is because applications of information and communications technologies (ICTs) might promote government, commerce and democracy but also hold the threat of increasing surveillance over persons and groups, thus raising the spectre of 'Orwell' in the midst of the realisation of 'Athenian' ideals (Lyon, 1994b; Van de Donk and Tops, 1992).

STATING THE ARGUMENT

Before looking at the issues in greater detail, the main thrust of the argument should be indicated. The claim that democracy and privacy reinforce each other means that the information-openness of democracy is not necessarily achieved at the expense of privacy's information-restriction. It is not that we can have either democracy or privacy – more of one implying less of the other – or some balance between two supposedly opposing forces. The development of accountable democratic institutions and privacy-protecting processes cannot take place in separate compartments, for each is an important condition of the other. Effective 'rules of the road' for treating non-personal and personal information are necessary if both democracy and privacy are to be enhanced – or at least not damaged – by advanced ICT, even though the precise future shape of electronic (multi)media cannot easily be foreseen or regulated.

Democracy both presupposes and supports liberty of expression and communication amongst citizens and between them and the state. Official secrecy and censorship contradict such liberties. Yet free speech may be limited in a democratic society, for example in wartime; and libel, defamation and obscenity, for example, also do not enjoy legal protection. Many see censorship in cyberspace as less justifiable and claim that the exclusion of certain participants from Internet discussion groups throws into question the open-discourse quality of the ISH; but Kapor (1991) points out that the ambiguity of the public or private status of these groups makes controversies likely over the permissible extent of free speech. Beyond informal regulation of this kind lies legislation promoting, for example, 'communications decency', as in the United States. These matters of law and etiquette inhabit a grey area concerning the applicability of rules and norms, and the permissibility of surveillance.

Intruding upon privacy, surveillance may impede democratic liberties because of its 'chilling' effect on communication or expression. Surveillance thrives in authoritarian regimes that are not exposed to public debate and criticism. When surveillance is employed in political systems that are considered democratic, it is legitimised and restricted on grounds of necessity and special justification; as with censorship, surveillance is seen as the exception, not the rule. Any covertness or unaccountability in its use is taken to signify incipient authoritarianism, and libertarians argue for safeguards. Thus legal requirements surround wire-tapping, and some form of democratic accountability for such practices helps – even if uneasily – to reconcile covert surveillance with democracy.

The isolative effect of surveillance disrupts social intercourse and communication. Isolation is far different from the solitude and privacy that individuals may wish to choose for themselves. Democracy is incompatible with isolation; it can, however, flourish where privacy exists. Democratic institutions and practices such as the secret ballot or the ability of political groups to discuss their internal affairs in conditions of intimacy underline this connection; so, too, does the right to distribute controversial political viewpoints anonymously.[1] ICT can promote communication, political expression and action amongst citizens who cannot meet in person, provided that they can trust the security of electronic media and their integrity against surveillance. But if it appears, or is convincingly suspected, that messages are being monitored by authorities, that participants with unorthodox opinions are being targeted and profiled, or that personal information disclosed for one purpose is used otherwise without one's knowledge or consent, then the ISH's potential as a reliable democratic tool is damaged.[2]

But where stands the proposition concerning the symbiosis of democracy and privacy when surveillance enjoys popular or political support, thus setting democracy at odds with liberty? Democracy is then in danger of becoming popular tyranny. Contemporary surveillance devices such as video cameras in public places (CCTV) pose this dilemma, although the aim is normally crime control and not political repression. But their careless, arbitrary or unaccountable use, especially when the object changes to the control of political protest or to the targeting of suspect social groups, makes surveillance inconsistent with democracy. The police have sometimes been reluctant to wield wide surveillance powers, and have even resisted identity card schemes for fear of becoming alienated from society unless certain democratic accountability rules are also in place. Although these scruples may be overcome, a crucial distinction between democratic and authoritarian systems is that they are never even entertained in the latter, whereas their relaxation in a democracy may result from lengthy debate and the decisions of the institutions of democracy, including an independent judiciary.

The idea of *consent* underlines the affinity between democracy and privacy, for it is important in the discourses of both domains. Democratic theory holds that authority is sustained by the consent of the governed; similarly, privacy protection involves the individual's consent to the use of her or his information, although this is far from easy to exercise. Consent to government's authority is more confidently given where government is publicly accountable and its actions reasonably transparent. This is why 'open government', or 'freedom of information', is seen as necessary. To the extent that electronic media make much more non-personal information available to many more people, they may be a significant asset to democracy (Dutton *et al.*, 1994; Raab *et al.*, 1996). Democracy requires transparency about the use of *personal* data as well. Similarly, data protection systems assume that consent to others' use of one's personal information may be genuine only to the extent that data users are transparent, and thus accountable, about what they are doing with it. Mellors aptly argues that 'the best safeguard is not that they know less about us, but that we know more about them; and that we are aware of what they know about us and how they use such information' (1978: 109). But transparency notwithstanding, limits on who can know what about whom are also required. Although cyberspace makes these limits much more problematical, it makes privacy safeguards all the more necessary for practical reasons.

DEMOCRACY

The argument for the mutuality of privacy and democracy requires elaboration, and its concepts of democracy and privacy need to be clarified. The abundance of definitions complicates this. Considering democracy: apart from definitions, there are also many adjectival and other forms and models, including pluralist, participatory, associational, social, liberal, direct, representative, and so on (for example, Dahl, 1982; Held, 1987; Held and Pollitt, 1986; Hirst, 1994; Holden, 1988; Pateman, 1970; Ware,

1992). No elaboration of these is attempted here,[3] but privacy claims and rights inhabit the realm of liberal-democratic discourse especially, providing an important rationale for limiting the scope of collective decision and government intervention. A general definition of liberal democracy is that of 'a political system in which the people make the basic political decisions, but in which there are limitations on what decisions they can make' (Holden, 1988: 12) Although Ware (1992) has reservations about this, its relevance is that it connects democracy with various liberties, both of them providing the preconditions for people to make decisions and for restricting government.

Holden (1988) distinguishes between two conceptions of the relationship between 'the people' and government. In one, they are separate and potentially hostile bodies; in the other, government is the agent of the people. In the first, the people have power to the extent that they can limit government: 'limited government exists *by virtue of* popular power. Democratic government *is* limited government and liberty is necessarily maintained by democracy' (Holden, 1988: 20; emphasis in original). In the second conception the link between democracy and liberty is made instead through the idea of the free, self-determined and self-governing individual achieving liberty by participating in government activity. Liberalism can therefore be seen not only as a source of limitation on, but as a component of democracy. The inventory of individual freedoms is among the liberal components that Beetham identifies as essential to democracy: 'without the guaranteed right of all citizens to meet collectively, to have access to information, to seek to persuade others, as well as to vote, democracy would be meaningless' (1992: 41).

Although the latter moves from liberal towards more participatory or direct forms of democracy, it is fairly obvious that both types of democracy implicate dimensions of privacy.[4] Limited government by definition involves keeping government away from matters deemed private; these matters would include individual (or group) privacy, and keeping government at bay thus entails freedom from state surveillance and the protection of one's personal information. But also, in its way, participatory democracy emphasises the capacity to act politically through freedom of choice, including free elections. 'There cannot be freedom of choice in the absence of freedom of speech, organisation and assembly' (Holden, 1988: 37). The crucial point is that these participatory freedoms require a degree of privacy for their exercise; this is pointed up by the association of free elections with the institution of the secret ballot, which promotes the making of uncoerced political choices (Mackenzie, 1958: chap. 15; Reeve and Ware, 1992: chap. 5).

Moreover, the other freedoms can only be truly exercised where the institutions of civil society through which people organise, assemble and communicate are not spied upon (Schoeman, 1992); that is, where people can control the terms and the means for implementing these freedoms, including controlling the flow of information about who participates, how, when and why. On this interpretation, it is none of the state's business who belongs to a legitimate political group and what they talk about behind closed doors. For Beetham, the separation of the private and public spheres in a limited state is necessary in a liberal democracy, which 'cannot in practice subsist without an autonomous sphere of citizen will-formation separate from the state' (1992: 42).

Taking a step further, Bryant notes that

> Privacy and privatisation figure prominently in the antinomy of freedom: the right of *individuals* to *privacy* and to freedom of speech, assembly, etc., can only be defended in *public* and in *concert* . . . . Privacy is double edged. It is dear to us but it must not become so dear that we are unwilling to sacrifice all or part of it in the defence of civil liberties . . . . [P]olitical action may secure rights to privacy but at the cost of some loss of privacy to the political activist.
>
> (1978: 77; emphasis in original)

Further, 'excessive regard for private life endangers civil liberties by leaving the body politic unattended. Individual privacy is a social right with attendant social responsibilities' (Bryant, 1978: 80).

This brings us closer towards considering the information and communication correlates of liberal or participatory democracy. In contrast to authoritarian or totalitarian systems, democracy in principle allows, facilitates, but does not coerce persons to interact politically with each other and with the state through mechanisms that are not restricted in their availability or controlled by the state or by any group. These interactions may be safeguarded through legally protected rights such as freedom of assembly, freedom of speech and freedom of the press. 'Freedom of information' also expresses this democratic principle in regard to interactions between persons and the state; arguments for its establishment explicitly appeal to democratic norms.

Arterton claims that '[c]ommunication, dialogue and information exchange are . . . the cornerstone of an informed body politic' (1987: 21). Reinforcing this point, some writers emphasise the necessity of certain communication conditions for democracy. Swabey observes that '[m]ore than once democracy has been called government by discussion' (1939: 129), and Benn and Peters even insist that '[f]reedom of discussion is thus not merely a safeguard against the abuse of authority in a democracy, but a condition for democracy itself' (1959: 352). Going further, Cassinelli explains the presence of civil liberties in a representative democratic state in terms of their being 'the direct result of the uncoerced periodic elections used to select the highest government officials' (1961: 56–7). This is because contestants must communicate freely with the electorate, whilst the electorate must be able to discuss this information among themselves, implying the freedom to assemble, organise, write and communicate. Moreover, outside the context of elections, the predication of democracy upon the existence of a well-informed public supports the idea of open government and freedom of information, or 'transparency'. Government transparency, or public access to information, plays a central part in any specification of the information conditions of democracy and may be greatly facilitated by the provisions made available along the ISH.

PRIVACY

The absence of surveillance and the protection of privacy are necessary conditions for both liberal and participatory democracy. The literature on privacy seems to support this point, and is not exclusively concerned with individualistic values in, or in some tension with, democracy. Westin (1967), on the one hand, considers the place of privacy in totalitarian and democratic societies. He notes its absence in the former, where '[a]utonomous units are denied privacy, traditional confidential relationships are destroyed, surveillance systems and informers are widely installed, and thorough dossiers are compiled on millions of citizens' (Westin, 1967: 23). In contrast, liberal democracy, seen in terms of limited government, maintains strong bastions of privacy and limits surveillance. Westin sees the private realm – for individuals and groups – as a necessary retreat from a totally politicised life and from the citizenship role, and he, too, instances the secret ballot as an institution.

But 'privacy' can be construed in various ways. If the argument is also to be extended to the more active forms of democracy, on what concept of privacy is this tenable? Velecky proposes that it is 'the state of a person who in the pursuit of the good justifiably can choose the nature and the duration of contact with others' (1978: 21). This is close to Westin's (1967: 7) famous definition that involves one's control over the communication of one's information to others. Flaherty (1989: 7–8) lists thirteen 'privacy interests', the ultimate values upon which to construct data-protection systems, but settles on a working definition drawn from Westin. Notions such as these are at what might be called the social or political end of a range of definitions, because they envisage the possibility of interaction with others, not just withdrawal. Other writers take up this possibility.

Solitude, intimacy, anonymity and reserve are the four 'states' of privacy identified in Westin's (1967: 31–2) classic formulation. Intimacy and anonymity are of particular relevance to democracy, whether liberal or participatory. Intimacy concerns the ability to exclude outsiders from a small unit of two or more persons, thus protecting a close and frank relationship. How small is 'small' is a relevant question in political contexts, for political parties, clubs or pressure groups may desire this sort of relationship, albeit with rather larger numbers. Whether that can be achieved outside the context of face-to-face interactions, such as 'virtual' groups in communication through electronic media, is an important question in the 'information polity'. Nevertheless, the means to an intimate relationship involve 'corporate seclusion' (Westin, 1967: 31). Therefore, where such seclusion obtains – whether through legal protection of information or a group culture of closed communications – the question of size may be irrelevant; the notion of a 'Whitehall village' underlines this point, as does Freemasonry.

Anonymity, or 'public privacy' (Westin, 1967: 32), is particularly pertinent in a political context. It

> occurs when the individual is in public places or performing public acts but still seeks, and finds, freedom from identification and surveillance . . . . Knowledge or fear that one is under systematic observation in public places destroys the sense of relaxation and freedom that men [sic] seek in open spaces and public arenas.
>
> (Westin, 1967: 31)

But beyond this sense of psychic well-being lies the relevance of anonymity to political efficacy:

> Here the individual wants to present some idea publicly to the community or to a segment of it, but does not want to be universally identified at once as the author – especially not by the authorities, who may be forced to take action if they 'know' the perpetrator.
>
> (Westin, 1967: 32)

As Flaherty observes, 'knowing that participation in an ordinary political activity may lead to surveillance can have a chilling effect on the conduct of a particular individual' (1989: 9). For the same reason, Van Stokkom concludes that '[t]he protection of the private domain is therefore one of the most elementary conditions for public activity' (1995: 57) Simitis claims that

> Neither freedom of speech nor freedom of association nor freedom of assembly can be fully exercised as long as it remains uncertain whether, under what circumstances, and for what purposes, personal information is collected and processed. In view of these implications of automated data processing, considerations of privacy protection . . . determine the choice between a democratic and an authoritarian society.
>
> (1987: 734)

This relates particularly to the quality of democracy for the individual, but *associational* privacy should be taken into consideration because, as we have seen, democratic participation is not only a question of individual ballots and political expression, but also involves the conditions under which groups can function as political actors. Westin recognises the necessity for anonymity and intimacy for groups outside government as consistent with democratic values when he concludes that '[p]rivacy is thus not a luxury for organizational life; it is a vital lubricant of the organizational system in free societies' (1967: 51).

The drift of this argument resonates with Schoeman's (1992) discussion of the contribution of privacy to *social* freedom, rather than to individual autonomy. This view is particularly important for the argument of this chapter.[5] The classical antinomy of the state and the individual neglects a position that does not depend upon the liberal defence of the individual against the state, but which recognises that

> Most of our protections from a monolithic social and political tyranny depend on participation in associations . . . . The practice of privacy, not as a right but as a system of nuanced social norms, modulates the effectiveness of social control over an individual . . . . [P]rivacy is important largely because of how it facilitates association with people, not independence from people.
>
> (Schoeman, 1992: 3, 6, 8)

In this light, autonomy is seen as a value that promotes self-expression within interpersonal relationships, and not individual disengagement from others.

Thus privacy and intimacy are the relevant concepts for such an interpretation of autonomy: 'The point of the restrictions on access is in large part not to isolate people but to enable them to relate intimately or in looser associations that serve personal and group goals' (Schoeman, 1992: 21). Effectiveness as a social actor depends upon associational ties that are protected by privacy norms of self-expression within a relationship, but the limited scope of each association over the individual's life is important for freedom. This points in the direction of pluralism and diversity of groups; social freedom involves the existence of 'functionally focused associations' in place of 'monolithic social hegemony' (Schoeman, 1992: 151), and entails respect for privacy between the different groups to which one has ties: 'Information exposed to one community should be private relative to another' (Schoeman, 1992: 154). Thus there is 'privacy from' – emphasising inter-group barriers – as well as 'privacy for' – emphasising the scope for self-expression and interchange within each group (Schoeman, 1992: 156).

These conceptual distinctions are germane to a consideration of privacy and democratic freedoms in an environment of advanced ICT.

INFORMATION AND REGULATION OF CYBERSPACE

The extent to which privacy can be preserved in the 'information age' or the 'networked economy' has been a prominent question in many discussions. As Lyon remarks, 'Sooner or later debates about the social impacts of ICT come round to the question of "Big Brother" (1988: 93). Our concern here is not with the privacy effects of the use of ICT in commerce or public administration. However, these challenge privacy in so far as the massive processing and transmission of personal data by profit-seeking interests in marketing and entertainment, and for state purposes in the form of electronic service delivery, are powerful driving-forces. In addition, whilst the electronic dissemination of official, non-personal information may make bureaucracies more transparent, some 'public service' applications of this may involve interactions that create risks to anonymity.

Focusing, however, on the implications of ICT for democracy: these are as keenly debated in the 1990s, as were previous dramatic developments in communications,[6] and recent discussions are not unequivocally sanguine. The bringing of governments 'on-line' has gathered pace, although unevenly across and within countries. Official documentation is increasingly available, more elected representatives are in touch with their constituents, and a greater volume of election campaign material is disseminated through the new media. Yet Zourdis (1995), whilst emphasising ICT's contribution to open government and democracy through better public access to information, sounds a note of caution. Government secrecy, rather than openness, could result through deliberate manipulations by a secrecy-minded administrative culture, or through gaps in the law. Other research also points to a cool conclusion about the democratic possibilities of ICT and also helps to avoid the determinist fallacy of forgetting that technologies are themselves shaped by the political contexts and purposes in which they are used (Arterton, 1987; Dutton, 1992; McLean, 1986; Van de Donk and Tops, 1992).

Nevertheless, cyberspace is seen by many in two ways. It is itself a democratic phenomenon, a realm of discussion about public affairs which actually or prospectively presents few obstacles to participation. But it also potentially serves particular democratic political systems not only by disseminating political and governmental information, but through its uses for testing public opinion or for enabling pressure groups to recruit support and exert influence. The extent to which ICT can fulfil these aims rather than increase the gap between 'haves' and 'have-nots' is questionable. Advocates of 'teledemocracy' explore the promise of ICT for strengthening, deepening and broadening public participation in elections and in collective decision-making. Perhaps, as Arterton (1987: chap. 9) concludes, only modest democratic gains can be made through electronic means, and some amelioration of inequalities in participation. Examples abound, both in the literature and in the daily experience on the Internet and its specialist subscriber groups, of 'grass-roots' discourse about public political issues and of attempts to organise political pressure upon elected representatives and governmental institutions. In some respects, and albeit only in 'virtual' terms, there is a proliferation of associational ties (Schoeman, 1992) amongst individuals for political purposes.

Interestingly – although maybe only with marginal effect at present – some of this activity also illustrates the use of technologies for democratic political action aimed at the protection of privacy and, self-referentially, in defence of the openness of the highway itself.[7] There is much debate, through these channels, on the questions of free speech, censorship, pornography, the accessibility of officials and politicians through electronic mail, intellectual property rights, the legal position and liabilities of anonymous remailers, the ability to dispose of secure encryption, and the facilities afforded by secure ISH networks to drug-traffickers and money-launderers. Blue ribbons and black screens were displayed in protest on a wide range of sites on the World Wide Web after the passage of the Communications Decency Act in the USA, accompanied by critical anti-censorship comment. The United States is the prime locus of these Internet debates, but many of them are international and global, and the values at stake are not peculiar only to one country.

It is still an open question whether groups outside government can enjoy anonymity and intimacy on the ISH whilst using it for democratic purposes, but answers are not easily found. Traditional broadcast media, which do not mainly capture personal data on listeners and watchers, do not raise many questions about the invasion of privacy. In contrast, transactional modes of electronic service delivery require the collection of personal details that may or may not be safeguarded by data protection principles, codes and regimes. Where these details circulate across the boundaries of services, organisations or countries, transparency and individuals' ability to exercise some control, or to consent, become difficult and are easily overridden by arguments for efficiency and effectiveness (Raab *et al.*, 1996).

In addition, the capture of personal data in interactive polling may increase the potential for surveillance and requires safeguards for anonymity. The same reasons that underpin the institution of the secret ballot in traditional elections also apply to electronic means of registering votes or opinions, and to politically relevant communications that do not necessarily involve governments themselves, such as discussions and debates within 'virtual' groups and amongst the general population. The apocalyptic 'Orwellian' scenario of state collection of personal information for control purposes goes far beyond the occasions when citizens participate in electronic politics. But for purposes of the present argument, the important point is that the truly democratic potential of ICT will be inhibited without adequate privacy safeguards that replicate the spirit of the secret ballot or of the intimate group in cyberspace.

This challenge is being met to various degrees in current ISH development programmes, although arguably very insufficiently (Raab, 1995). In national and international forums some thought as well as policy-formation is being devoted to establishing regulatory regimes that are robust enough to afford privacy protection for the 1990s and beyond, building upon national systems and international guidelines for privacy protection that have already been established since the 1970s – mainly with computers and 'data banks' in mind, and therefore outpaced by technological change.

The technical, legal and organisational means of providing safeguards deserve comment, although the issues go beyond the question of privacy-in-*democracy* as such. Information privacy laws are difficult enough to achieve in single states, although there has been a great development of these in many countries since 1970 (Bennett, 1992; Flaherty, 1989; Nugter, 1990). Although these have converged upon commonly accepted principles of privacy protection, implementation differences coupled with national differences in administrative use of personal data and in the configuration of commercial competitive positions in international trade have made harmonisation difficult to achieve even when confined only to the European Union (Raab and Bennett, 1994).

Second, legislation strengthens individual rights and organisational responsibilities but it is only as good as the machinery with which it is enforced. Vigorous regulatory agencies and commissions are required for this (Flaherty, 1989; Simitis, 1987), as well as for inserting privacy issues in political agendas and in public consciousness. In many countries, regulatory leadership has played an indispensable part in the privacy protection system. But it is of considerable strategic importance to reassess the aims, scope, organisation and workload of such commissions, which were not designed to regulate the increasingly sophisticated and global environment of the ISH.

Current thinking favours the further development of sectoral codes of practice to tailor privacy protection more precisely to the information systems and practices of industries or of parts of the public sector such as health care, policing and welfare services. The debates and negotiations that bring codes into being concentrate attention on issues involved in the use of personal data, and codes bring data-protection principles to bear upon specific practices. Conflicts are exposed and ways of resolving them are canvassed. For example, the desire to make public services more effective and efficient may suggest that many personal details should be collected, matched and shared across organisations, but anonymity requires limits on these operations. This may be frustrating to administrators and technicians, but their interests are not the only ones to be taken into account in designing ICT systems. Codes help to arbitrate such differences by specifying the ground rules for permissible activity in particular contexts; they also make processes more transparent.

The voluntary-code approach has much to commend it; lessons may be learned from the adoption of codes with varying degrees of formality in the data-protection systems of the Netherlands, the UK and other countries. There is also an important Canadian development of a model privacy standard for the private sector (Canadian Standards Association, 1995). However, codes by themselves are not the whole answer. Their relationship to statutes, in terms of legal rights and responsibilities, is also important. In addition, codes must be enforced and conflicts adjudicated or negotiated in several kinds of relationship: between the industries that seek to police their own ICT practices and the official regulatory bodies; between industry-wide associations and their constituent members; and between the industry and the public. Privacy regulatory authorities as well as data users may have to re-learn and re-tool. There is therefore space for applying a 'social technology' or 'organisational technology' in and between the bodies concerned, in order to implement codes at the level of the customer or citizen, where privacy violations occur in spite of the organisation's policy or the strictures of codes.

One problem is the identification of relevant 'industries' or 'sectors' as the appropriate ones to adopt and implement codes. Multimedia opportunities for providing services and goods blur conventional conceptions or boundaries, affecting the applicability of codes and standards. This is especially worrisome in so far as the constitutive networks and 'networks of networks' of cyberspace are amorphous, anarchic and global; much of their appeal, in fact, lies in this decentralised flexibility. Many users of personal data on the ISH may elude or evade the applicability of self-regulatory mechanisms and principles; law and litigation, rather than self-policing, may be the better means of control, albeit very difficult to invoke. Current attempts to regulate privacy internationally, as with the resolution of knotty issues of copyright and intellectual property in electronic publishing, must come to grips with problems of this order.

Possibly because of problems with state regulation or sectoral self-regulation, technological solutions placed in the hands of individuals, such as public-key encryption, are finding favour (Chaum, 1992). Once again, however, they cannot address all the problems of privacy protection on the information superhighway, because that requires more than physical security, authentication and the authorisation of access which technological solutions handle. Privacy safeguards should ideally be built in, rather than bolted on, to new technologies and their applications. Privacy impact assessments and their consideration in public forums could make a valuable contribution. Whether individuals should take primary responsibility for protecting their own privacy,[8] whether they should bear the costs of privacy, and whether privacy should be considered a luxury affordable only by some are, of course, large public policy and economic issues to be tackled in deciding upon the role of technologically related solutions.

The governance of cyberspace for privacy and for democratic politics requires the involvement of elected politicians and the public in deciding issues such as these, entailing their education in the often obscure ins-and-outs of information technology and privacy. Representative politics is not sufficiently equipped or informed to deal with these issues beyond the level of the special pleading with which it is presented by interest groups. Governments, privacy commissions, industries, the media and educational institutions could play a part in informing public debates. The unspecialised mass media often seem to be adept at alternating between highlighting cyberspace horror stories, and singing the praises of ICT for industry, consumerism, services, entertainment and policing. There is less attention paid to analyses of ICT's part in organisational change, in the effects on the public in terms of democracy and privacy values, and on the pros, cons and possibilities of regulation.

The responsibilities of individuals, self-regulating sectors or organisations, and official agencies are shared (Ippel *et al.*, 1995; Raab, 1993). Privacy protection may ideally be the result of collaboration among differently placed participants, with different interests, but whose activities might synergise their interests rather than taking them necessarily or always as mutually antagonistic. Legal, self-regulatory and technological approaches to privacy are complementary and intertwined: for example, the citizen (or customer) can be helped in self-protection by government's laws and by industry's facilitation; the litmus test of a code of practice is the extent to which it gains the public's trust as well as the confidence of official privacy regulators; and a privacy commission or a government armed with statutes needs the co-operation both of industrial sectors and of an informed and vigilant public, given the limitations upon policing, supervision and legal sanctions.

But there remain conflicts over privacy and surveillance that are difficult to resolve, because interests do not neatly dovetail. Conflicts can also be seen in regard to the other side of the coin, the provision of information in a more open system of democracy. Here, too, is a world of statute, voluntary codes of openness, and individual activity to wrest information from secretive governments and business firms. Some of this information consists of one's personal data to which these data 'subjects' seek access, bolstered in many countries by statutory rights, but requiring individual initiative and the good practices that codes may enjoin upon data users. But as was argued earlier, the public availability of other, non-personal, information is closer to the centre of the 'freedom of information' that is associated with democracy. ICT mechanisms for providing it are increasingly employed, but they cannot work as citizens' technological levers unless public and private organisations accede to their use within a legal and/or self-regulatory framework, provide the lanes and route maps for the public information highway, and place at risk some of the power that comes from information control.

SUMMARY AND CONCLUSION

No elaborate conclusion is needed. Electronic information processes throw up many political issues of control at the individual and collective levels. The discourse on democracy typically deals with rules of access to non-personal information, whereas the discourse on privacy concentrates upon rules of access to personal information. But these are not separate realms, for the ability to engage in the flow of non-personal information for democratic purposes (including, incidentally, the framing of policies for privacy protection) is affected by one's ability to control the flow of one's personal information; and the availability of such controls is affected by the availability of such engagements. Thus Simitis draws the connection: 'the protection of privacy must be accompanied by an equally efficient, guaranteed access to the information necessary to follow and evaluate social processes' (1987: 734–5).

ICT and the ISH alter the conditions of both democracy and privacy, providing possibilities for better engagements and better controls. Simitis argues that, '[w]hen the relationship between information processing and democracy is understood, it becomes clear that the protection of privacy is the price necessary to secure the individual's ability to communicate and participate' (1987: 746). The interrelated values of democracy and privacy are not, as yet, primary ones in the exploration and exploitation of ICT. However, governance requires the formation of information policies and regulations that pay attention to both, whilst being grounded in theories of privacy and democracy that take a rounder view of these than has often been the case in policy circles. It would be too crude and rhetorical simply to say that the better the privacy, the better the democracy, and vice versa (and the better the provision of commercial or governmental outputs as well), and to talk about minimum prerequisites for each assumes that it is possible to measure the extent of privacy safeguards and of democracy, a problem that is discussed elsewhere (Raab and Bennett, 1996).

ICT can be applied in ways that facilitate 'efficient, guaranteed' public access to government information, as, for example, in the provision of sites for the publication of documents and other material on the World Wide Web, and in two-way communication links between members of the public and their elected representatives. Cyberspace can also enable 'lateral' dissemination of information amongst different groups, and members of groups, in civil society for political purposes, provided that privacy requirements are met. Conventions, understandings, norms and informal sanctions are evolving; the ropes are there for newcomers to learn, but also are modified as developments unfold. But government secrecy, the unclarity of laws involving intellectual property, as well as pressure to commodify and sell public information profitably, are obstacles to be confronted at the level of law and public policy; 'who owns information?' (Branscomb, 1994) is a thorny question.

On the privacy side, anonymity and intimacy are at risk in cyberspace, but legal, policy and practical action are required at all levels, as well as privacy-enhancing technologies and individual awareness. However, none of these may prove to be sufficiently robust to match ISH developments presenting new risks that are not easily assessable or amenable to existing regulatory practices. In addition, privacy protection is often seen as a costly impediment on the ISH, and as a danger to a lawful and orderly world. The force of these arguments cannot always be easily countered, nor can the powerful interests that stand behind them be ignored in practice. But, as with democracy, the rules and methods for allowing and regulating privacy claims and counter-claims require continuous reformulation to meet, and preferably to shape, new developments. And such reformulation, as with the politics of any other field, in turn presupposes privacy-protected, democratic discourse through which positions can be moulded and debated.

NOTES

1 See the US Supreme Court's decision in *McIntyre* v. *Ohio* (1995).
2 So, too, may be its reliability in providing services or goods, where such transactions involve personal data. ISH proponents consider privacy and data security to be important for administrative and commercial activities including electronic credit-card payments, licence applications, benefit claims and the like (Raab *et al.*, 1996). A crucial problem is the establishment and maintenance of trust amongst participants. Trust is also an essential property of democracy.
3 Among other things, one should consider the 'cyberspace' effects on each form of democracy – the contribution that ICT can make to it, the dangers to its realisation, and the other values that might be affected by 'informatisation'. The literature addresses some of these issues (for example, Arterton, 1987; Dutton, 1992; Edwards, 1995; Laudon, 1987; Van de Donk and Tops, 1992), and considers the implications of ICT administration and policy outputs (for example, Dutton *et al.*, 1994; Taylor and Williams, 1991; Van de Donk *et al.*, 1995).
4 Bennett associates privacy only with Lockian liberal democracy and limited government: 'Information privacy is . . . a precondition not of democracy per se but of a particular type of democracy, one that is individualistic, noncommunitarian, possessive, perhaps market-oriented' (1992: 32). He rejects, as an intellectual antecedent to privacy, the alternative set of democratic values of co-operation, community consciousness and active participation that is inspired by Rousseau. But participatory democracy should not be confused with total politicisation. See also the discussions of libertarian, communitarian and republican positions in Van Stokkom (1995) and Vorstenbosch (1995).
5 See especially Schoeman (1992: chaps 1, 6, 7 and 9). The argument is also reflected in Vorstenbosch (1995).
6 There is no space here to review this history, but in the same year that Hitler rolled over Poland, Swabey – sounding remarkably in tune with today's cyberspace discourse – thought that radio and other 'mechanical facilities for combining personal privacy with public information' (1939: 129–30) would

mark the opening of an entirely new era in politics. By its means something like the classic ideal of direct democracy becomes realizable on an undreamt-of scale. The classic unities of time and place seem reestablished, and the way opened to convene immense popular assemblies. Through the instrumentality of the radio, telephone, and television, simultaneous audition and communication become possible to a community of millions scattered over thousands of miles. By these devices leaders can speak directly to their constituents at any time on important matters . . . . Politics, suddenly freed from confinement within party clubs, convention halls, and newspaper columns, becomes all-pervasive. Already it is taking advantage of the new intimacy . . . . By the electric arts of light and sound, opportunities of sharing impressions and ideas have increased a thousandfold . . . . Information and amusement rove the ether for any ear to catch.

(1939: 128)

But Swabey saw the dangers of propaganda, and worried about broadcasting in the era before the advent of phone-ins:

Democratization is entering a new phase – yet with a difference. For in place of the old face-to-face local groups there is growing up a new national, even world-wide, community conferring through disembodied sights and sounds. Fleeting images from machines are displacing the richness of immediate contacts. What is stranger, the stream of communication is at present largely one way. The auditor or spectator has no choice but to be passive; there is no give-and-take, no chance for discussion with a radio voice or a silhouette on a screen. Despite the unprecedented facilities for intercourse, members of the new community seem paradoxically condemned to a greater passivity, anonymity, and isolation than ever.

(1939: 128–9)

7 For example, see the Electronic Privacy Information Center (EPIC) home page at http://epic.org/.
8 Simitis (1987) and Vorstenbosch (1995) are justifiably sceptical about this.

Chapter 11

The future of cryptography

Dorothy E. Denning

A few years ago, the phrase 'crypto anarchy' was coined to suggest the impending arrival of a 'brave new world' in which governments, as we know them, have crumbled, disappeared and been replaced by virtual communities of individuals doing as they wish without interference. Proponents argue that crypto anarchy is the inevitable – and highly desirable – outcome of the release of public key cryptography into the world. With this technology, they say, it will be impossible for governments to control information, compile dossiers, conduct wire-taps, regulate economic arrangements and even collect taxes. Individuals will be liberated from coercion by their physical neighbours and by governments. This view has been argued recently by Tim May (1995).

Behind the anarchists' vision is a belief that a guarantee of absolute privacy and anonymous transactions would make for a civil society based on a libertarian free market. They ally themselves with Jefferson and Hayek, who would be horrified at the suggestion that a society with no government control would be either civil or free. Adam Ferguson once said: 'Liberty or Freedom is not, as the origin of the name may seem to imply, an exemption from all restraints, but rather the most effectual applications of every just restraint to all members of a free society whether they be magistrates or subjects.' Hayek opens *The Fatal Conceit: The Errors of Socialism* (1988) with Ferguson's quote. Although May limply asserts that anarchy does not mean lawlessness and social disorder, the absence of government would lead to exactly these states of chaos.

I do not want to live in an anarchistic society – if such could be called a society at all – and I doubt many would. A growing number of people are attracted to the market liberalism envisioned by Jefferson, Hayek and many others, but not to anarchy. Thus, the crypto anarchists' claims come close to asserting that the technology will take us to an outcome that most of us would not choose.

This is the claim that I want to address here. I do not accept crypto anarchy as the inevitable outcome. A new paradigm of cryptography, key escrow, is emerging and gaining acceptance in industry. Key escrow is a technology that offers tools that would assure no individual absolute privacy or untraceable anonymity in all transactions. I argue that this feature of the technology is what will allow individuals to choose a civil society over an anarchistic one. I will review this technology as well as what it will take to avoid crypto anarchy. First, however, I will review the benefits, limitations and drawbacks of cryptography and current trends leading towards crypto anarchy.

CRYPTOGRAPHY'S BENEFITS, LIMITATIONS AND DRAWBACKS

The benefits of cryptography are well recognised. Encryption can protect communications and stored information from unauthorised access and disclosure. Other cryptographic techniques, including methods of authentication and digital signatures, can protect against spoofing and message forgeries. Practically everyone agrees that cryptography is an essential information security tool, and that it should be readily available to users. I take this as a starting assumption and, in this respect, have no disagreement with the crypto anarchists.

Less recognised are cryptography's limitations. Encryption is often oversold as the solution to all security problems or to threats that it does not address. For example, the headline of Jim Warren's op-ed piece in the *San José Mercury News* reads 'Encryption could stop computer crackers' (Warren, 1995). Unfortunately, encryption offers no such aegis. Encryption does nothing to protect against many common methods of attack, including those that exploit bad default settings or vulnerabilities in network protocols or software – even encryption software. In general, methods other than encryption are needed to keep out intruders. Secure Computing Corporation's Sidewinder™ system diffuses the forty-two 'bombs' (security vulnerabilities) in Cheswick and Bellovin's book *Firewalls and Network Security* (1994) without making use of any encryption (Secure Computing Corporation, 1994).

Moreover, the protection provided by encryption can be illusory. If the system where the encryption is performed can be penetrated, then the intruder may be able to access plaintext directly from stored files or the contents of memory or modify network protocols, application software or encryption programs in order to get access to keys or plaintext data or to subvert the encryption process. For example, PGP (Pretty Good Privacy) could be replaced with a Trojan horse that appears to behave like PGP but creates a secret file of the user's keys for later transmission to the program's owner much like a Trojan horse login program collects passwords. A recent penetration study of 8,932 computers by the Defense Information Systems Agency showed 88 per cent of the computers could be successfully attacked. Using PGP to encrypt data transmitted from or stored on the average system could be like putting the strongest possible lock on the back door of a building while leaving the front door wide open. Information security requires much more than just encryption – authentication, configuration management, good design, access controls, firewalls, auditing, security practices and security awareness training are a few of the other techniques needed.

The drawbacks of cryptography are frequently overlooked as well. The widespread availability of unbreakable encryption coupled with anonymous services could lead to a situation where practically all communications are immune from lawful interception (wire-taps) and documents from lawful search and seizure, and where all electronic transactions are beyond the reach of any government regulation or oversight. The consequences of this to public safety and social and economic stability could be devastating. With the government essentially locked out, computers and telecommunications systems would become safe havens for criminal activity. Even May himself acknowledges that crypto anarchy provides a means for tax evasion, money laundering, espionage (with digital dead drops), contract killings and implementation of data havens for storing and marketing illegal or controversial material. Encryption also threatens national security by interfering with foreign intelligence operations. The United States, along with many other countries, imposes export controls on encryption technology to lessen this threat.

Cryptography poses a threat to organisations and individuals too. With encryption, an employee of a company can sell proprietary electronic information to a competitor without the need to photocopy and handle physical documents. Electronic information can be bought and sold on 'black networks' such as Black-Net (May, 1995) with complete secrecy and anonymity – a safe harbour for engaging in both corporate and government espionage. The keys that unlock a corporation's files may be lost, corrupted or held hostage for ransom, thus rendering valuable information inaccessible.

When considering the threats posed by cryptography, it is important to recognise that only the use of encryption for confidentiality, including anonymity, presents a problem. The use of cryptography for data integrity and authentication, including digital signatures, is not a threat. Indeed, by strengthening the integrity of evidence and binding it to its source, cryptographic tools for authentication are a forensic aid to criminal investigations. They also help enforce accountability. Because different cryptographic methods can be employed for confidentiality and authentication, any safeguards that might be placed on encryption to counter the threats need not affect authentication mechanisms or system protocols that rely on authentication to protect against system intrusions, forgeries and substitution of malicious code.

THE DRIFT TOWARDS CRYPTO ANARCHY

Crypto anarchy can be viewed as the proliferation of cryptography that provides the benefits of confidentiality protection but does nothing about its harms. It is government-proof encryption which denies access to the government even under a court order or other legal order. It has no safeguards to protect users and their organisations from accidents and abuse. It is like an automobile with no brakes, no seat belts, no pollution controls, no licence plate and no way of getting in after you've locked your keys in the car.

The crypto anarchist position is that cyberspace is on a nonstop drift towards crypto anarchy. Powerful encryption algorithms, including the Data Encryption Standard (DES), triple-DES, RSA and IDEA, are readily available at no charge through Internet servers as stand-alone programs or as part of packages providing file or electronic mail encryption and digital signatures. Among these, PGP, which uses RSA and IDEA for encrypting files and electronic mail messages, has become particularly popular. Software that will turn an ordinary PC into a secure phone is posted on the Internet for free downloading. These systems have no mechanisms for accommodating authorised government decryption. Export controls have little effect as the programs can be posted in countries that have no such controls.

In addition to the free encryption programs being distributed on the Net, encryption is becoming a basic service integrated into commercial applications packages and network products. The IP Security Working Group of the Internet Engineering Task Force has written a document that calls for all compliant IPv6 (Internet Protocol, version 6) implementations to incorporate DES cryptography.

Anonymous remailers, which allow users to send or post messages without disclosing their identity or host system, have also become popular on the Internet. May (1995) reports that there are about twenty cypherpunk-style remailers on the Internet, with more being added monthly. These remailers allow unlimited nesting of remailing, with PGP encryption at each nesting level. Anonymous digital cash, which would provide untraceability of electronic payments, is on the horizon.

The potential harms of cryptography have already begun to appear. As the result of interviews I conducted in May 1995, I found numerous cases where investigative agencies had encountered encrypted communications and computer files. These cases involved child pornography, customs violations, drugs, espionage, embezzlement, murder, obstruction of justice, tax protesters and terrorism. At the International Cryptography Institute held in Washington in September 1995, FBI Director Louis Freeh reported that encryption had been encountered in a terrorism investigation in the Philippines involving an alleged plot to assassinate Pope John Paul II and bomb a US airliner.[1]

AccessData Corp., a company in Orem, Utah, which specialises in providing software and services to help law enforcement agencies and companies recover data that has been locked out through encryption, reports receiving about a dozen and a half calls a day from companies with inaccessible data. About one-half dozen of these calls result from disgruntled employees who left under extreme situations and refused to co-operate in any transitional stage by leaving necessary keys (typically in the form of passwords). Another half dozen result from employees who died or left on good terms, but simply forgot to leave their keys. The third half dozen result from loss of keys by current employees.

THE EMERGENCE OF KEY ESCROW AS AN ALTERNATIVE

The benefits of strong cryptography can be realised without following the crypto anarchy path to social disorder. One promising alternative is key escrow encryption, also called escrowed encryption.[2] The idea is to combine strong encryption with an emergency decryption capability. This is accomplished by linking encrypted data to a data recovery key which facilitates decryption. This key need not be (and typically is not) the one used for normal decryption, but it must provide access to that key. The data recovery key is held by a trusted fiduciary, which could conceivably be a governmental agency, court or trusted and bonded private organisation. A key might be split among several such agencies. Organisations registered with an escrow agent can acquire their own keys for emergency decryption. An investigative or intelligence agency seeking access to communications or stored files makes application through appropriate procedures (which normally includes getting a court order) and, upon compliance, is issued the key. Legitimate privacy interests are protected through access procedures, auditing and other safeguards.

In April 1993, as response to a rising need for and use of encryption products, the Clinton Administration announced a new initiative to promote encryption in a way that would not prohibit lawful decryption when investigative agencies are authorised to intercept communications or search computer files.[3] Government agencies were directed to develop a comprehensive encryption policy that would accommodate the privacy and security needs of citizens and businesses, the ability of authorised government officials to access communications and data under proper court or other legal order, the effective and timely use of modern technology to build the National Information Infrastructure, and the need of US companies to manufacture and export high technology products. The goal was not to prevent citizens from having access to encryption or 'to stigmatize cryptography as something only criminals would use' (Thomas, 1995). As part of this encryption initiative, the government developed an escrowed encryption chip called the Clipper Chip.

Each Clipper Chip has a unique key that is programmed onto the chip and used to recover data encrypted by that chip. This key is split into two components, and the two components are held by two separate government agencies: the National Institute of Standards and Technology and the Department of Treasury Automated Systems Division. Clipper's data encryption algorithm, SKIPJACK, is a classified algorithm designed by the National Security Agency.[4] It has a key size of 80 bits. The general specifications for the Clipper Chip were adopted in February 1994, as the Escrowed Encryption Standard (EES) (National Institute for Standards and Technology, 1994), which is a voluntary government standard for telephone communications, including voice, fax and data. Implementations of the EES are required to use tamper-resistant hardware in order to protect the classified algorithms. The chip and associated key escrow system have been designed with extensive safeguards, including two-person control and auditing, to protect against any unauthorised use of keys (Denning, 1994, 1995a). Clipper's key escrow system does not provide user data recovery services.

The National Security Agency also designed a more advanced chip called Capstone as part of the Multilevel Information System Security Initiative (MISSI). Capstone implements the EES plus algorithms for the Digital Signature Standard (DSS) and for establishing session keys. It has been embedded in the Fortezza card (a PCMCIA card), where it is used to provide the cryptographic services needed for communications and file security. The private keys used for key establishment and digital signatures, which are stored on the Fortezza card, are not stored in Clipper's key escrow system. They are, however, escrowed with the user's public-key certificate authority so that they can be recovered in case the card becomes corrupted. This allows encrypted files and previously received electronic mail messages to be read. Fortezza cards are available with or without a modem capability. The modem cards allow encryption and decryption to be performed as part of the communications protocols or as independent service calls (for example, for encrypting the content of an email message or file).

The government has not been alone in its pursuit of key escrow technology. Some type of key escrow is a feature or option of several commercial products, including Fisher Watchdog®, Nortel's Entrust, PC Security Stoplock KE, RSA Secure™ and TECSEC Veil™. Escrowing is done within the user's organisation and serves primarily to protect against data loss.

Several companies have proposed designs for commercial key escrow systems where the escrow agents could be trusted third parties that provide emergency decryption services for both registered users and authorised government officials. Such escrow agents might be licensed, with licences granted to organisations demonstrating the capability to administer key escrow encryption and safeguard keys and other sensitive information. Some of the proposed systems have been designed with the objective of being suitable for international use.

One such example is a proposal from Bankers Trust for an international commercial key escrow system for secure communications (Bankers Trust Electronic Commerce, 1995). Their proposal uses a combination of hardware and software, unclassified algorithms and public-key cryptography for key establishment and key escrow functions. Each user has a trusted encryption device, a public–private signature key pair and a public–private encryption key pair that is used for establishing session keys and for data recovery. The private encryption keys are escrowed through a device registration process, and may be split among several escrow agents.

Trusted Information Systems (TIS) has proposed a commercial software key escrow system intended primarily for file encryption (Walker *et al.*, 1996). A commercial entity serves as a key escrow agent and operates a data recovery centre. To use the services of a particular centre, a user must register with the centre. Emergency decryption is possible through a key that is private to the centre. The key is not released to users or the government; instead, the centre participates in the decryption of each file that is encrypted under a distinct file encryption key. TIS would franchise their data recovery centres to interested organisations. National Semiconductor and TIS have jointly proposed Commercial Automated Key Escrow (CAKE), which combines a

CAKE-enabled PersonaCard™ token (National's PCMCIA cryptographic card) with a TIS data recovery centre (Sweet and Walker, 1995). The goal is an exportable, strong encryption alternative using accepted public encryption algorithms such as DES, triple DES and RSA.

Under current US export regulations, encryption products with key lengths greater than 40 bits are not generally exportable when used for confidentiality protection. One of the attractions of key escrow encryption is that by providing a mechanism for authorised government decryption, it can enable the export of products with strong encryption. For example, Clipper/Capstone devices are generally exportable, even though the encryption algorithm is strong and uses 80-bit keys. Commercial key escrow approaches that use some form of hardware token are good candidates for export as they can provide reasonable protection against modifications to bypass the key escrow functions. The Bankers Trust and National/TIS proposals take that approach. Fortress U & T Ltd also has proposed a token-based approach to key escrow (Gressel *et al.*, 1995).

Hardware encryption generally offers greater security than software. Nevertheless, there is a large market for software encryption. On 17 August 1995, the Clinton Administration announced a proposal to allow ready export of software encryption products with key lengths up to 64 bits when combined with an acceptable key escrow capability. This policy would allow export of DES, for example, which uses 56-bit keys, but not triple DES. Keys would be held by government-approved trusted parties within the private sector, where they would support both user data recovery and legitimate government decryption. In July 1996, the administration further proposed to allow ready export of any encryption product that uses an escrowed key management infrastructure, regardless of algorithm, key length or hardware or software implementation.[5] The key could be held within the US or in any country which has a government-to-government key agreement with the US.

Key escrow encryption has been a topic of growing interest in the research community. Silvio Micali's proposal for 'fair cryptosystems' (1994) has influenced several designs, including the Bankers Trust proposal. Karlsruhe University's TESS system uses smart cards for user keys which are escrowed (Beth *et al.*, 1994). A proposal from Royal Holloway – University of London integrates escrow with the trusted third parties that serve as certificate authorities (Jefferies *et al.*, 1995).

Some type of escrow facility might be used to control anonymity services as well as encryption. For example, escrow could be used with digital cash and anonymous remailers to ensure traceability when there is a court order or other legal authorisation for information about the originator of a transaction. Ernie Brickell, Peter Gemmell and David Kravitz propose a system for electronic cash that would incorporate trustee-based tracing in an otherwise anonymous cash system (Brickell *et al.*, 1995).

ALTERNATIVES TO KEY ESCROW

Key escrow is not the only way of accommodating authorised government access. Another approach is weak encryption. The data encryption keys are short enough that a key can be determined by trying all possibilities. From the user's perspective, key escrow encryption has an advantage over weak encryption of allowing the use of strong encryption algorithms that are not vulnerable to attack. However, for applications where such a high level of security is not needed, weak encryption offers a less costly alternative. A disadvantage of weak encryption (unless it is extremely weak) from a law enforcement perspective is that it can preclude real-time decryption in an emergency situation (for example, kidnapping).

A third approach is link encryption. Communications are encrypted between network nodes but not across nodes. Thus, plaintext communications can be accessed in the network switching nodes. One major advantage of link encryption is that it allows someone with a cellular phone to protect the over-the-air connection into the phone system without requiring that the other party have a compatible encryption device or, indeed, use any encryption at all. Global System for Mobile (GSM), a worldwide standard for mobile radio telecommunications, encrypts communications transmitted over the radio link, but they are decrypted before being transmitted through the rest of the network. The disadvantage of link encryption is that plaintext data are exposed in, potentially, many intermediate nodes. By contrast, key escrow encryption can support secure end-to-end encryption.

CRYPTO ANARCHY IS NOT INEVITABLE

In the United States, there are no restrictions on the import, manufacture or use of cryptographic products (except that government agencies are required to use government standards). The question is: are such controls needed or will voluntary key escrow, combined with weak encryption and link encryption where appropriate, be sufficient to avoid crypto anarchy?

Several factors will facilitate the adoption of key escrow. Because key escrow products will be exportable, under appropriate conditions, vendors will have a strong incentive to adopt key escrow, as it will enable them to integrate strong cryptography into a single product line for both domestic and international sales. Currently, vendors must either install weak cryptography, which does not meet the needs of many customers, or develop two sets of products, which greatly increases costs and prohibits interoperability between domestic and foreign customers. Users will have an incentive to purchase key escrow products, because such products will protect them against lost or damaged keys. The government's own commitment to key escrow will ensure a large market for escrowed encryption products. As the market develops, many users will choose key escrow products in order to communicate with those using such products. Concern over the social consequences of crypto anarchy will also motivate some people to develop or use key escrow products. Finally, the adoption of key escrow might be facilitated by legislation that would specify the qualifications, responsibilities and liabilities of government-approved escrow agents. This legislation could define unlawful acts relating to the compromise or abuse of escrowed keys (for example, deliberately releasing a key to someone who is not authorised to receive it). Such legislation could ensure that at least approved escrow agents satisfy the requirements of users and the government. It also could allay the privacy concerns of those using approved escrow agents.

International interest in key escrow will also contribute to its success. There is growing recognition on the part of governments and businesses worldwide of the potential of key escrow to meet the needs of both users and law enforcement. In addition to providing confidentiality and emergency backup decryption, escrowed encryption is seen as a way of overcoming export restrictions, common to many countries, which have limited the international availability of strong encryption in order to protect national security interests. With key escrow, strong exportable cryptography can be standardised and made available internationally to support the information security needs of international business. Key escrow could be a service provided by trusted parties that manage the public-key infrastructure and issue X.509 certificates. Some products and proposals for key escrow use this approach

At a meeting sponsored by the Organisation for Economic Development (OECD) and the International Chamber of Commerce (ICC) in December 1995 in Paris, representatives from the international business community and member governments agreed to work together to develop encryption policy guidelines based on agreed upon principles that accommodate their mutual interests. The INFOSEC Business Advisory Group (IBAG) issued a statement of seventeen principles that they believe can form the basis of a detailed agreement.[6] IBAG is an association of associations (mostly European) representing the information security interests of users.

The IBAG principles acknowledge the right of businesses and individuals to protect their information and the right of law-abiding governments to intercept and lawfully seize information when there is no practical alternative. Businesses and individuals would lodge keys with trusted parties who would be liable for any loss or damage resulting from compromise or misuse of those keys. The trusted parties could be independently accredited entities or accredited entities within a company. The keys would be available to businesses and individuals on proof of ownership and to governments and law enforcement agencies under due process of law and for a limited time-frame. The process of obtaining and using keys would be auditable. Governments would be responsible for ensuring that international agreements would allow access to keys held outside national jurisdiction. The principles call for industry to develop open voluntary, consensus, international standards and for governments, businesses and individuals to work together to define the requirements for those standards. The standards would allow choices about algorithm, mode of operation, key length and implementation in hardware or software. Products conforming to the standards would not be subject to restrictions on import or use and would be generally exportable.

EUROBIT (European Association of Manufacturers of Business Machines and Information Technology Industry), ITAC (Information Technology Industry Association of Canada), ITI (Information Technology Industry Council, USA), and JEIDA (Japan Electronic Industry Development Association) also issued a statement of principles for global cryptography policy at the OECD meeting.[7] The quadripartite group accounts for more than 90 per cent of the worldwide revenue in information technology. Acknowledging the needs of both users and governments, their principles call for harmonisation of national cryptography policies and industry-led international standards.

It is conceivable that domestic and international efforts will be sufficient to avoid crypto anarchy, particularly with support from the international business community. However, it is possible that they will not be enough. Many companies are developing products with strong encryption that do not accommodate government access, standards groups are adopting non-key escrow standards, and software encryption packages such as PGP are rapidly proliferating on the Internet, which is due, in part, to the crypto anarchists, whose goal is to lock out the government. Since key escrow adds to the development and operation costs of encryption products, the price advantage of unescrowed encryption products could also be a factor which might undermine the success of a completely voluntary approach. If escrow is integrated into the public-key infrastructure, however, cost might not be a significant factor.

Considering the explosive growth of telecommunications and the encryption market, it will be necessary to closely watch the impact of encryption on law enforcement. If government-proof encryption begins to seriously undermine the ability of law enforcement agencies to carry out their missions and fight organised crime and terrorism, then legislative controls over encryption technology may be desirable. One possibility would be to license encryption products but not their use. Licences could be granted only for products that reasonably satisfy law enforcement and national security requirements for emergency decryption and provide privacy protections for users. The exact requirements might be those that evolve from the current efforts of the OECD and international business community to develop common principles and standards. The manufacture, distribution, import and export of unlicensed encryption products would be illegal, but no particular method of encryption would be mandated. Individuals would be allowed to develop their own encryption systems for personal or educational use without obtaining licences, though they could not distribute them to others. France and Russia have adopted licensing programmes, though of a somewhat different nature. France requires licences to use encryption when keys are not held by licensed parties.

Under this licensing programme, commercial encryption products, including programs distributed through public network servers, would comply with government regulations. These products would not support absolute privacy or completely anonymous transactions. Mainstream applications would assure accountability and protect societal and organisational interests. Although non-compliant products might be distributed through underground servers and bulletin boards, such products would not interoperate with licensed ones, so their use would be limited.

Such an approach would not prevent the use of government-proof encryption products by criminals and terrorists. They could develop their own or acquire the products illegally. But an approach of this type would make it considerably more difficult than it is at present. Had such controls been adopted several years ago – before programs such as DES and PGP were posted on the Internet – the encryption products on the market today would support key escrow or some other method for government access. It would not be possible to acquire strong, government-proof encryption from reputable vendors or network file servers. The encryption products available through underground servers and the black market would most likely not possess as high a quality as products developed through the legitimate market. Underground products could have security vulnerabilities or be less user-friendly. They would not be integrated into standard applications or network software.

CONCLUSION

Crypto anarchy is an international threat which has been stimulated by international communications systems, including telephones and the Internet. Addressing this threat requires an international approach that provides for both secure international communications crossing national boundaries and electronic surveillance by governments of criminal and terrorist activity taking place within their jurisdictions. The adoption of an inter-national approach is critical in order to avoid a situation where the use of encryption seriously endangers the ability of law enforcement agencies, worldwide, to fight terrorism and crime. The result will not be worldwide suppression of communica-tions and encryption tools, as May asserts, but rather the respon-sible use of such tools lest they lead to social disorder. Our information superways require responsible conduct just as our interstate highways require it.

Key escrow encryption has emerged as one approach that can meet the confidentiality and data recovery needs of organisa-tions while allowing authorised government access to fight ter-rorism and crime. It can facilitate the promulgation of standards and products that support the information security requirements of the global information infrastructure. The governments of the OECD nations are working with the international business com-munity to find specific approaches that are mutually agreeable.

NOTES

1 Louis J. Freeh, Keynote talk at International Cryptography Institute, Sept. 1995. Available through http://www.fbi.gov/crypto.htm.
2 For a description of the characteristics of key escrow encryption systems and different proposals, see Denning and Branstad (1996). More detailed descriptions of thirty systems can be found through http://www.cs.georgetown.edu/~denning/crypto. See also Denning (1995b, 1995c).
3 Statement by the Press Secretary, the White House, 16 April 1993.
4 Because the algorithm is classified and not open to public review, outside experts were invited to examine the algorithm and report their findings to the public. See Ernest F. Brickell, Dorothy E. Denning, Stephen T. Kent, David p. Maher and Walter Tuchman, 'The SKIPJACK Review, Interim Report: The SKIPJACK Algorithm', 28 July 1993; available through http://www.cs.georgetown.edu/~denning/crypto.
5 Administration Statement on Commercial Encryption Policy, 12 July 1996, and 'Enabling Privacy, Commerce, Security and Public Safety in the Global Information Infrastructure', Office of Management and Budget, 17 May 1996. Both papers are available through the Cryptography Project: http//www.cs.georgetown.edu/~denning/crypto.
6 INFOSEC Business Advisory Group (IBAG) Statement. Available through http://www.cs.georgetown.edu/~denning/crypto.
7 EUROBIT-ITAC-ITI-JEIDA Statement. Available through http://www.cs.georgetown.edu/~denning/crypto.

Chapter 12

Multimedia information products and services
A need for 'cybercops'?

Puay Tang

INTRODUCTION

This chapter addresses the problems that multimedia information services and products pose for copyright and the technological solutions that are being adopted to deal with them. It argues that the development of these technologies will result in higher costs of access to electronic information and this, in turn, is likely to create a society of information rich and information poor. Available evidence shows that, currently, the use of these services is largely concentrated in the hands of 'big business', and to a much lesser degree utilised by small and medium sized companies, the educational community and the home consumer (Mansell and Tang, 1994). The chapter concludes by suggesting that government policies must actively promote public awareness of intellectual property laws, and implement the use of multimedia services, thereby demonstrating the benefits of access to a vast range of information.

This chapter focuses on CD-ROMs and databases that are transmitted electronically through telecommunication networks and the role of copyright. Information available on CDs, which was once considered expensive to reproduce, is becoming easier and cheaper to copy with the introduction of new technologies. Electronic databases are flourishing as more users recognise their inherent advantages, and they are readily available through various on-line services and the Internet. The relatively plodding growth of 'roaming' data communication networks will give a further boost to the use of electronic databases as they will be accessible from any location.

Multimedia services and information products are based on

concepts associated with the convergence of computer, telecommunication and broadcasting technologies that process and transmit digital combinations of sound, text and video images (generically treated as information) and allow interactivity between the user and the electronic information product. The frenzied hype over multimedia has led businesses involved in content development, production and distribution of information-based products to emphasise the need for new laws and methods to ensure the appropriation by owners of intellectual property embedded in these products.

Legislation lags behind technological advancement and businesses involved in multimedia fear that legal remedies are unlikely to be very helpful or too slow to be implemented. This is largely because of the rapid pace of technological innovations and because multimedia products do not fit neatly into any pre-existing category for copyright protection.[1] In the looming digital age, pundits have begun to attest that the dynamic and expeditious technological advancements are creating too many works, too many users, and too many uses. While 'too many users' has yet to be substantiated, it is nonetheless observable that there is a growing irrelevance of traditional copyright law. This, therefore, poses a legal challenge to redefine copyright, which, in turn, may imply that copyright as we know it today will become obsolete. Some have suggested that copyright will become a system of compulsory licences; others have said that it will degenerate into a right of 'equitable remuneration' for publishers, developers and creators of digital information products (Oman, 1993). Inherent in any of these suggestions is a notion of increasing cost as the producer-community continues to ensure the sanctity of their rights through the development of technologies of control or technological solutions, and the law, of course. The White Paper on intellectual property prepared by the National Information Property Working Group in 1995 for the Clinton Administration expanded rights for copyright owners (Information Infrastructure Task Force, 1995). If the recommendations advanced by the White Paper, such as those suggesting browsing and 'pay-per-use' rules, are incorporated into the yet to be debated National Infrastructure Copyright Protection Act, there will be implications of rising cost for access and use of the information.

At the same time, producers want wide diffusion of their

works. So how content-providers can protect their works and how users can gain access to such works by affordable and practical means are issues that are moving to centre stage in the formulation of the 'superhighway code'. These issues are in keeping with the original purpose of intellectual property protection, which was to make intellectual property available to the public so that it could be used. What has changed is the medium; and the digital medium is confounding the system. Multimedia technologies are enabling widespread infringement of the copyrights of creators and developers as a result of the voluminous reproduction and manipulation of digital information-based products. Despite their appeal for legislative remedies, creators, developers and providers of electronic information are concentrating on the development of technologies to safeguard their intellectual property. They claim that new copyright laws and the technologies of protection are necessary to foster the growth of the multimedia industry and the realisation of the 'information superhighway'.

In short, the issues surrounding intellectual property and technology are governed by three forces: those of the law; business relationships between the producers, owners and users of intellectual property; and technology. These issues prompt a rethinking of intellectual property, how to define these properties, how to value them and how to protect them (Baron, 1993). Stated differently, multimedia products are bringing about a new paradigmatic shift, from that of a once-clearly categorised system of intellectual property protection towards one of 'organised chaos' in which these products and services do not fit neatly, but only somewhat, into any of the categories.

MULTIMEDIA TECHNOLOGIES: THEIR ATTRIBUTES

Multimedia technologies are fundamentally different from print technologies, just as the printed word is different from the digital word. Digital photocopiers, audio and video tape machines, optical scanners, CD-Recordable machines and computers have reduced replication costs and decentralised copying processes so dramatically that rights holders are no longer assured of control of the production and integrity of their intellectual property. Electronic transmission of information has exacerbated the reproduction problem. Similarly, the availability of broadcast works simultaneously with their reproduction makes arrangements for the collection of royalty payments unwieldy and pro-hibitively expensive. These features have helped to encourage 'digital' piracy.

Seven characteristics of multimedia technology are collect-ively confounding existing copyright laws:

1 The falling costs of replication technologies and of reproduc-tion are reflected in the decreasing costs of optical storage, together with the increasing speed at which replications and 'perfect' copies can be made.

2 Speedy, simultaneous access to centralised sources of informa-tion means that the number of users who are privy to them 'before the ink is dry' is growing. At the same time, the moni-toring and controlling of onward transmission of copyrighted material are proving to be monumental problems.

3 The decentralisation and pervasiveness of fast and powerful home and business computers equipped with CD-drives, modems and Internet connection is encouraging widespread access to on-line database services and CDs. The interconnect-edness of machines allows works to be transferred with impunity and without the knowledge of their creators.

4 The versatility of multimedia technologies facilitates the stor-age and transmission of any combination of text, audio signals and video images. Digital information is malleable. This induces 'information buffs' to download copies and to 'experi-ment' with all forms of manipulation of information. There are opportunities for exploitation of freedom of access such as the intent to trade in the manipulated and reproduced infor-mation products. For example, computerised music databases, or 'digital jukeboxes', include massive catalogues of record-ings and allow users to select a particular recording, listen to it and obtain a history of the recording and the recording artist. If it is on-line and access is relatively cheap, it can be downloaded by any user for his or her own use. There is also nothing to prevent a record store from using it for commercial purposes.

5 Since computers can be interconnected privately, works can be created interactively and joint authorship need not be limited by physical distance. Interactivity can make it difficult to cre-ate an authoritative work, and works produced in this way present problems for the attribution of authorship.

6 Machines can mask original authorship through the use of sophisticated software.

7 More and more information can be stored digitally with advances in storage and compression technologies. This will provide much value to users and cost savings to creators, developers and distributors of multimedia products, for example CD-ROMS. This type of concentration of value, however, is Janus-faced; while on the one side it provides savings, on the other the density of storage also raises the stakes in the battle against reproduction and infringement, 'from piracy for profit to copying for convenience' (Goldberg, 1993).

MULTIMEDIA INFORMATION SERVICES: WHAT COPYRIGHT PROBLEMS?

Copyright is arguably the biggest issue that will affect markets for the production and use of digitally transmitted works. Copyright was introduced as a result of a technological challenge – the Gutenberg printing press. It made the dissemination of information easier, but the printing press also made it easier to copy and steal information. In the face of these misdemeanours, copyright was formulated specifically to deal primarily with the flow and use of information and information-based products so as to protect and reward authors and creators of literary works through various forms of compensation. Thus, it is to copyright rather than to other intellectual property protection provisions, such as trade secrets or patents, that the creators, developers, producers and distributors of electronic information are looking primarily in their efforts to gain legislative protection for their information-based works.

As noted above, copyright, historically, has been awarded to authors and creators of paper-based original 'literary works'. It was the responsibility of the author or creator to detect infringement and prevent unauthorised use of a work. The photocopier complicated the process of uncovering infringement, and laws enforcing copyright protection were introduced. Despite the implementation of these laws, it was difficult to patrol the 'paper chase'. Nonetheless, on the whole, the laws worked. Though they are still in place, the use of combinations of technologies in a digitally mediated environment is confounding the process of copyright protection and subverting the mechanisms that governed the system.[2] Digital works are not tangible products; one cannot 'see' a digital product, unless it is processed and projected through a microprocessor-controlled device. This peculiar characteristic of digital information lends enormous potential for manipulation, alteration, mixing, modification and combination of information, whereby the arrangement of contents can conceal original authorship and to present a new 'original' product.

Thus a major problem is the identification of authorship. The difficulty of determining authorship in a networked, interconnected environment in which everyone can work simultaneously on an article also creates a large problem. Since copyright is awarded to authors of 'original' works, how should legislation deal with this? Furthermore, whether information that is automatically written or compiled by a computer can be construed as a 'work of authorship' is a highly controversial matter. Electronic assemblers and compilers, in some cases, have taken over the task of compiling computer code from high-level language to machine-readable form (Congress of the United States, Office of Technology Assessment, 1986). Developments in natural language processing eventually may enable computer systems to 'understand' documents written within a database and then to produce written abstracts in response to a user's query and eventual use of the abstracted information. Where does authorship lie? Similarly, artificial intelligence and neural networks can create, manipulate and analyse digitally recorded objects (Johnson-Laird, 1990). Such technological developments test the definition of 'authorship'.

Identifying infringement of copyright is also creating a portentous problem. The increased communications capacity in terms of speed, volume and distance allows the rapid transmission and distribution of incredible amounts of information at a rate of 100 average-length pages in a second (Congress of the United States, Office of Technology Assessment 1986). This allows the creation of huge libraries of information with 'universal' access. Even if the initial distribution of information is lawful, it is virtually impossible to control its redistribution, onward transmission or reproduction.

Similarly, a piece of technology, for instance, called an anonymous remailer prevents the disclosure of anyone posting information on a bulletin board service. This technology is simply a computer connected to the Internet that forwards electronic mail or files to other addresses on the network. It strips the 'header' part of the messages, which shows where they came from, and who sent them. All the receiver can tell about the message's origin is that it passed through the remailer (Arthur, 1995). This makes infringement immensely difficult to detect.

The issue of what can, and cannot, legally be used in the compilation of specialised information in CD or electronic form raises the issue of 'derivative products'.[3] Electronic derivative products comprise an important segment of electronic publications, either as stand-alone works or as part of other works. They are not very different in concept from derivative products of traditional publishing, such as abridgements, abstracts, digests, condensations or catalogues. An example of a derivative product is a digital specialised bibliographical source, or specialised data, using material which is already published. A derivative product also can be an abridgement of a book or volumes of books, such as *The Joy of Cooking* or *An Anthology of American Poetry*. A derivative product can also originate from another derivative product.

The already mentioned capabilities of information and communication technologies to morph, transform and conceal originality and ownership of digital information are often harnessed in the publication of electronic derivative products. On the one hand, since copyright law confers upon the holder the right to benefit from *all* subsequent works based on the original work and prevents commercial copying, it could inhibit the use and production of secondary material, if inclusion of copyrighted works cannot duly reward the rights holders. On the other hand, as David Vaver has argued, the uncertainty surrounding the practical application of copyright law with respect to such works can be prejudicial to their production because 'risk-averse' producers will simply pay what is demanded by the source work owner, thereby increasing the price of such products (Vaver, 1995).

The avoidance of copyright infringement and the establishment of copyright protection are central concerns with the production of derivative products. Producers must know how to separate ideas from expressions (the former is not protected whereas the latter is), and unprotectible expression (such as functionality of the database programme) from protectible expressions (such as the particular means of expressing the database; for instance, a customised database programme or format) (*Copyright Law Journal*, 1994). To avoid infringement, producers must know the scope of protection of the information used in their derivative products. Furthermore, producers also must be aware that quantitatively *insignificant* copying from the source material may still be construed as infringement, if the copied material is a qualitatively important part of the owner's copyrighted work.

Data by themselves are not copyrighted, but when supplied as electronic text, for instance as a computer database, they are protected and copyrightable. Therefore, derivative products produced from such electronic text can only contain licensed information. Copyright in the electronic data used in derivative products must be retained by the holder and its ownership is to be identified and protected throughout. A derivative product produced from a derivative product must define the subject matter of copyright protection and clearly reference and list the respective data owners so that permission to use the data is obtained. Furthermore, an electronic publisher of derivative products adds value and sometimes more data to the 'core' or source data. Therefore the nature of his/her intellectual property right should be specified and differentiated from the 'core' data copyright holders in order for the derivative work to be copyrighted. This may prove very difficult or complicated in practice with each step of added value. These legal complexities can foster inadvertent infringement and, in some cases, deliberate infringement on the pretext of ignorance or misunderstanding.

While electronic specialised databases, a common example of derivative works, are assigned copyright protection in the UK, this is the exception rather than the rule in other countries. The 1993 Directive on the *Legal Protection of Databases* from the European Commission, which was unanimously accepted by Member States in December 1995 and subsequently by the Council of Ministers on 26 February 1996, is an example of the vital importance of this matter. The driving force behind this directive came mainly from the publishing industry, which noted that large-scale pirated copies and adaptations of digital works were being sold openly on the market. Publishers, who felt that their market was being systematically eroded by what they claimed were unlawful acts, lobbied their governments to take legislative measures to stem the tide of unauthorised replication and 'illegal' derivative products. This Directive is to be enacted into national law and will introduce a *sui generis* right to protection for intellectual works produced in the European Union that do not now fit into any copyright category.[4]

If identifying infringement of electronically networked copyrighted material is becoming more complicated, then the ability to enforce compliance is in double jeopardy. Existing legislation is perceived to have lost its teeth in enforcing compliance and this is precipitating further violations. As noted above, increased communication capacity permits the storage and distribution of copious amounts of information. Once this capability is in place in the network, it could lead to the creation of huge private or public centralised libraries, downloading of information, or trading of information without the knowledge of copyright holders is possible. Furthermore, copies can be written over or removed in no time.

No 'copyright squad' will have the ability to detect these occurrences as they were able to do when they were sent out on surprise missions to school libraries, for example, to check on the reproduction of books and the number of unauthorised copies being made without permission of authors. This may be possible, however, if 'superhighway cops' are posted along the network routes in the form of 'video monitors' tracking all electronic transmissions. This undoubtedly would provoke accusations of transgressions of personal privacy, as well as incur an intimidating cost for development and installation of these 'video monitors', if they are at all possible.

Although copyright holders seem to be besieged by the versatility and capabilities of multimedia technologies, these same technologies can also serve their interests well by playing the role of 'cybercops'. 'Electronic books', for example, can be brought under the control of the author. Since the author no longer has to sell her or his books via a distributor, wholesaler, retailer or in hard copy, she or he is, in effect, in control of sales. This means that authors can set the terms of sale. The implication is the escalating cost of information, but the author is in less of a danger of losing the benefit of copyright in this case, provided she/he employs the services of 'cybercops'.

MULTIMEDIA TECHNOLOGIES: CYBERCOPS

To borrow a now famous phrase, 'the solution to the machine is in the machine', 'cybercops' can be employed to patrol the electronic beat (Clark, 1994). There are several varieties of technologies of control available to prevent unauthorised use of intellectual works. Many are targeted at preventing the copying of software, broadcast video signals and audio and video recordings, as there are developments aimed at preventing the copying of on-line and CD-based databases, and detecting infringement. This chapter will focus on encryption, as it is widely regarded as the 'mother of all' cybercops, and on a sample of other kinds of cybercops.[5]

Encryption

Encryption is the most widely used method of securing information from piracy. It also can be used for monitoring the use of information and creating proprietary channels for the distribution of information. Encryption involves scrambling information so that it is not accessible until a 'key' is applied. Encryption methods are not fail-safe. According to the US Defense Information Systems Agency, a Pentagon computer security agency, US Defense Department computers containing non-classified but sensitive data were attacked 250,000 times in 1995, in which hackers succeeded in penetrating the computers in an estimated 160,000 incidents (Keyhoe, 1996). Nevertheless, encryption is reputed to be an effective deterrent against copying as the effort and cost required to unscramble the encryption codes often outweigh the benefits of copying. The quest for a uniquely powerful encryption method of protecting information on the networks that is not excessively expensive and time-consuming for users to use, according to publishers and software developers, has become a commercial priority. This is evidenced by the developments in the US, the European Union and elsewhere.

Encryption serves various purposes: for publishers, it is used to protect their intellectual property and that of their authors; for manufacturers it is used to ensure that their software-based processes and applications are safe from tampering and theft; for researchers and librarians it is used to protect the integrity of a document or to demonstrate its authenticity. Governments encrypt for security purposes and they need to be able to decrypt for surveillance purposes. National security needs complicate the commercial implementation of 'perfect' encryption techniques as individuals who want to close network transmissions to third parties must open them to the government. On the whole, however, users and suppliers of information want technology to help enforce the law rather than to break it.

There are several forms of encryption which may be used in a document delivery context. Private key encryption involves a pre-established relationship between the user and the source before the encrypted document is transmitted. This kind of encryption is limited to each transmission, and is therefore regarded as costly, time-consuming and complex, particularly by traders of electronic information. Public key encryption involves encryption by the information vendor, who then sells the release keys or codes to members of the public who wish to become users. The disadvantage of this system is that users may exchange keys with other users or the communication of keys between the vendors and users may be interrupted or 'hacked into', thereby establishing access to a key illegally. To counter this some argue for the development of 'electronic notaries' on the network to validate keys in current use and prevent the resale of old or superseded keys (Worlock, 1994).

Another method is the 'RSA standard', named after its creators, Rivest, Shamir and Adleman, at MIT. This method is a public-key system and can be used for encryption and authentication. The sender uses the public key (which belongs to the recipient and which is available in a directory) to encrypt data. The second key, which belongs to the recipient, is a private and secret key and is used to decrypt the same data. To authenticate the message, the sender attaches his or her digital signature (which is done computationally) to the message. The signature, which is composed of data, cannot be forged. Verification of the signature by the recipient is also done computationally. This form of encryption is being applied commercially by Apple, Hewlett Packard, Sun, Bank America and Lockheed on their trading networks, and by CommerceNet, which runs on the Internet. The weakness of this system lies in the possibility of reproduction once a document is re-transmitted to a third party.

Another variant of encryption is found in the linking of the published material to the computer that contains the code, which enables one to view the text and graphics, or listen to music. To view text and graphics, one needs a to have a 'viewer'; to listen to music, one needs a 'player.' To gain access to these software programs, one needs to have a special key to be a legitimate viewer of the information, or listener of the music. The special key is either a password or a personal identification number (PIN).

London-based Cerberus Sound and Vision is a commercial outfit distributing music through the Internet. It is one for the first developers of this system. Subscribers' details are entered into the company's central computer. When a subscriber logs onto the Internet, the software will connect them to the Cerberus computer, which encrypts the information of the application onto the 'player' software. The player and PIN are then sent to the subscriber. When the subscriber requests a piece of music, a message is sent to the Cerberus computer, where it then searches for and extracts the music requested, works out which artists should be paid, and then compresses and encrypts the data (Lawrence, 1993). This method is not foolproof, and development on data compression is continuing to improve its 'fool-proofness'. Some experts claim that hackers can still break into the software and find a means of 'stealing' the song digitally as it is played. This could be done, for example, by intercepting the digital feed between the processor in the customer's computer and sound card on the computer, or even by digitally recording the output. Nonetheless, the UK's Mechanical Copyright Protection Society has approved the system and the Performing Rights Society is interested in the system for collecting royalties. The video industry is reported to be interested in the system as well (Lawrence, 1993).

Encryption as a means of protection is also being studied through various programmes by the European Union. Its first project was Copyright in Transmitted Electronic Documents (CITED), which focused on special software to gain access to the copyrighted material and to decode it. This is done through keying in a password. In addition to encryption, CITED's proposals included a vital aspect of protection: how to protect the information *after* it had been decoded. Its solution was to build a piece of tamper-proof software which recorded everything that happens to the copyrighted material. The recordings are then stored in a database on a central computer. Through this mechanism, the movements of a copyrighted material can be tracked.

In collaboration with another European project, Computer Ownership Protection in Computer Assisted Training (COPI-CAT), the combined team is currently testing a copyright management system to deal with the nettlesome issues of 'digital' copyright protection and onward transmission. Preliminary trials of various methods are being undertaken, one of which involves embedding features into the software which disable the 'copy' and 'save' features, thereby preventing duplication. COPI-CAT wrapped material can be protected according to the level of protection required. The inbuilt Copyright Management System can monitor usage and control both access authorisation as well as the information necessary for subsequent royalty and licence collections. The most recent initiative of the European Commission is IMPRIMATUR, which aims to devise and recommend methods and processes to protect all types of intellectual property. This is an international project and involves US, Japanese and European participants.

Encryption is also being used in the CD-ROM marketplace. CD-ROM publishers use encryption software packages to protect their disks or to limit access to specified groups of users. Typically, users ring the CD-ROM publisher's hot line after having reviewed sample material and are given release or password keys after paying for the material.[6] The decryption software looks for an embedded 'signature' stored on the CD-ROM, which it must have in order to decipher the encrypted data. C-Dilla, a UK-based company, has developed a way of putting the signature onto a pressed CD-ROM so that it cannot be copied onto a blank CD. Detection of infringement or reproduction occurs this way. At the start of a CD, there is an electronic index which lists all the data files on the disk and their locations. Although a CD-ROM drive must read the index before it can read the files on the disk, it will not deliver the index to the CD recorder. What happens, instead, is that the recorder creates a new index for the new disk as the data files are transferred. The incriminating signature, however, is not copied.

Other cybercops

An associated method of legally demonstrating originality (or detecting infringement) that is gaining the interest of publishers is 'fingerprinting' of digital images, which involves embedding originator-specific data-within-data. Each digital image is coded with fingerprints and identification (ID) sentences containing letters and dates. These fingerprints and ID remain in the image after manipulation or duplication, enabling copyright holders to identify and prove ownership. This method can also be used to detect which parts of a composite image have fingerprints and whether an image has been changed. As with the above, this method does not prevent reproduction.

'Watermarking' copyrighted material with a code number or word is also being developed to help copyright protection. Thorn EMI (UK) have designed an inaudible code word into audio of any kind, and this technology is being trialled throughout 120 monitoring sites across the US. The company also has developed a technology to insert invisible coded information into an image. This technology is independent of the medium by which the image is stored or transmitted. When the image is printed on paper or displayed on the screen, the code is invisible, but can be retrieved using the same technology (Fox, 1996).

Holograms are starting to be used by electronic publishers against software pirates.[7] The hologram, a holographic disk, is buried inside a CD or CD-ROM, without limiting data storage. Previously, the holographic disks could not hold a hologram and data in the same section, thereby limiting data storage capacity. 'Holographic' CDs make detection of infringement easier; they do not, however, prevent the reproduction of CDs with a CD-Recordable machine.

System-based methods of ensuring payment for copyrighted material on the Internet are also being developed. For instance, authors will be provided with a computer program that 'wraps around' any work they want to make available on the Internet. Potential customers will have to go through the program, which will then check if the interested party (or parties) have already paid a royalty. If they have not, it will demand some form of electronic payment, or access to the work is denied. The company providing this 'wrap around' programme will monitor use of the various copyright works, collect payments and distribute them to the authors or creators (Kleiner, 1995).[8]

While encryption methods appear to be used increasingly as 'cybercops', a few important obstacles stand in the way of widespread implementation. First, governments must permit universal adoption, for example, and encryption systems must be standardised internationally. While encryption is purportedly the most effective means of protection of information, its export is prohibited as most countries regard it as a form of munition. Philip Zimmermann, a US citizen, was charged by the US Department of Justice and to be tried by the US Supreme Court for violation of the International Traffic and Arms Regulations (ITAR, controls the export of encryption as it is regarded as munition) because his easy-to-use and secure encryption software program 'Pretty Good Privacy' was placed on the Internet and became widely downloaded. The Department of Justice subsequently dropped its charges against Zimmerman before the US Department of State finally amended ITAR allowing individuals to use and export strong encryption material without a special licence. This incident, however, illustrates the potential severity of exporting encryption programs without permission. When exported, governments must be assured, on national security grounds, that they have the means to decrypt the information. Use of encryption is allowed domestically in most countries, but under restricted conditions.

Second, the user community must be persuaded to accept the cost and 'inconvenience' of encryption if there is to be tamper-free and authentic information. Therefore, encryption will need to obtain widespread support from users. Industry observers agree that the cost of information will increase with the development of technologies of protection. Despite their increasing adoption, these technological solutions have yet to gain industry-wide acceptance. A major problem lies in the diverse encryption import and export controls and requirements of countries which affect usage and licensing arrangements, which are very often restrictive.

Third, 'Joe Citizen Users' need to be instilled with a sense of *noblesse oblige* with respect to intellectual property rights as much as they will need to be convinced that intellectual property laws are implemented for the benefit of society. The above

notwithstanding, experimentation and the development of technologies of control are continuing at rapid pace.

MULTIMEDIA SERVICES: THE NEED FOR 'SUPERHIGHWAY' POLICIES

Most of the technological 'fixes' imply an increase in the cost of
gaining access to information, at least in the short to medium
term. Paradoxically, in their attempts to forge ahead, multimedia
services producers risk the possible loss of opportunities to
increase the use of their services. In most cases, increased costs
suppress use and this, in turn, is likely to restrain public enthusiasm for the 'information superhighway'. If policy-makers believe
in the sanctity of copyright to provide incentives for the creation
and use of information, then they will need to consider how
existing policies will affect the multimedia sector.

One approach would be to encourage public education with
respect to the impact of intellectual property laws. For example,
intellectual property education programmes or curricula could
be developed by schools, public libraries and educational organisations. Law schools and universities, through government
sponsorship, could offer special classes on intellectual property
to the public. Support for the development of extra-mural activities (continuing education) on these issues in public libraries
could also spread user awareness of them. The US government
has identified the importance of informing the public on the
multiple issues that digital technologies have confronted existing
intellectual property regimes with in order that a balance is
maintained between reward for innovation, and use and free
flow of digital information (Congress of the United States, Office
of Technology Assessment, 1986; Information Infrastructure Task
Force, 1995). Similarly, American industry organisations and
interest groups have been instrumental in launching 'intellectual
property rights in the digital age' programmes.

Alternatively, public–private sector sponsorship of meetings
between intellectual property holders and the user community
would also be useful. Co-operative efforts between the government and industry could involve training seminars and workshops on intellectual property-related issues for smaller firms to
elevate their awareness of the constraints on, and business opportunities arising from, the derivative use of digital information.

Courses on the penalties resulting from deliberate and non-deliberate infringement of copyright also could be conducted.

Finally, to demonstrate the benefits of multimedia services, the public sector also could increase its use of multimedia services through the Internet and enhance public access to them at a reasonable rate as a form of 'practice run'. Through its use, the government could achieve four broader purposes: (1) to assist the general public in overcoming its perceived fear of the 'esotericness' of digital technologies; (2) to raise public awareness of information technology and electronic information products; (3) to generate demand for multimedia information services which the information superhighway is envisaged to deliver abundantly; and (4) to demonstrate the value and importance of information for the benefit of the general economy.

A law-abiding user-community does not mean that 'cyber-cops' will be redundant; rather it means a more ready acceptance of copyright controls by users and a higher cost of information. The policy challenge, however, is to ensure that a higher cost of information does not result in a society in which the much touted information superhighway ends up as a province of the affluent and educated.

CONCLUSION

This chapter has argued that the cost of access to multimedia services will likely increase with the introduction of technological 'fixes' to protect rights in information, thus creating problems for the realisation of the information superhighway. The increasing costs of gaining access to commercial services on the Internet are harbingers of this trend. Governments will need to establish policies to encourage the use of advanced multimedia services in a continual attempt to educate the public to their benefits. Although the cost of using many of these commercial services will be beyond the ambit of regulatory 'price fixing' or governmental control, the cost of access to public electronic services at reasonable rates may well be an incentive to smaller and medium-sized businesses, organisations, the educational community and the home consumer to use these services.

Equally importantly, there must be policies to help implement and organise courses that will improve and widen public awareness of intellectual property laws so as to prevent the abuse of digital information, thereby stimulating the necessity of more cybercops. In the absence of these concerted moves, the realisation of the information superhighway and the notion of 'cyberspace' will be no more than a quixotic pursuit by a few, a subject for academic discourse and a form of 'tribalism' among a select group of 'cyberpunks'.

As noted earlier, copyright as it is known today, will become increasingly obsolete. Originally developed for the paper-based written word, copyright is continually under siege, not only by the technical attributes of multimedia technologies, but also by the fact that a popular medium for the written word is no longer paper-based, but digital. The non-tangibility and dynamism of digital products have changed dramatically the traditional static notion of copyright. Furthermore, as noted in this chapter, new technologies have transformed the concepts of the written word and authorship. It seems likely, therefore, that copyright will be replaced by a combination of various system-based mechanisms – cybercops – to effectively deter and reduce copying and manipulating of information.

To sum up, the 'cyber dance' between the law and technology continues; technology is leading it. Yet how densely cyberspace will be 'populated' ultimately will be the consumer's decision; too many cybercops may discourage residence. H.G. Wells's phrase 'the shape of things to come' provides an appropriate concluding remark to this chapter: cyberspace is still shaping up.

NOTES

1   The four categories of publishing are books, films, computer software and music. Multimedia products can be conveniently described as an offspring of a combination of these four categories.
2   For an overview of some of the problems, see Congress of the United States, Office of Technology Assessment (1986), Motyka (1992) and the National Science Foundation (1993).
3   Section 101 of the US Copyright Act defines a derivative work as not only familiar acts of adaptation (translation and condensation), but 'any other form in which a work may be recast, transformed or adapted'.
4   A *sui generis* right to protection awards copyrightability to works that have not been considered as having such a right in a majority of Member States of the European Union.
5   The discussion of these methods, however, does not claim to be comprehensive, given rapid technological developments and space constraint.

6   Presentation by Barry Neuman, chief executive, C-Dilla, a UK-based company that develops encryption software, at a conference 'CD-ROM and Security', London, 7 February 1995.

7   Conversation with David Tidmarsh, chief executive, Applied Holographics, a leading UK-based manufacturer of holograms. See also Fox (1995).

8   A company in Arkansas, the Intellectual Property Licensing Agency, is developing this software and claims that when it has controlled enough material, it will issue blanket licensing rights to companies that provide services on the Internet.

Chapter 13

The Far Right on the Internet

Michael Whine

INTRODUCTION

The increasing utilisation of the Internet by extremists is of concern to me and to other researchers. Our concern is fuelled by the knowledge that the Internet is being used by neo-Nazis to spread race hate material. Such extremists seek to exploit the Internet to avoid legal sanctions which might make racist propaganda (in the form of publications, video and audio cassettes) illegal in most countries. The Internet is accessed by a youthful and impressionable audience, whose obvious technology and communications skills mark them as potential leaders of the next generation, and it is an area with enormous growth potential.

Racist material on the Internet is seldom subject to supervision, regulation or sanction. If it continues unchecked, then it is likely that a vicious cycle of increasingly extreme material will develop both in scale, and content. The Internet allows easy fast and cheap communication on a one-to-one, one-to-many and many-to-many basis. Amongst other things this allows for new alliances. It allows those who would previously have been 'observers' to become more active.

An important feature of the Internet has been to allow the free exchange of information, unfettered and unhindered by government-imposed restraint. However this very freedom also attracts those who would use it to promote race hatred. It is in the nature of radicalism and extremism to propagate by all available means. The Internet represents a previously undreamed of possibility for both propagating racism and allowing racists to access each other's ideas and resources.

Its use by political extremists is not yet overwhelming; it has not yet grown to the level where it is out of control or is beyond monitoring, but it is growing, as the Internet grows.

According to a recent article in *Marketing Business*, it is thought that the current users of the Internet number somewhere between 25 and 30 million, but the rate of growth is exponential and phenomenal. The Web, reportedly the fastest growing part of the Internet, grew by a staggering 443,931 per cent in 1991, although this slowed to only 1,713 per cent in 1994 (Schofield, 1995). Of concern is that it is in the nature of the system that it is difficult to monitor anyway; its size and the ease by which the origins of messages can be disguised ensure that no agency is yet prepared to devote significant time or resources to investigate hate material. The FBI as late as 1989 stated that it was not monitoring race hate bulletin boards and the Metropolitan Police have recently confirmed that they are also not in a position to do so, despite internal discussion on the matter (Stills, 1989). However, as has become apparent, American government agencies have only recently investigated, somewhat belatedly, the publication of bomb-making manuals published on the Net (Stills, 1989). The German Office for the Protection of the Constitution (BfV) has noted the use being made of the Internet, and other electronic means of communication, to evade state surveillance so it may be assumed that they are now monitoring it for counter-terrorism purposes (Werthebach, 1994).

For the purposes of this chapter it is necessary to define what we mean by the Far Right. The term is generally used to describe extra-parliamentary groups with a neo-Nazi or radical national-ist and racist ideology. Many of these groups see themselves as the successors to the Nazi regime of Hitler's Third Reich; others, especially in America, are more influenced by the radical racist nationalism of such national revolutionaries as Julius Evola, Georg and Gregor Strasser, or the 'leaderless resistance' ideology of Louis Beam and William Pierce, the American author of *The Turner Diaries*, who, in his fictional writings, forecasts an American civil war, in which autonomous groups of white citi-zens wage guerrilla warfare against Blacks, Jews and a liberal-leaning government.

Skinheads retain a somewhat less intellectual view of their surroundings. They see a world in which Jews, anti-fascists, for-eign workers, are all regarded as 'scum', to be harassed, expelled or murdered. The vilification of 'others' is used in order to define their own identity, in an ever-changing world.

The Far Right sees the Internet as the information route for the future:

> The unique nature of the Internet makes this *the* information battle-ground of the future . . . by contrast, television and radio require the creation of broadcast quality programmes, and reaching listeners and viewers is tied to the amount of money one can afford to spend. Books, magazines and other printed materials are durable and inexpensive, but no way near so freely available, and can be confiscated by oppressive Governments . . . . Internet users, though, enjoy free access to virtually all the information on the system and new features are becoming available to allow researchers to equip to find everything on the Internet in their areas of interest.[1]

Again, today, skinhead rock remains the movement's most important propaganda tool. But followers are discovering that the PC provides what the music can't – connectivity. Skinhead Bulletin Board Services (BBSs) let users meet one another on-line, share information and plan events – social and otherwise. They help skinheads turn ideology into action (Stills, 1989).

The author of a Canadian article, Chad Skelton (1994), believes that 'hate' BBSs date back to at least 1985, but since then the number has increased dramatically. During a two-month investigation the author found at least eleven such Bulletin Boards, seven of which continue to operate. During his search he gathered over 600 pages of BBS transcripts. He noted that the hate BBSs come equipped with off-line mail readers, high-quality BBS programmes, and extensive file areas that include not only text files, but digitised pictures of everyone from David Duke (American Ku Klux Klan leader) to Adolf Hitler.

The systems he found did not actively promote themselves to BBS users who did not share their point of view, but others, like Dan Gannon's Banished CPU, are available to all. He listed Cyberspace Minutemen from Chicago, Stormfront from West Palm Beach, Florida, Logo Plex from Richmond, Virginia, New Age from Denver, and others.

According to Cyberspace Minutemen's mission statement, which is viewed after logging onto the system:

Cyberspace Minutemen is a meeting place for those coura-
geous men and women fighting to preserve their Northern
European culture, Nordic ideals and freedom of speech and
association – a forum for planning strategies for victory and
forming political and social groups to defeat the enemies of
our race.

(cited in Skelton, 1994: 10)

Hans Hackmeister (an alias), System Operator of Cyberspace
Minutemen, adds that 'Cyberspace Minutemen is a white power
board dedicated to helping [members of the white race] survive
and to fighting the disastrous demographic changes concerning
this once great country turning it into a multicultural slum'
(cited in Skelton, 1994: 10). Don Black, System Operator of
Stormfront, and a former KKK leader, states that his system provides 'an additional way for white activists to communicate as
well as to acquaint others with our worldview' (cited in Skelton,
1994: 10).

The Transponder for Raising Consciousness, while promoted
by the white supremacist National Alliance, insists that they are
not a hate BBS:

'This is not a hate BBS', reads a system message. Instead the
System Operator, Vance (an alias), suggests that his system
supports 'racial idealism' which is 'based on the love of one's
people. It means placing the interests and welfare of the racial
community to which you belong ahead of your own personal
interests and desires . . . . This is a warning to those who live
in a fantasy of multi-cultures, the truth displayed within may
disturb you. Gay loving, bleeding heart, politically correct
sheep will not like what they read here, and there is no place
for their misguided views.'

(Skelton, 1994: 10)

HOW THE FAR RIGHT IS USING THE INTERNET

Holocaust denial is the link which binds many Far Right organisations. The denial of history, and the Nazi's crimes against
humanity, have been made a priority by today's neo-Nazis, who,
fifty years after the end of the war, seek once again a political
legitimacy. The Nazi's crimes deny them this legitimacy, and

therefore they deny the crimes, or belittle them, in order to gain the political support of a new generation.

Web pages, electronic mail and newsgroups

The Institute for Historical Review (IHR) in California is the major promoter of Holocaust denial. The Institute, with its pseudo-academic pretensions, and its annual seminars, which attract the likes of David Irving, Ahmed Rami, Robert Faurisson and others, has made the Internet a priority.

> So far only a few IHR leaflets and selected IHR journal articles are available on the Internet WWW (although new items are being added as time permits). Also available is a listing of every article that has appeared in the Journal, allowing callers to quickly search for titles and authors. The multi media nature of the World-Wide Web means that IHR materials are available in a very readable and even attractive layout and style. Internet users around the world can also save copies of IHR material on their personal computers for later study, or for reprinting and distribution . . . .
>
> We are seeking funds to make this an IHR priority, so that eventually just about everything that's appeared in 14 years of the *Journal of Historical Review* will be available on the Internet.[2]

The IHR gives instructions on how to access its material on the Internet.

> Every computer user with full Internet access was invited to access IHR materials on the World-Wide Web. Currently, sub-scribers to information providers such as CompuServe, Prodigy, America On Line, and GEnie have only partial access to the Internet. The best method is to use graphical Web soft-ware such as Netscape (available free in both Macintosh and Windows versions from ftp.mcom.com), although this requires a SLIP or PPP connection, or a dial-up connection running TIA. Alternatively, Internet users with character-based accounts can read IHR material on-line using Lynx. The Universal Resource Locator (URL) for IHR materials is http://www.kaiwan.com/-greg.ihr. Electronic mail can be sent to the IHR at greg.ihr@kaiwan.com.[3]

Holocaust denial material now has its own newsgroup: alt.revisionism. Denial material also appears on various alt.politics and talk.politics newsgroups. Mark Weber of the IHR published a series of articles in 1991 in talk.politics entitled 'The Holocaust: Let's hear both sides. Revisionists challenge extermination story'.

Intense Holocaust denial propaganda coupled with vehement anti-semitism were published by two particular people using the aliases 'Fritz Goldman' and 'Oskar Andersson' on the Swedish FidoNet BBS during 1993. The former also uploaded a denial file to several BBSs, which included an accurate Swedish translation of the Leuchter Report. This report is a major denial publication by Fred Leuchter, a self-proclaimed gas chamber expert who claimed to have carried out a forensic examination of the gas chambers at Auschwitz, from which he concluded that there were insufficient traces of cyanide for there ever to have been mass gassings of Jews – a lie that was exposed by a subsequent court case in his home state of Massachusetts (*Commonwealth of Massachusetts* v. *Fred A. Leuchter Jr, 1991*). Leuchter has since been expelled from Britain, and a short time later was fined and expelled from Germany. He was subsequently due to stand trial in Mannheim in September 1994 on other charges, but failed to return from America.

Holocaust denial material has now begun to appear in other newsgroups. For example, Michael A. Hoffman II, a well-known American denier, together with an Alan R. Critchley, recently published an article 'Spielberg Commits Fraud in film Schindler's List' in the soc.culture.palestine newsgroup (21 March 1995). In their article they attempt to prove that *Schindler's List*, and the book on which it is based, *Schindler's Ark*, is no more than a sophisticated hoax. They state that portions of their article first appeared in *Revisionist Researcher Magazine*, published in New York.

Bulletin Boards

A second source for Far Right material is the hotlines and BBSs, the means of communication between Far Right groups. Email and the Internet are now used extensively, providing local and international communications for the price of a local call. According to a recent press article, two leading figures in the Scottish Anti-Nazi League were subjected to a campaign of telephone death threats from neo-Nazis after their names appeared on-line. This appears to be the first instance that the Internet has been used in Britain in this way.[4]

British neo-Nazis tend to be markedly less sophisticated and organised than their foreign counterparts. There are, however, indications that they are catching up. A recent posting by the International Third Position, a breakaway group from the old National Front, announced that messages to and about them on the uk.politics newsgroup can be 'anonymised' to aid the sender to avoid state surveillance.[5]

German neo-Nazis are known to have been developing inter-computer communications since 1980. The so-called Thule Network was developed specifically to allow different German neo-Nazi groups to communicate with one another.[6] The computer magazine *Chip* estimates that about 1,500 German Far Right extremists are active on the Thule Network. This consists of at least a dozen Bulletin Boards, and derives its name from the small élite 1920s movement considered to be the forerunner of the Nazi party. Names of anti-fascist activists, code named '*Zecken*' (ticks), as well as undesirable judges and journalists can also be obtained. Code names such as '*schöne Mädchen*' (beautiful girls) have also been used to refer to the police (*Antisemitism World Report*, 1995).

It is believed that the Thule Network is located in Baden-Württemberg, Bavaria and North Rhine-Westphalia. The precise planning of German Nazis, and their planned strategy of remaining in small groups, enabling new ones to be formed rather than amalgamating with one or two large umbrella organisations, has been facilitated by the use of the Internet.

> Police have recently been baffled by the precise, military-style planning of neo-Nazi actions. Provided with passwords, such as Germania or Endsieg (final victory), from a post office box, personal computer schemes will display a calendar of forthcoming neo-Nazi events and list contact numbers of leading right wingers . . . . On Remembrance Sunday police saw in action, for the first time, computer planned co-ordinated neo-Nazi action, involving the widespread use of secret codes and radio communication . . . . 'The advantage of electronic mail boxes is that they are free of censorship

and bug-proof,' said Karl-Heinz Sendbühler of the National Democratic Party.[7]

The stated aims of the Resistance Bulletin Board Service networks are to strengthen links between German neo-Nazi groups, rally support for their cause and raise funds for their neo-Nazi 'political prisoners'. They are said to operate through a telephone line in the Bavarian town Erlangen and can only be accessed by use of coded passwords.[8]

A Norwegian neo-Nazi group, Fedrelandspartiet Youth (FLP), stated in 1994 that its sponsored Bulletin Board, Nasjonal Allianse BBS, was used to establish links with the German Thule in order to exchange regular reports. When the BBS was exposed in the *Aftenposten* daily newspaper, Arnljot Moseng, the FLP leader, panicked and closed it down.[9]

A message defending the British National Party's banning of Combat 18 in 1994 appeared on the Internet, and originated from Norway, but no further details are known. It appeared to be the means by which Britain's largest neo-Nazi group was announcing to foreign neo-Nazis its proscription of this small violent group. In the article it was suggested that

> there is growing evidence that C18 has been heavily infiltrated and probably taken over by Government agents who are acting as 'agents provocateurs' in order to incite nationalists into criminal activities, thereby making them vulnerable to arrest and imprisonment.

The article ends:

> the banning of C18 does not mean that the BNP 'has gone soft' on defending itself against violent attack. The party will continue to hit back against any assault by the opposition – and hit back hard. But we are in the business of serious politics; we are not a street gang or a 'secret army'.

Liberty Lobby, a major American racist organisation which funds other groups, sponsors the Logo Plex BBS. The most active American BBS appears to be Cyberspace Minutemen, which is said to act as a connecting point for much of the Far Right in the USA, and possibly Europe. The neo-Nazi British National Party has a contact on it, who uses the name D Man 1.[10]

Lists and hate articles

Norwegian Nazis recently published an international contact list giving the country, Bulletin Board names, System Operators, contact numbers, and so on, for over forty neo-Nazi groups in Sweden, Germany and the USA. It also listed two Internet newsgroups used by neo-Nazis and racists; alt.revisionism, and alt.skinheads, as well as alt.politics.radical-left. An American Nazi sympathiser calling himself Markus Maximus published in alt.politics.nationalism.white, in February 1995, several lists of neo-Nazi and white racist groups, including skinhead organisations in America and elsewhere.

A recent listing in alt.politics.whitepower entitled 'This Damned Group', published on 8 February 1995 from Don Black, was published in response to a question from a correspondent who asked for more information on white power groups. Black gave nineteen pages of names, addresses, contact numbers of white power groups throughout America and Canada, followed by details of neo-Nazi short-wave and satellite broadcasts on AM and FM radio stations throughout America.

A similar entry on 17 February 1994 appeared from a Jason.Smith@freenet.carleton.ca. In his response to a request for information, he stated: 'I am a nationalist skinhead, and I would be happy to provide you with some addresses to write to in order to get the information from the source.' He then lists various American neo-Nazi organisations, as well as the address of the Afrikaner Resistance Movement in Pretoria, an Australian skinhead group and the British National Party.

The Net is also being used to publish 'hate' articles. A recent example entitled 'Rothschild the Head of the Beast' attacks the Rothschild family in terms similar to that used in classic anti-semitic pre-war texts.

> You must realise too that Rothschild agents are like cockroaches crawling around your home. These cockroaches crawl all over Europe, they are everywhere. They are all around the world; in United States, in Europe, Asia, Africa, Japan and the Orient. They are constantly manoeuvring and working for the Rothschild purposes . . . . When this source speaks of the Rothschild purposes, it refers also to those cohorts, the other 12 superworld families that associate or ride the coat tails of the Rothschild.[11]

The Swedish Jewish community reported that anti-semitic messages dominated approximately fifteen to twenty neo-Nazi BBSs active in Sweden in 1993. It may be assumed that this figure will have grown considerably since then (*Antisemitism World Report*, 1994).

A message on alt.skinheads downloads (16 March 1995) appears to be a nasty diatribe in which someone called 'Les' taunts 'Heebie', a Vietnamese, about the Vietnam war.

That is only because there was stupid Rules of Engagement imposed on American soldiers by their friendly Jew, Henry Kissinger, so that you little rickshaw-runners could retreat into Cambodia whenever it looked like you would get your yellow asses kicked.

Members of the Jewish community in Britain have been plagued by anti-semitic hate-mail for the past six years. These letters frequently appear on the forged notepaper of a local synagogue or a church and provide quotations, taken out of context, or what appear to be quotations, but which are in fact rubbish, with an air of authenticity. Detectives at Scotland Yard are now investigating the origins of these, and during the first half of 1995 several homes were searched as a consequence. Similar material is now appearing on the Internet, although it originates in America.

A message on 22 March 1995 entitled 'Jewish Bigotry' appeared in the alt.revisionism newsgroup:

Although the Holy Bible is readily available in many, many languages, the Jewish Talmud, on the other hand, is hidden and secretive, and English translations, although they exist, are definitely hard to come by. In the following quotations, you will see the word 'GOY'. It serves several meanings; 'non-Jew', 'cattle', 'filthy', etc. Here are some quotes from the Talmud:

'To communicate to a GOY about our religious relations would be equal to the killing of all Jews, if the GOY knew what we teach about them, they would kill us openly' (Book of Libbre David, 37). Every GOY who studies TALMUD, and every Jew who HELPS HIM in it OUGHT TO DIE (Sanhedryn 59a Aboda Zora 8–6, Szagiga 13). The ears of the GOYS are filthy, their baths, houses, countries are filthy (Tosefta

Mikwat,VI). . . . [A] Jew may rob a GOY, he may cheat him over a bill, which should not be perceived by him, otherwise the name of G-d would become dishonoured (Schulchan Aruch, Choszen Hamizszpat 348). . . . If a GOY killed a GOY or a Jew he is responsible, but if a Jew killed a GOY he is NOT responsible (Tosefta, Aboda Zara, VIII).

According to the American Holocaust denier Tom Marcellus, the most actively used service is GEnie, the major public subscription and computer Bulletin Board Service owned by General Electric. Another Bulletin Board used for this purpose is Prodigy.[12] This is confirmed by the Simon Wiesenthal Centre of California, which states that the most complaints about racist and anti-semitic messages were those on Prodigy, which has an estimated 2 million subscribers.

Racist computer games

Racist computer games have been widely publicised and, although not strictly available on the Net, are worth mentioning. They first came to public attention in Austria in 1988, although it is believed that the games themselves originated around 1986. Early press reports suggested that they were a popular pastime for Austrian youth.

The games themselves are believed to originate in Germany, although some initial reports suggested that they might have been produced in Sweden, and others pointed to the American Gary Rex Lauck, of the National Socialist German Workers' Party (NSDAP-AO), who was arrested in Denmark in early March 1995. Following his arrest, German police searched the homes of German Nazis with whom he was in contact, and seized computers as well as other material.

The neo-Nazi video games are produced on a clandestine basis and sold or swapped on the black market; there has never been evidence to show that they are openly available. The Austrian and German governments denied any knowledge of their existence until about 1988, a consequence of the underground mode of distribution. Had the videos been available on the open market the manufacturers would almost certainly have been charged under existing German or Austrian legislation, which forbids the glorification of the Nazi era, bans overt display of Nazi symbols, and forbids denial of the Holocaust.

Not all the games are anti-Jewish; some are anti-Turk, or anti-immigrant. It is believed that they are now into the second and possibly third generations and that they are both sophisticated and interactive.

There is no evidence that the games are available in Britain. Should they become available, they would appear to fall within the scope of sections 18 and 19 of the Public Order Act. In May 1992, Glyn Ford MEP, Rapporteur of the European Community's Commission on Racism and Xenophobia, reported *Amiga Format* magazine (a computer journal) to the Crown Prosecution Service for advertising the sale of an anti-Arab computer game, 'Operation Thunderbolt', which allowed the player to play at killing Arab soldiers. In the event the CPS took no action in this case.[13]

Originally produced as interactive video games, they are now said to be available on disk, and details are now appearing on BBSs. A survey of 165 children by researchers at the University of Regensburg discovered that games had fallen into the hands of seven children. They included 'Concentration Camp Manager', in which players have to decide whether Turks (the largest ethnic minority group in Germany) should be put in labour camps or immediately gassed. 'Achtung Nazi' is set in Auschwitz concentration camp and the name of the game is to gas as many Jews as possible. Other names are said to be: 'Aryan Test', 'Hitler-Diktator 1' and 'Anti-Turk Test'.

According to Helmut Lukesch, Professor of Psychology at Regensburg:

> The games are technically excellent quality and they cost nothing. The distributors have no commercial interests, only ideological ones. They build a world view with these games that children cannot protect themselves from.[14]

The Bonn-based Bundesprufstelle, the Federal Government agency for monitoring comics, magazines and videos for their suitability for children and adolescents, has placed on its index 107 games which promote racial hatred, racial incitement and glorification of violence, and banned a further thirty.[15] The examiners in Bonn were said to be convinced, however, that they had only dealt with the tip of the iceberg.

Bomb-making manuals have also been transmitted by computer links, although it is not certain if it was via the Internet. What is certain is that much of the material emanates from the USA, where the NSDAP-AO transmitted plans in its magazine *Endsieg* by modem to Austria, Germany, France and the Netherlands and that one issue featured a home bomb-making manual. It may have been this manual which was used by Austrian Nazis to construct the bombs that were used in the wave of terror attacks that took place throughout Austria in 1994 and early 1995, in retaliation for the imprisonment of Austrian Nazi leader Gottfried Kussel.

Other bomb-making manuals are more readily available on the Internet. 'The Big Book of Mischief – The Terrorist's Handbook' is available in the newsgroup rec.pyrotechnics. Originally produced in 1991 by the Chicago group 'Chaos Industries', it is now distributed by John Cormier of the University of Manitoba, Winnipeg. However, it is believed to have originated with anarchists rather than with the Far Right. In this instance, warnings are given that the instructions given are merely for 'reading enjoyment, and is not intended for actual use'. The material has long been available, however, through neo-Nazi organisations in Britain and America. An undated file entitled 'ARYAN GUERRILLA RESISTANCE WARFARE – Guidelines For Resistance to Tyranny' states that this file is taken from Army Field Manual 31–31 Guerrilla Warfare and Special Forces Operations. The article lists tactical aspects of guerrilla warfare and states that a free copy of the Hard Core Survival Skills Book Catalogue can be obtained from Gaddis Publications, PO Box 411476-CM, Los Angeles, CA 90041. Gaddis are believed to be a Far Right publisher.

New developments

A new development during mid-1995 was heralded by Milton John Kleim Jnr in his paper 'On Tactics and Strategy for USENET':

> USENET offers enormous opportunity for the Aryan Resistance to disseminate our message to the unaware and the ignorant. It is the only relatively uncensored (so far) free-forum mass medium which we have available. The State

cannot yet stop us from 'advertising' our ideas and organisations on USENET, but I can assure you this will not always be
the case. NOW is the time to grasp the WEAPON which is the
Net, and wield it skilfully and wisely while you may still do
so freely. Crucial to our USENET campaign is that our message is disseminated beyond 'our' groups: alt.politics.nation-
alism.white,   alt.politics.whitepower,   alt.revolution.counter,
alt.skinheads, and, to a certain extent, alt.revisionism . . . . We
MUST move out beyond our present domain, and take up
positions on 'mainstream' groups. Each USENET 'cyber guerrilla' must obtain a listing of all Net newsgroups that are
available on their system, and search through the list for
groups suitable for our posts. Don't overlook foreign orientated and language newsgroups. Find groups that require 'tailored' messages: rec. groups concerning food would be
suitable for our 'kosher tax' message; alt., soc., and talk.
groups concerning politics and society would be suitable for
our message about the Jewish-controlled media . . . .
Remember: our overall USENET strategy must be to repeat
powerful themes OVER AND OVER AND OVER. We cannot
compete with the Jewsmedia, of course, as our propaganda
dissemination is but a very small fraction of the everywhere
pervasive leftist propaganda. However, our ideas possess an
energy that truth alone contains . . . . If you have the time
and money to spend, monitor the Enemy's groups, such as
soc.culture.jewish, and other groups where his ideas have
complete reign, such as soc.culture.german.[16]

Kleim's suggestion that neo-Nazi groups should publish their
own material and invade other sites was taken up enthusiastically by the Far Right in Britain during 1995. Among the first on
scene was the British National Party, which announced in
October that it was now on the Internet:

The British National Party has now established itself on the
Internet, the international computer network, with a site at:
http://ngw wmall.com/frontier/bnp/. A second site is in the
testing stage. The sites carry a condensed version of *British
Nationalist*, the party's newspaper, and general information on
the party and its Book Service. It will shortly also carry selected articles from *Spearhead* . . . . Patriots in the USA have pioneered the use of the Internet to put over news, articles and

letters from beleaguered Whites. Media censorship is completely by-passed. So why scrape around trying to get tiny quotes into the national news media, within articles and programmes of unbelievable bias, when one can put one's case at leisure to a world audience through the Internet ?[17]

The International Third Position also announced its presence in uk.politics, as did the National Democrats, publishers of *England My Country*, who stated that they were going worldwide on the Internet.[18] Similarly 'The Third Way', another Third Positionist (national revolutionary) breakaway faction from the National Front announced, in September 1995, that it, too, was going on the Internet, and Patrick Harrington, its leader, has since posted several articles.[19] The BNP in particular sees the Internet as the route for the future, and one on which it can both compete on equal terms and evade the publicity restrictions it normally encounters.

> The significance of the Internet for us is primarily as a rival news and propaganda medium to television . . . . A medium in which the BNP has unrestricted access and is able to address a large and growing audience, uncensored and on equal terms with the other parties (their emphasis) . . . .[T]he lack of centralisation and lack of control means that the 'little guy' has a chance to compete with the biggest in the world . . . . Thus the British National Party can for instance compete on the Internet on equal terms with either Labour or the Tories.
>
> (Lecomber, 1995: 8)

LEGAL REMEDIES

The Internet's global reach presents a seemingly insurmountable challenge to would-be regulators. At present, the Internet relies on the sensibilities of users to deal with those who 'abuse' its self-proclaimed ethos for their own unacceptable ends. This anarchic situation neither allows the deletion of supposedly unacceptable messages, nor does it prevent further unacceptable messages from being posted.

However, as the author of a recent article in *MacUser* argued, cyberspace is not set apart from society, it is a part of it. 'Virtual conferencing has real world results. Organised groups of fascists may be operating in a virtual environment but they intend actual physical harm to other people. That's why there should be no place for these groups in Cyberspace.' She goes on to argue that users should use the freedom that is being defended to exercise some direct control. 'If there are Nazis in a conference you are enjoined to drive them out.'[20]

The suggestion that the senders of hate messages be 'flamed out' by other users, that is, that their machines be bombarded with thousands of messages, even blank pages, thus tying up their phone lines, exhausting their fax machines, and ultimately disabling their computers, is no long-term solution, although it has its appeal:

> The other day I encountered my first neo-Nazi on the 'Net', a madman shouting hate. You know what happened? A bunch of Internet citizens ran him out of town. Chased him away, sent him packing. Gave him the big heave-ho.[21]

The practice of 'flaming' is

> a dangerous invitation to digital vigilantism and promiscuous computer violence. It turns cyberspace into a rude, lawless, frontier town in which everyone carries a six-shooter and exacts his own revenge . . . . There is no discourse when everyone is free to interrupt and no-one is appointed to keep order. No human activity can long remain unregulated . . . . The Internet, too, is a form of human behaviour. Computers and modems do not remove them from the human orbit.
>
> (Littman, 1995)

Clearly the scenario that has occurred recently, where racists have broken into electronic mail accounts and fired off racist messages, falls within the terms of the Computer Misuse Act 1995 in Britain. A professor at Texas A&M University reported in 1993 that someone had broken into his electronic mail account and sent out racist messages from the neo-Nazi National Alliance to 20,000 computer users in four states. Again, at Middlesex University in March 1995, the email account of the university's Jewish Society was broken into and racist messages transmitted throughout the campus. In an internal memorandum Professor Michael Driscoll, Dean of the University, threatened disciplinary action, including exclusion, for the culprits.

Governments are now starting to legislate against hate mail. The recent Telecommunications Decency Act 1996 (CDA) provides penalties of up to two years in jail for using a modem to send 'any comment, request, suggestion, proposal, image or other communication which is obscene, lewd, lascivious, filthy or indecent'. Although dedicated to banning pornography on the Internet, the concept may have a relevance to hate mail.

Opposition, however, comes from two lobbies: those who believe it might prevent more restrictive and effective legislation by individual states, as was argued at the Computers, Freedom and Privacy conference in San Francisco in 1991; and others, such as the Electronic Frontier Foundation, who wish to extend to cyberspace the freedom granted by the First Amendment to the US Constitution.[22]

On 12 June 1996, a panel of federal judges granted a preliminary injunction against the CDA. The judges ruled unanimously that the CDA would unconstitutionally restrict free speech on the Internet. The US government has appealed to the Supreme Court, but the earliest an appeal could be heard is October 1996, with an eventual decision in 1997.

The US Supreme Court decision in *R.A.V.* v. *City of St Paul Minnesota* in 1992 strengthened the First Amendment obstacle to banning or curbing hate expression, and the legal fight against racism in the United States has now increasingly turned towards adopting other statutes in which a content 'neutrality' is maintained, but the racial bias selection of the target is the basis of the offence (Roth, 1995).

Discussions with academic and practising lawyers and the police in Britain lead the author to believe that the provisions of Part III of the Public Order Act 1986 might be relevant where hate material, or Holocaust denial material, is transmitted with the intention of inciting hatred against a group defined by reference to their colour, race or nationality, ethnic or national origins, for example Jews. Section 19 makes it an offence to publish or distribute written material where the intention is to stir up racial hatred; section 21 makes it an offence to distribute visual images likely to stir up racial hatred; section 22 makes an attempt to broadcast threatening, abusive or insulting visual images or sounds on a cable programme service an offence; section 23 makes it an offence to possess written material which is threatening, abusive or insulting or recording of visual images or sounds which are abusive or insulting, where it is intended that racial hatred be stirred up.

The Malicious Communications Act 1988 makes it an offence to send to another person:

(a) a letter or other article which conveys:
   (i)   a message which is indecent or grossly offensive;
   (ii) a threat; or
   (iii) information which is false and known or believed to be false; or
(b) any other article which is, in whole or part, of an indecent or grossly offensive nature.

Moreover, section 43 (1) of the Telecommunications Act 1984 makes it an offence to send by means of a public telecommunications system a message that is grossly offensive or of an indecent, obscene or menacing character. While there is no case law on the matter, the view of those consulted is that the medium by which the insulting message is transmitted is immaterial, and that a criminal prosecution of material on the Internet might be pursued provided that all evidential requirements are met. This view was confirmed by the Home Secretary to a Board of Deputies' delegation on 4 December 1995.

Again the view of those consulted is that the holding of prosecutable information on a computer in the UK would be an offence, and therefore the owners of such host machines would have to consider their legal positions. The sending of such email either internally or from this country abroad, whilst technically an offence, would be hard, if not impossible, to monitor, and therefore unlikely to result in a prosecution. Likewise, the receipt in this country of material sent from abroad would similarly be an offence, albeit hard, if not impossible, to prosecute. If, however, the material is subsequently transmitted or distributed by non electronic methods, or if a UK-based recipient complains, a prosecution might be possible. The storage of such material in a physical computer might be considered akin to being in the public arena, as are paper, video tapes and audio tapes, whereas the use of the Internet for communication is more ephemeral (compare telephone and face-to-face conversations).

Denial of the Holocaust, the glorification of the Nazi Third Reich, the falsification of history and the publication of Nazi and or racist literature are all illegal in different European legislations. An examination of each domestic legislation would be necessary to ascertain whether the definition of the mode of distribution includes or excludes email and the Internet. There is no case-law in international law, but both the International Covenant on Civil and Political Rights, and the Convention on the Elimination of all Forms of Racial Discrimination prohibit the incitement of race hatred, and these would also apply to the Internet.

NOTES

1 *IHR Update*, February 1995, Institute for Historical Review, California.
2 Ibid.
3 Ibid.
4 'Neo-Nazis Use Computer Linking in Campaign against Left', *The Scotsman*, 1 June 1994.
5 Anonymous forwarding service/state infiltration of anti-fascist groups, TP, uk.politics, 17 September 1995.
6 'L'extrême droite se met sur ordinateur', *Le Figaro*, 21 May 1994.
7 'Neo-Nazi's Go Hi-Tech with Electronic Mailboxes', *The Guardian*, 19 November 1993.
8 'Neo-Nazis Use Computer Games of Hate to Recruit', *Evening Standard*, 14 May 1993.
9 'The Far Right in Norway', Antirasistisk Senter, Oslo, 31 December 1993.
10 'Combat 18 Banned from BNP Norwegian BBS', undated, but received by author in October 1994.
11 Newsgroup alt.fan.rumpole, 24 October 1994.
12 IHR Newsletter, May 1992, Institute for Historical Review.
13 Correspondence sent to Board of Deputies, Glyn Ford MEP, 15 May 1992.
14 *Times Educational Supplement*, 17 February 1995.
15 *The Guardian*, 24 November 1988, *The German Tribune*, 29 January 1989.
16 J.M. Kleim Jr, 'On Tactics and Strategy for USENET', undated posting [1995] at 66 748 @freenet.carleton.ca.
17 'BNP Now on Internet', *Spearhead*, 320, October 1995, p. 22.
18 *England My Country*, 52, August 1995.
19 For example, Patrick Harrington, 'Prostitution: Coping with the Oldest Profession', uk.politics, 21 September 1995.
20 Caroline Bassett, 'Censors in Space', *MacUser*, 8 July 1994.
21 Jim Carrol, 'I Know the Internet, and It's Not a Cauldron of Evils', *The Globe and Mail*, 21 March 1995.
22 Andrew Brown, 'Free-Speech Battle as Congress Declares Global War on Cyberporn', *The Independent*, 3 April 1995.

Glossary

Baud A unit of data transmission speed, or the maximum speed at which data can be sent down a channel.

BBSs Bulletin Board Services. A shared file where users can enter information for other users to read or download. Many bulletin boards are set up according to general topics and are accessible throughout a network.

Bit A contraction of binary digit. A bit is the smallest unit of information a computer can hold. The speed at which bits are transmitted or bit rate is usually expressed as bits per second or bps.

Byte This is a number of bits used to represent a character. Eight bits is equivalent to a byte.

Client A computer or computer program that is one side of the client–server communication.

CMC Computer-mediated communication.

CSCW Computer-supported cooperative working.

Cyberspace A term coined by William Gibson, a science fiction writer, to refer to a near-future computer network where users mentally travel through matrices of data. The term is now usually used to describe the Internet and other computer networks.

Flame An abusive message which, when placed publicly in a newsgroup, can provoke a flame war as people trade insults.

FTP File Transfer Protocol is a protocol that allows the transfer of files from one computer to another. FTP is also the verb used to describe the act of transferring files from one computer to another.

Gopher A distributed information system similar to the World Wide Web, but less versatile and generally used only for text files.

Home page This term is used loosely. It can refer to the top or main page of an organisation, company or personal page for an individual.

HTML An acronym for HyperText Markup Language, HTML codes are interpreted by the Web browser to format documents in a particular way.

HTTP The abbreviation for Hypertext Transfer Protocol, a protocol used to transfer documents on the World Wide Web.

ICTs Information and communications technologies.

Information superhighway A future symmetrical switched broadband network which the Internet may evolve into. Not the Internet today.

Internet The collection of networks and gateways that use the IP Protocol suite and function as a single, co-operative virtual network. The Internet reaches many universities, government research labs and military installations.

MUDS Multi-User Dungeons: imaginary worlds in computer databases where people interact to improvise melodramas, build worlds and all the objects in them, and play games.

Netiqette A corruption of network etiquette, that is, a generally accepted guide to 'good manners' when talking to other people on the Internet. Abuses of netiquette will generally result in you being flamed.

Netscape A graphical Web browser.

RAM Random Access Memory needed for running programs such as Netscape.

Server A computer or computer program that manages and delivers information for client computers.

TCP/IP The basic protocols controlling communication on the Internet.

URL This is the abbreviation for Uniform Resource Locator. The addressing system used in the World Wide Web and other Internet resources. The URL contains information about the method of access, the server to be accessed and the path of any file to be accessed.

VR Virtual reality: a system that creates an alternate representation of data in a dynamic form. Data representation is in the form of an interactive system that models in three dimensions and allows the participant to move about in an unrestricted manner to examine it from any perspective. Images are generated by a computer and projected in any number of fashions. VR systems range from aircraft flight simulators to Web browsers.

WAIS The abbreviation for Wide Area Information Service, WAIS is a Net-wide system for looking up specific information in Internet databases.

Web browser A type of software that allows you to navigate the Web.

Web page An HTML document that is accessible on the Web.

World Wide Web Also known as WWW, or W3, is a way that information is moved around the Internet, the world-wide network of computer networks, providing text, files, graphics, sounds and moving pictures. It is a hypertext-based Internet service used for browsing Internet resources.

Bibliography

Abell, P. (1987) 'Rational Equitaritarian Democracy. Minimax Class and the Future of Capitalist Societies: A Sketch Towards a Theory', *Sociology*, 21, 4/5, pp. 567–90.

Agassi, J. (1985) *Technology: Philosophical and Social Aspects*, Dordecht: D. Reidel.

Antisemitism World Report (1994, 1995) Institute of Jewish Affairs, London.

Arterton, F. (1987) *Teledomacy*, Newbury Park, CA: Sage.

Arthur, C . (1995) 'Identity Crisis on the Internet', *New Scientist*, 11 March, pp. 14–15.

Baddeley, S. (1995) 'Internal Polity', *Human Relations*, 48, 6. pp. 1073–103.

Bankers Trust Electronic Commerce (1995) 'Private Key Escrow System', paper presented at the SPA/AEA Cryptography Policy Workshop, 17 August, and at the International Cryptography Institute, 'Global Challenges', 21–2 September.

Barlow, J.P. (1996a) 'Thinking Locally, Acting Globally', *Cyber-Rights Electronic List*, 15 January.

—— (1996b) 'Declaration of the Independence of Cyberspace', *Cyber-Rights Electronic List*, 8 February.

Baron, D. (1993) 'Digital Technology and the Implications for Intellectual Property', paper delivered at the WIPO Worldwide Symposium on the Impact of Digital Technology on Copyright and Neighbouring Rights, Harvard University, 31 March–2 April.

Baudrillard, J. (1983) 'The Ecstacy of Communication', in H. Foster (ed.), *The Anti-Aestheic: Essays on Postmodern Culture*, Port Townsend, WA: Bay Press.

—— (1988) *Selected Writings*, edited by M. Poster. Cambridge: Polity Press.

Bauman, Z. (1988) *Freedom*, Milton Keynes: Open University Press.

—— (1992) *Intimations of Postmodernity*, London and New York: Routledge.

Baym, N. (1995) 'The Emergence of Community in Computer-Mediated Communication', in S. Jones (ed.), *Cyber Society: Computer-Mediated*

Communication and Community, London and Thousand Oaks, CA: Sage.

Beetham, D. (1992) 'Liberal Democracy and the Limits of Democratization', *Political Studies*, 40, Special Issue, pp. 40–53.

Bekkers, V.J.J.M. and Frissen, P.H.A (1992), 'Informatization and Administrative Modernization in the Netherlands', in P.H.A. Frissen, V.J.J.M. Bekkers, B.K. Brussard, I.T.M. Snellen and M. Walters (eds), *European Public Administration and Informatization*, Amsterdam, Oxford, Washington and Tokyo: IOS Press.

Bellamy, C. and Taylor J.A. (eds) (1994) 'Towards the Information Polity? Public Administration in the Information Age', *Journal of Public Administration*, 72, 1.

Beniger, J.R. (1986), *The Control Revolution*, Cambridge, MA, and London: Harvard University Press.

Benn, S. and Peters, R. (1959) *Social Principles and the Democratic State*, London: George Allen and Unwin.

Bennahum, D. (1996) 'Call for Comments from Around the World', *MEME*, 2 March.

Bennett, C. (1992) *Regulating Privacy*, Ithaca, NY, and London: Cornell University Press.

Beth, T., Knobloch, H.-J., Otten, M., Simmons, G.J. and Wichmann, P. (1994) 'Clipper Repair Kit – Towards Acceptable Key Escrow Systems', *Proceedings 2nd ACM Conference on Communications and Computer Society*, New York: ACM.

Boden, M. (1977) *Artificial Intelligence and Natural Man*, Hassocks: Harvester.

Boehme. E. (1994) 'Piebald and Strange', *Times Literary Supplement*, 2 December.

Bollas, C. (1993) *Being a Character: Psychoanalysis and Self-Experience*, London: Routledge.

Boswell, J. (1970) *Life of Johnson*, London: Oxford University Press (first published 1791).

Bradford City Council (1995) Horizon Open ITeC Initiative, *Open Learning for Disadvantaged Groups 1992–94*, Bradford: Bradford City Council.

Branscomb, A. (1994) *Who Owns Information?*, New York: Basic Books.

Brickell, E., *et al.* (1995) 'Trustee-based Tracing Extensions to Anonymous Cash and the Making of Anonymous Change', *Proceedings of the Sixth Annual ACM–SIAM Symposium on Discrete Algorithms*.

Bricken, M. and Byrne, C. (1992) 'Summer Students in Virtual Reality: A Pilot Study on Educational Applications of Virtual Reality Technology' (unpublished paper).

Brook, J. and Boal, I. (1995) *Resisting the Virtual Life*, San Francisco: City Lights.

Bryant, C. (1978) 'Privacy, Privatisation and Self-Determination', in J. Young (ed.), *Privacy*, New York: Wiley.

Bukatman, S. (1993) *Terminal Identity*, London: Duke University Press.

Burrows, R. (1996) 'Cyberpunk as Social Theory: William Gibson and the Contemporary Sociological Imagination', in S. Westwood and J. Williams (eds), *Imagining Cities*, London: Routledge.

Byrne D. (1994) 'Planning for and against the Divided City', in R. Burrows and B. Loader (eds), *Towards a Post-Fordist Welfare State?*, London: Routledge.

Cadigan, P. (1987) *Mindplayers*, New York: Bantam/Spectra.

—— (1991) *Symmers*, New York: Bantam Books.

—— (1992) *Fools*, New York: Bantam/Spectra.

Cage, J. (1961) *Silence*, Middletown, CT: Wesleyan University Press (first published 1939).

Calhourn, C. (1992) 'The Infrastructure of Modernity: Indirect Social Relationships, Information Technology and Social Integration', in H. Haferkamp and N. Smelser (eds), *Social Change and Modernity*, Berkeley: University of California Press.

Campbell, B. (1993) *Goliath: Britain's Dangerous Places*, London: Methuen.

Canadian Standards Association (1995) *Model Code for the Protection of Personal Information*, CAN/CSA-Q830–1995. Rexdale: Canadian Standards Association.

Carey, J. (1993) 'Everything that Rises Must Diverge: Notes on Communications, Technology and the Symbolic Construction of the Social', in P. Gaunt (ed.), *Beyond Agendas*, Westport, CT: Greenwood. Press.

Cassinelli, C. (1961) *The Politics of Freedom*, Seattle: University of Washington Press.

Cerf, V. (1993) 'How the Internet Came to Be', in B. Aboba (ed.), *The On-Line User's Encyclopaedia*, New York: Addison Wesley.

Chapman, B. (1970) *Police State*, New York and London: Praeger.

Chaum, D. (1992) 'Achieving Electronic Privacy', *Scientific American*, 267, pp. 96–101.

Cherry, C. (1971) *World Communication: Threat or Promise? A Socio-technical Approach*, London: Wiley-Interscience.

Cherryh, C.J. (1988) *Cyteen*, New York: Warner Books.

Cheswick, W.R. and Bellovin, S.M. (1994) *Firewalls and Network Security*, Reading, MA: Addison Wesley.

Clark, C. (1994) 'The Publisher in the Electronic World', paper presented at the International Publishers' Copyright for the Third IPA International Copyright Symposium, Turin, 23–5 May.

Clarke, R. (1994) 'The Digital Persona and its Application to Data Surveillance', *The Information Society*, 102, 2.

Commission of the European Communities (1993) *Draft Directive on the Protection of Computer Databases*, Brussels.

Commune di Bologna (1995) 'Manifesto on the Mobility of People and Knowledge – Cities as Actors of the European Development', Bologna.

Congress of the United States, Office of Technology Assessment (1986) *Intellectual Property Rights in an Age of Electronics and Information*, Washington, DC: United States Government Printing Office.

Conrad, J. (1947) *Almayer's Folly*, London: Dent (first published 1895).
Copyright Law Journal (1994) 'Apple Computer v. Microsoft', VIII, 6, pp. 62–7.
Crook, S., Pakulski, J. and Waters, M. (1992) *Postmodernization: Change in Advanced Society*, London: Sage.
Dahl, R. (1982) *Dilemmas of Pluralist Democracy*, New Haven, CT: Yale University Press.
Davenport, T.H. (1993), *Process Innovation: Reengineering Work through Information Technology*, Cambridge MA: Harvard Business School Press.
Davies, S. (1996) *Big Brother*, London: Pan Books.
Davis, M. (1990) *City of Quartz* London: Verso.
—— (1992) *Beyond Blade Runner: Urban Control, the Ecology of Fear*, Westfield, NJ: Open Magazine Pamphlets.
De Sola Pool, I. (1983) *Technologies of Freedom*, Cambridge, MA: Bellknap/Harvard University Press.
Deakin, N. and Edwards, J. (1993) *The Enterprise Culture and the Inner City*, London: Routledge.
Demos Quarterly (1994) 'Liberation Technology', 4.
Denning, D.E. (1995a) 'The Case for the Clipper', *MIT Technology Review*, July, pp. 48–55.
—— (1995b) 'Key Escrow Encryption: The Third Paradigm', *Computer Security Journal*, Summer, p. 277.
—— (1995c) 'Critical Factors of Key Escrow Encryption Systems', *Proceedings of National Information Systems Security Conference*, October.
Denning, D. and Branstad, D.K. (1996) 'A Taxonomy of Key Escrow Encryption', *Communications of the ACM*, 39, 3, pp. 34–40.
Denning, D. and Smid, M. (1984) 'Key Escrowing Today', *IEEE Communications*, 32, 9, September, pp. 58–68.
Depla, P. (1995) *Technologie en de vernieuwing van de lokale democratie: Vervolmaking of Vermaatschappelijking* (Technology and the Renewal of Local Democracy). 's-Gravenhage: VUGA.
Derlien, H.U. (1993) 'Staatliche Steuerung in Perspektive: Ein Gesamtkommentar'. in K. König and N. Dose (eds), *Instrumente und Formen staatlichen Handelns*, Cologne *et al.*: Heymanns.
Dorling, D. and Tomaney, J. (1995) 'Poverty in the Old Industrial Region: A Comparative View', in C. Philo (ed.), *Off the Map: Social Geography of Poverty in the UK*, London: CPAG.
Dror, Y. (1989) 'Memo for System-Reforming Rulers', *Futures: A Journal of Forecasting, Planning and Policy*, 21, 4, pp. 334–43.
Durlach, N. and Mavor, A. (eds) (1994) *Virtual Reality: Scientific and Technological Challenges*, Washington, DC: National Academy Press.
Dutton, W. (1992) 'Political Science Research on Teledemocracy', *Social Science Computer Review*, 10, pp. 505–22.
Dutton, W., Taylor, J., Bellamy, C., Raab, C. and Pettu, M. (1994) *Electronic Service Delivery: Themes and Issues in the Public Sector*, Policy Research Paper No. 28, Programme on Information and

Communication Technologies, Economic and Social Research Council, Brunel University, Uxbridge.

Edelman, G. (1992) *Bright Air, Brilliant Fire*, New York: Basic Books.

Edwards, A. (1995) 'Informatization and Views of Democracy', in W. van de Donk, I. Snellen and P. Tops (eds), *Orwell in Athens: A Perspective on Informization and Democracy*, Amsterdam: IOS Press.

Ellenberger, H.F. (1994) *The Discovery of the Unconscious: The History and Evolution of Dynamic Psychiatry*, London: Fontana.

Emery, F.E. (1967) 'The Next Thirty Years: Concepts, Methods and Anticipations', *Human Relations*, 30, 3, pp. 199–237.

Escobar, A. (1994) 'Welcome to Cyberia – Notes on the Anthropology of Cyberculture', *Current Anthropology*, 35, 3, pp. 211–31.

Etzioni, A. (1993) *The Spirit of Community: Rights, Responsibilities, and the Communitarian Agenda*, New York: Crown.

EU (1993) 'Growth, Competitiveness, Employment: The Challenges and Ways Forward into the 21st Century', White Paper, Brussels.

—— (1994) 'Europe and the Global Information Society', Recommendations to the European Council, Brussels.

Featherstone, M. (1995) *Undoing Culture: Globalization, Postmodernism and Identity*, London: Sage.

Flaherty, D. (1989) *Protecting Privacy in Surveillance Societies*, Chapel Hill, NC: University of North Carolina Press.

Forster E.M. (1993) *Howard's End*, London: Penguin (first published 1910).

Foucault, M. (1965) *Madness and Civilisation: A History of Insanity in the Age of Reason*, translated by R. Howard, New York: Random House.

—— (1978) 'Governmentality', in G. Burchell, C. Gordon and P. Miller (eds), *The Foucault Effect: Studies in Governmentality*, Hemel Hempstead: Harvester Wheatsheaf, 1991.

—— (1980) *Power/Knowledge: Selected Interviews and Other Writings, 1972–77*, edited by C. Gordon, Brighton: Harvester.

—— (1982) 'The Subject of Power', in H.L. Dreyfus and P. Rabinow (eds), *Michel Foucault: Beyond Structuralism and Hermeneutics*, Brighton: Harvester.

—— (1984) *The History of Sexuality, Vol. 3: The Care of the Self*, translated by R. Hurley, London: Allen Lane.

Fox, B. (1995) 'Holograms Join War Against Digital Pirates', *New Scientist*, 18 February, p. 19.

——(1996) 'Hidden Watermark Traps Pictures', *New Scientist*, 3 June, p. 7.

Frank, J. (1963) *The Widening Gyre*, New Brunswick, NJ: Rutgers University Press.

Freud, S. (1962) 'The Question of Lay Analysis', in *Two Short Accounts of Psychoanalysis*, London: Penguin (first published 1910).

Frieden, J. (1991) 'Invested Interests: The Politics of National Economic Policies in a World of Global Finance, *International Organisation*, 45, 5.

Friedman, T. (1995) 'Making Sense of Software: Computer Games and Interactive Textuality', in S. Jones (ed.), *CyberSociety: Computer-*

Mediated Communication and Community, London and Thousand Oaks, CA: Sage.

Frissen, P.H.A. (1990) 'Besturingsconcepties, recht en wetgeving' (Steering Conceptions, Law and Law-Making), in *Recht doen door wetgeving*, Zwolle: W.E.J. Tjeenk Willink.

—— (1994) 'The Virtual Reality of Informatization in Public Administration', *Informatization and the Public Sector*, 3, 3/4, pp. 265–81.

Fukuyama, F. (1992) *The End of History and the Last Man*, London: Penguin.

Gandy, O. (1993) *The Panoptic Sort*, Boulder, CO: Westview Press.

Gibson, W. (1984) *Neuromancer*, New York: Ace.

—— (1991) 'Academy Leader' in M. Benedikt (ed.) *Cyberspace: First Steps*, Cambridge, MA: MIT Press.

—— (1993) *Virtual Light*, London: Viking.

Giddens, A. (1985) *The Nation-State and Violence*, Cambridge: Polity Press.

—— (1991) *Modernity and Self-Identity*, Cambridge: Polity Press.

Giedion, S. (1948) *Mechanization Takes Command*, New York: Oxford University Press.

Giles,W. (1994) 'The Virtual Divide: Conception and Consumption of Virtual Reality Entertainment', unpublished BSc thesis, Brunel Unversity.

Goldberg, M.D. (1993) 'Copyright and Technology: The Analog, the Digital, and the Analogy', paper delivered at the WIPO Worldwide Symposium on the Impact of Digital Technology on Copyright and Neighbouring Rights, Harvard University, 31 March–2 April.

Gressel, C., Granot, R. and Dror, I. (1995) 'International Cryptographic Communication without Key Escrow; KISS: Keep the Invaders (of Privacy) Socially Sane', paper presented at the International Crytography Institute, 'Global Challenges', 21–2 September.

Habermas, J. (1989) *The Structural Transformation of the Public Sphere*, Cambridge: Polity Press.

Hacking, I. (1983) *Representing and Intervening*, Cambridge: Cambridge University Press.

Haddon, L. (1993) 'Interactive Games', in P. Hayward and T. Wollen (eds), *Future Visions – New Technologies of the Screen*, London: British Film Institute.

Hamnett, C. (1994) 'Social Polarisation in Global Cities: Theory and Evidence', *Urban Studies*, 31, 3, pp. 401–24.

Haraway, D. (1985) 'A Manifesto for Cyborgs: Science, Technology, and Socialist Feminism in the 1980s', *Socialist Review*, 80, pp. 65–107.

—— (1990) 'A Manifesto for Cyborgs', in L. Nicholson (ed.), *Feminism/Postmodernism*, London and New York: Routledge.

Hardy, H.E. (1993) 'The History of the Net: How the Net Evolved from Cold War Project to Electronic Town Hall', master's thesis, School of Communications, Grand Valley State University, Michigan.

Harnard, S. (1992) 'Post-Gutenberg Galaxy: The Fourth Revolution in the Means of Production of Knowledge', *Public Access Computer Systems Review*, 2, 1, pp. 39–53.

Harvey, D. (1989) *The Condition of Postmodernity*, Cambridge and Oxford: Blackwell.

Hawkins, D.G. (1995) 'Virtual Reality and Passive Simulators: The Future of Fun', in F. Biocca and M. Levy (eds), *Communication in the Age of Virtual Reality*, Hillsdale, NJ: Lawrence Erlbaum.

Hayek, F. A. (1988) *The Fatal Conceit, The Errors of Socialism*, edited by W.W. Bartley III, Chicago: University of Chicago Press.

Held, D. (1987) *Models of Democracy*, Cambridge: Polity Press.

—— (1995) *Democracy and the Global Order*, Cambridge: Polity Press.

Held, D. and Pollitt, C. (eds) (1986) *New Forms of Democracy*, London: Sage.

Hirst, P. (1994) *Associative Democracy*, Cambridge: Polity Press.

Hoggett, P. (1994) 'The Politics of the Modernisation of the UK Welfare State', in R. Burrows and B. Loader (eds), *Towards a Post-Fordist Welfare State?*, London: Routledge.

Holden, B. (1988) *Understanding Liberal Democracy*, Oxford: Philip Allen.

Hollander, V. (1991) 'Cybernetic Deconstructions: Cyberpunk and Postmodernism', in L. McCaffrey (ed.), *Storming the Reality Studio: A Casebook of Cyberpunk and Postmodern Science Fiction*, Durham, NC: Duke University Press.

Hood, C. (1983) *The Tools of Government*, London and Basingstoke: Macmillan.

Horton, R. (1995) 'Infection: The Global Threat', *New York Review*, 6 April.

Hubbard, R. and Wald, E. (1994) *Exploding the Gene Myth: How Genetic Information is Produced and Manipulated by Scientists, Physicians, Employers, Insurance Companies. Educators and Law Enforcers*, Boston: Beacon Press.

Information Insfrastructure Task Force (1995) 'Intellectual Property and the National Information Infrastructure: The Report of the Working Group on Intellectual Property Rights', Washington, DC: United States Patent and Trademark Office.

Innis, H.A. (1964) *The Bias of Communication*, Toronto: University of Toronto Press.

Ippel, P., de Heij, G. and Crouwers, B. (1995) 'Thinking Watchdogs: Values and Practice', in P. Ippell, G. de Heij and B. Crouwers (eds), *Privacy Disputed*, The Hague: SDU.

Johnson-Laird, A. (1990) 'Neural Networks: The Next Intellectual Property Nightmare?', *The Computer Lawyer*, 7, 3 pp. 3–5.

Jones, S. (1995a) 'From Where to Who Knows', in S. Jones (ed.), *CyberSociety: Computer-Mediated Communication and Community*, London and Thousand Oaks, CA: Sage.

——(ed.) (1995b) *CyberSociety: Computer-Mediated Communication and Community*, London and Thousand Oaks, CA: Sage.

Kalawsky, R. (1993) *The Science of Virtual Reality and Virtual Environments*, Reading, MA: Addison Wesley.

Kant, I. (1900) *Dreams of a Spirit-Seer*, translated by E.F. Goerwitz and edited by F. Sewall, London: Swan Sonnenschein (first published 1766).

Kapor, M. (1991) 'Civil Liberties in Cyberspace', *Scientific American*, 265, pp. 116–20.

Karnow, C. (1993) *The Promise and Challenge of Virtual Reality*, paper delivered at the Computer Law Association International Annual Retreat Conference, Monterey, California, 22 October.

Katz, W. (1994) 'Military Networking Technology Applied to Location-Based, Theme Park and Home Entertainment Systems', *Computer Graphics*, 28, 2, pp. 110–12.

Kaufmann, W. (1968) *Nietzsche: Philosopher, Psychiatrist, Antichrist*, New York: Vintage Books.

Kellner, D. (1995) 'Mapping the Present from the Future: From Baudrillard to Cyberpunk', in *Media Culture*, London: Routledge.

Kelly, K. (1994) *Out of Control*, Reading, MA: Addison Wesley.

Kleiner, K. (1995) 'Sweet Sound of Cash Registers on the Internet', *New Scientist*, 3 June, p. 7.

Koestler, A. (1945) *The Novelist's Temptations: The Yogi and the Commissar*, London: Cape.

—— (1959) *The Sleepwalkers: A History of Man's Changing Vision of the Universe*, London, Hutchinson.

Kozel, S. (1994) 'Virtual Reality: Choreographing Cyberspace', *Dance Theatre Journal*, 11, 2, pp. 35–7.

Kramer, P.D. (1993) *Listening to Prozac: A Psychiatrist Explores Mood-Altering Drugs and the New Meaning of the Self*, London, Viking/Penguin.

Kristeva, A.J. (1994) *Strangers to Ourselves*, Hemel Hempstead: Harvester Wheatsheaf.

Kroker, A. and Weinstein, M. (1994) *Data Trash: The Theory of the Virtual Class*, Montreal: New World Perspectives.

Kuypers, P. , Foqué, R. and Frissen, P.H.A. (1993) *De lege plek van de macht* (The Empty Space of Power), Amsterdam: De Balie.

Lappé, M. (1994) *Evolutionary Medicine: Rethinking the Origins of Disease*, San Francisco: Sierra Club Books.

Lash, S. and Urry, J. (1994) *Economies of Signs and Space*, London: Sage.

Laudon, K. (1977) *Communications Technology and Democratic Participation*, New York: Praeger.

Lawrence, A (1993) 'Publish and be Robbed?', *New Scientist*, 18 February, pp. 33–7.

Leach, E. (1968) *A Runaway World*? London: BBC.

Lecomber, T. (1995) 'The Internet', *Spearhead*, 322, December, p. 8.

Lee, P. (1994) 'Limitations of the Population Census in Studying the Development of an Underclass', *British Urban and Regional Information Systems Asociation*, 115.

Lenk, K. (1994) 'Information Systems in Public Administration: From Research to Design'. *Informatization and the Public Sector*, 3, 3/4, pp. 305–24.

Littman, S. (1995) 'Some Thoughts on the Regulation of Cyberspace', Simon Wiesenthal Centre, Canada, 4 December.

Lyon, D. (1988) *The Information Society*, Cambridge: Polity Press.

Lyon, D. (1994a) *Postmodernity*, Minneapolis: University of Minnesota Press/ Buckingham: Open University Press.

—— (1994b) *The Electronic Eye: The Rise of Surveillance Society*, Cambridge: Polity Press/Minneapolis: University of Minnesota Press.

Lyon, D. and Zureik, E. (eds) (1996) *Computers, Surveilllance and Privacy*, Minneapolis: University of Minnesota Press.

Lyotard, J.-F. (1984) *The Postmodern Condition: A Report on Knowledge*, translated by G. Bennington and R. Massumi, Manchester: Manchester University Press.

McBeath, G. and Webb, S. (1996) 'Cities, Technoculture and Cyberspace', in S. Westwood and J. Williams (eds), *Imagining Cities*, London: Routledge.

McCaffery, L. (ed.) (1991) *Storming the Reality Studio: A Casebook of Cyberpunk and Postmodern Science Fiction*, Durham, NC: Duke University Press.

Macedonia, M., Zyda, M., Pratt, D., Barham, P. and Zeswitz, S. (1994) 'NPSNET: A Network Software Architecture for Large-Scale Virtual Environments', *Presence: Teleoperators and Virtual Environments*, 3, 4, pp. 265–87.

Mackenzie, W. (1958) *Free Elections*, London: George Allen and Unwin.

McLean, I. (1986) 'Mechanisms for Democracy', in D. Held and C. Pollitt (eds) *New Forms of Democracy*, London: Sage.

—— (1989) *Democracy and New Technology*, Cambridge: Polity Press.

McNeil, W.H. (1992) *The Global Condition: Conquerors, Catastrophes, and Community*, Princeton: Princeton University Press.

Manchester City Council (1994) 'Manchester – The Information City: Promoting Economic Regeneration Through the Use of Telematics', Manchester.

Mann, T. (1949) *Doctor Faustus: The Life of the German Composer Adrian Leverkühn as Told by a Friend*, translated by H.T. Lowe-Porter, London: Secker and Warburg.

Mansell, R. (ed.) (1994) *The Management of Information and Communication Technology*, London: Association for Information Management.

Mansell, R. and Tang, P. (1994) *Electronic Information Services: Competiveness in the United Kingdom. A Report prepared for the Department of Trade and Industry*, London: DTI.

May, T. (1995) 'Crypto Anarchy and Virtual Communities', *Internet Security*, April, pp. 4–12.

Mellors, C. (1978) 'Governments and the Individual – Their Secrecy and His Piracy', in J. Young (ed.), *Privacy*, New York: Wiley.

Micali, S. (1994) *Fair Cryptosystems*, MIT/LCS/TR-579.c, Cambridge, MA: MIT.

Michie, D. (1974) *On Machine Intelligence*, Edinburgh: Edinburgh University Press.

Miers, P. (1993) 'Connectionism and its Consequences', *Postmodern Culture*, 4, 1 (pmc@unity.ncsu.edu).

Miller, J. (1995) 'Going Unconscious'. *New York Review*, 20 April.

Mollenkopf, J. and Castells, M. (1991) *Dual City: Restructuring New York*, New York: Russell Sage Foundation.

Morningstar, C. and Farmer, R. (1991) 'The Lessons of Lucasfilm's Habitat', in M. Benedikt (ed.), *Cyberspace: First Steps*, Cambridge, MA: MIT Press.

Motyka, C (1992) 'US Participation in the Berne Convention and High Technology', in American Society of Composers, Authors and Publishers, *Copyright Law Symposium*, No. 39, New York: Columbia University Press.

Munro, J. (1895) *The Wire and the Wave: A Tale of Submarine Telegraph*, London: The Religious Tract Society.

Murdoch, I. (1992) *Metaphysics as a Guide to Morals*, London: Chatto and Windus.

Naipaul, V.S. (1991) 'Our Universal Civilisation', *New York Review*, 31 January.

National Institute for Standards and Technology (1994) *Escrowed Encryption Standard (EES)*, Federal Information Processing Standards Publication (FIPS PUB) No. 185.

National Science Foundation (1993) *Global Dimensions of Intellectual Property Rights in Science and Technology*, Washington, DC: National Academy of Sciences.

Neumann, F. (1957) *The Democratic and the Authoritarian State*, Glencoe, IL: Free Press.

Neumann, W.R. (1991) *The Future of the Mass Audience*, Cambridge: Cambridge University Press.

Nietzsche, F. (1974) *Beyond Good and Evil*, London: Penguin (first published 1885).

Nugter, A. (1990) *Transborder Flow of Personal Data Within the EC*, Deventer and Boston: Kluwer.

O'Brien, R. (1992) *The End of Geography*, London: Routledge.

Ogden, M.R. (1994) 'Politics in a Parallel Universe', *Futures: A Journal of Forecasting, Planning and Policy*, 26, 7, pp. 713–29.

Oman, R. (1993) 'Reflections on Digital Technology', paper delivered at the WIPO Worldwide Symposium on the Impact of Digital Technology on Copyright and Neighbouring Rights, Harvard University, 31 March–2 April.

Ornstein, R. (1986) *Multimind*, London, Macmillan.

Oz, A. (1994) *Fima*, translated by N. de Lange, London: Vintage.

Pahl, R. (1995) *After Success: Fin-de-Siècle Anxiety and Identity*, Cambridge: Polity Press.

Pateman, C. (1970) *Participation and Democratic Theory*, Cambridge: Cambridge University Press.

Pausch, R., Crea, T. and Conway, M. (1992) 'A Literature Survey for Virtual Environments: Military Flight Simulator Sickness', *Presence: Teleoperators and Virtual Environments*, 1, 3, pp. 344–63.

Peters, T. (1992) *Liberation Management: Necessary Disorganization for the Nanosecond Nineties*, London: Macmillan.

Phillips, A. (1994) *On Flirtation*, London: Faber.

Piercy, M. (1983) *Woman on the Edge of Time*, London: Michael Joseph.

—— (1992) *Body of Glass*, London: Michael Joseph.

Plant, S. (1995) *The Virtual Complexity of Culture*, Cultural Studies, Birmingham University.

Poster, M. (1989) *Critical Theory and Poststructuralism*, Ithaca, NY: Cornell University Press.

—— (1990) *The Mode of Information: Poststructuralism and Social Context*, Cambridge: Polity Press.

—— (1995a) *The Second Media Age*, Cambridge: Polity Press.

—— (1995b) 'Postmodern Virtualities', *Body and Society*, 1, pp. 3–4.

Proust, M. (1954) *Contre Sainte-Beuve*, Paris: Gallimard (English edn, *By Way of Sainte-Beuve*, translated and edited by J. Sturrock, London: Penguin, 1994).

Provenzo, E. (1991) *Video Kids: Making Sense of Nintendo*, Cambridge, MA: Harvard University Press.

Raab, C. (1993) 'Co-producing Data Protection: the Role of the State, Civil Society and the Market', paper delivered at the European Consortium for Political Research, Joint Sessions of Workshops, Leiden, 2–8 April.

—— (1995) 'Connecting Orwell to Athens? Information Superhighways and the Privacy Debate', in W. van de Donk, I. Snellen and P. Tops (eds), *Orwell in Athens: A Perspective on Informization and Democracy*, Amsterdam: IOS Press.

Raab, C. and Bennett, C. (1994) Protecting Privacy Across Borders: European Policies and Prospects', *Public Administration*, 72, pp. 95–112.

—— (1996) 'Taking Measure of Privacy: Can Data Protection be Evaluated?', *International Review of Administrative Sciences*, 62, 4.

Raab, C., Bellamy, C., Taylor, J., Dutton, W. and Peltu, M. (1996) 'The Information Polity: Electronic Democracy, Privacy, and Surveillance', in W. Dutton (ed.), *Information and Communication Technologies – Visions and Realities*, Oxford: Oxford University Press.

Rafaeli, S. (1988) 'Interactivity: From New Media to Communication', in R. Hawkins and J. Wiemann (eds) *Advancing Communication Science: Merging Mass and Interpersonal Processes*, Newbury Park, CA: Sage.

Ranson, S. (1990) 'Towards Education for Citizenship', *Educational Review*, 42, 2, pp. 151–66.

Reed, D.K. (1985) *The Novel and the Nazi Past*, New York: Peter Lang.

Reid, E. (1995) 'Virtual Worlds: Culture and Imagination', in S. Jones (ed.), *CyberSociety: Computer-Mediated Communication and Community*, London and Thousand Oaks, CA: Sage.

Reeve, A. and Ware, A. (1992) *Electoral Systems*, London and New York: Routledge.

Rheingold, H. (1991) *Virtual Reality*, London: Secker and Warburg.

—— (1993) 'A Slice of My Life in Virtual Community', in L. Harasim (ed.), *Global Networks: Computers and International Communication*, Cambridge MA: MIT Press.

—— (1994) *The Virtual Community*, London: Secker and Warburg.

Robins, K. (1996) 'Cyberspace and the World We Live In', in M. Featherstone and R. Burrows (eds), *Cyberspace/Cyberbodies/Cyberpunk: Cultures of Technological Embodiment*, London: Sage.

Roche, M. (1992) *Rethinking Citizenship: Welfare, Ideology and Change in Modern Society*, Cambridge: Cambridge University Press.

Rogers, E. (1986) *Communication Technology: The New Media in Society*, New York: Free Press.

Roizman, B. and Hughes, J.M. (1995) *Infectious Diseases in an Age of Change*, Washington, DC: National Academy of Science.

Rojek, C. (1995) *Decentring Leisure*, London; Sage.

Ronfeldt, D. (1992) 'Cyberocracy, Cyberspace and Cyberology: Political Effects of the Information Revolution', *The Information Society*, 8, 4, pp. 243–96.

Roth, S. (1995) 'The Legal Fight Against Antisemitism: Survey of Documents in 1993', in *Israel Yearbook on Human Rights*, Tel Aviv University.

Rowan, J. (1990) *Subpersonalities: The People Inside Us*, London: Routledge.

Rushkoff, D. (1994) *Cyberia: Life in the Trenches of Hyperspace*, London: Routledge.

Sabine, G. (1957) *A History of Political Theory*, London: Harrap.

Samuels, A. (1989) *The Plural Psyche*, London: Routledge.

—— (1994) *The Political Psyche*, London: Routledge.

Sassen, S. (1991) *The Global City: New York, London, Tokyo*, Princeton: Princeton University Press.

Schalken, K. and Flint, J. (1995) *Handboek Digitale Steden* (Manual Digital Cities), Amsterdam: Stichting De Digitale Stad.

Schoeman, F. (1992) *Privacy and Social Freedom*, Cambridge: Cambridge University Press.

Schofield, J. (1995) *Marketing Business*, March, pp. 10–12.

Schroeder, R (1993) 'Virtual Reality in the Real World: History, Applications, Projections', *Futures: A Journal of Forecasting, Planning and Policy*, 25, 9, pp. 963–73.

—— (1994) 'Cyberculture, Cyborg Postmodernism and the Sociology of Virtual Reality Technologies: Surfing the Soul in the Information Age', *Futures: A Journal of Forecasting, Planning and Policy*, 26, 5, pp. 519–28.

—— (1995a) 'Disenchantment and its Discontents: Weberian Perspectives on Science and Technology', *Sociological Review*, 47, 2, pp. 227–50.

—— (1995b) 'Virtual Environments and the Varieties of Interactive Experience: An Analysis of Legend Quest', *Convergence: The Journal of Research into Media Technologies*, 1, 2, pp. 45–55.

—— (1995c) 'Learning from Virtual Reality Applications in Education', in *Virtual Reality: Research, Development and Applications*, 1, 1, pp. 33–40.

Schroeder, R., Giles, W. and Cleal, B. (1994) 'Virtual Reality and the Future of Interactive Games', in H.-J. Warnecke and H.-J. Bullinger (eds), *Virtual Reality '94: Anwendungen und Trends*, Berlin: Springer.

Scott, M. (1992) *Dreamships*, New York: Tom Doherty Associates/Tor Books.

—— (1994) *Trouble and Her Friends*, New York: Tor Books.

Secure Computing Corporation (1994) *Answers to Frequently Asked Questions About Network Security*, Roseville, MN, October.

Seidman, S. (ed.) (1992) *The Postmodern Turn: New Perspectives on Social Theory*, Cambridge and New York: Cambridge University Press.

Sherman, B. and Judkins, P.H. (1992) *Glimpses of Heaven, Visions of Hell: Virtual Reality and Its Implications*, London: Hodder and Stoughton.

Simitis, S. (1987) 'Reviewing Privacy in an Information Society', *University of Pennsylvannia Law Review*, 135, pp. 707–46.

Skelton, C. (1994) 'Network of Hate: The Dark Side of Cyberspace', *id Magazine*, 3, 2, pp. 9–12.

Smith, N. and Williams, P. (eds) (1986) *Gentrification of the City*, London: Allen and Unwin.

Snellen, I.T.M. (1987) *Boeiend en geboeid. Ambivalenties en ambities in de bestuurskunde* (Fascinating and Captivated), Alphen aan den Rijn: Samsom.

—— (1994) 'ICT: A Revolutionizing Force in Public Administration?', *Informatization and the Public Sector*, 3, 3/4, pp. 283–304.

Spiller, N. (1996) *Digital Dreams: The Architecture of Cyberspace*, London: Ellipsis.

Steiner, G. (1971) *In Bluebeard's Castle: Some Notes Towards the Re-definition of Culture*, London: Faber.

—— (1991) *Real Presences*, Chicago: University of Chicago Press.

Stephenson, N. (1992) *Snow Crash*, New York: Bantam Books.

Sterling, B (1986) *Mirrorshades: The Cyberpunk Anthology*, London: Paladin.

—— (1994) *The Hacker Crackdown*, Harmondsworth: Penguin.

Sterling, B. and Gibson, W. (1993) 'Literary Freeware – Not for Commercial Use: Speeches to the National Academy of Sciences Convocation on Technology and Education, May 10th, Washington, DC', *Computer Underground Digest*, 5, 54.

Stevenson, R.L. (1985) *The Strange Case of Dr Jekyll and Mr Hyde*, Harmondsworth: Penguin (first published 1886).

Stewart, J.D. (1995) *Innovation in Democratic Practice*, Birmingham: Inlogov.

Stills, P. (1989) 'Dark Contagion – Bigotry and Violence Online: Neo-Nazi Bulletin Board Services', *TC Computing*.

Storace, P. (1994) 'In the Promised Land', *New York Review*, 26 May.

Swabey, M. (1939) *Theory of the Democratic State*, Cambridge, MA: Harvard University Press.

Sweet, W.B. and Walker, S.T. (1995) *Commercial Automated Key Escrow (CAKE): An Exportable Strong Encryption Alternative*, Sunnyvale, CA.

Taylor, C. (1991) 'Shared Divulgent Values', in R. Watts and D. Brown (eds), *Options for a New Canada*, Toronto: Toronto University Press.

Taylor, J.A. and Williams, H. (1991) 'Public Administration and the Information Polity', *Public Administration*, 69, pp. 171–90.

Thiele, L.P. (1990) *Friedrich Nietzsche and the Politics of the Soul*, Princeton: Princeton University Press.

Thomas, T.A. (1995) 'Can the FBI Stop Private Cryptology?', *Internet Security*, April, pp. 13–14.

Toulmin, S. and Goodfield, J. (1967) *The Discovery of Time*, London: Pelican.

Tribe, L.H. (1991) 'The Constitution in Cyberspace: Law and Liberty Beyond the Electronic Frontier', keynote address at the First Conference on Computers, Privacy and Freedom, Computer Professionals for Social Responsibility, 26 March (available from Jim Warren – jwarren@well.sf.ca.us).

University of Manchester (1996) 'The Birth of the Baby: The First Stored Program Computer', Manchester.

Van de Donk, W.B.H.J. and Frissen, P.H.A. (1990) 'Informatization and Administrative Ambition', in P.H.A. Frissen and I.T.M. Snellen (eds), *Informatization Strategies in Public Administration*, Amsterdam, New York, Oxford and Tokyo: Elsevier Science Publishers.

Van de Donk, W. and Tops, P. (1992) 'Informatization and Democracy: Orwell or Athens?', *Informatization and the Public Sector*, 2, pp. 169–96.

Van de Donk, W., Snellen, I. and Tops, P. (eds) (1995) *Orwell in Athens: A Perspective on Informization and Democracy*, Amsterdam: IOS Press.

Van Paassen, C. (1981) 'The Philosphy of Geography: From Vidal to Hägerstrand', in *Space and Time in Geography: Essays dedicated to Torsten Hägerstrand* ,Lund: Gleerup.

Van Stokkom, B. (1995) 'Citizenship and Privacy: A Domain of Tension', in P. Ippel, G. de Heij and B. Crouwers (eds), *Privacy Disputed*, The Hague: SDU.

Vattimo, G. (1992) *The Transparent Society*, Baltimore: John Hopkins University Press

Vaver, D. (1995) 'Abridgements and Abstracts: Copyright Implications', *European Intellectual Property Rights*, 5, pp. 225–35.

Velecky, L. (1978) 'The Concept of Privacy', in J. Young (ed.), *Privacy*, New York: Wiley.

Virilio, O. (1993) 'Marginal Groups' *Diadalos*, 50, pp. 72–80.

Vorstenbosch, J. (1995) 'Privacy and Autonomy: Conflicting Theories', in P. Ippel, G. de Heij and B. Crouwers (eds), *Privacy Disputed*, The Hague: SDU.

Walker, S.T., Lipner, S.B., Ellison, C.M. and Balenson, D.M. (1996) 'Commercial Key Escrow', *Communications of ACM* 39, 3, pp. 41–7.

Ware, A. (1992) 'Liberal Democracy: One Form or Many?', *Political Studies*, 40, Special Issue, pp. 130–45.

Warren, J. (1995) 'Is Phil Zimmermann Being Persecuted? Why? By Whom? Who's Next?', *Internet Security*, April, pp. 15–21.

Werthebach, E. (1994) 'Verscharfen sich Extremismus / Terrorismus in einem Europa ohne Grenzen?', Bundesamt für Verfassungsschutz, September.

Westin, A. (1967) *Privacy and Freedom*, London: Bodley Head.

White, O.F and McSwain, C.J. (1990), 'The Phoenix Project: Raising a New Image of Public Administration from the Ashes of the Past', in H.D. Kass and B.L. Catron (eds), *Images and Identities in Public Administration*, Newbury Park, CA, London and New Delhi: Sage.

Wilkinson, H. and Mulgan, G. (1995) *Freedom's Children: Work, Relationships and Politics for 18–34 Year Olds in Britain Today*, London: Demos.

Winner, L. (1987) *Political Ergonomics: Technological Design and the Quality of Public Life*, IIUG discussion paper 1987/7, Berlin: Wissenschaftszentrum Berlin.

Woolley, B. (1992) *Virtual Worlds*, London and New York: Blackwell.

Worlock, D (1994) 'Intellectual Property Rights: Technologies of Control', *Online Proceedings*, February, pp. 357-65.

Young, K. (1993) 'People, Places and Power – Local Democracy and Community Identity', *Belgrave Papers*, No. 8, London: Local Government Management Board.

Zourdis, S. (1995) 'Information Technology, Openness of Government and Democracy', in W. van de Donk, I. Snellen and P. Tops (eds), *Orwell in Athens: A Perspective on Informization and Democracy*, Amsterdam: IOS Press

Zuboff, S. (1988) *In the Age of the Smart Machine: The Future of Work and Power*, New York: Basic Books,

Zuurmond, A. (1994) *De infocratie: Een theoretische en empirische heroriëntatie op Weber's ideaaltype in het informatietijdperk (The Infocracy)*, Phaedrus, 's-Gravenhage.

Index